Crime-Related Events Identification Based on Text Analytics Approach

As modern society is extremely dependent on the Internet, social networks, and developing technologies, a threat to the security of both the individual and society as a whole has emerged. The openness and global nature of the Internet create opportunities both for criminals, who can use the available information for criminal purposes, and for law enforcement officials. Police officers, in turn, can deal with the preventive processing of data from the Internet in order to prevent crimes. This type of data analysis can detect illegal or criminal actions even at the stage of their formation. *Crime-Related Events Identification Based on Text Analytics Approach* describes the possibilities of extracting crime-related facts from semi-structured information from various Internet sources so that crime can be combatted. This book is aimed at police officers and IT professionals working in online investigations.

Crime-Related Events Identification Based on Text Analytics Approach

Orken Mamyrbayev, Nina Khairova and Waldemar Wójcik

Routledge
Taylor & Francis Group
LONDON AND NEW YORK

Cover Image: Shutterstock

First published 2025
by Routledge
4 Park Square, Milton Park, Abingdon, Oxon OX14 4RN

and by Routledge
605 Third Avenue, New York, NY 10158

Routledge is an imprint of the Taylor & Francis Group, an informa business

British Library Cataloguing-in-Publication Data
A catalogue record for this book is available from the British Library

ISBN: 978-1-032-95789-0 (hbk)
ISBN: 978-1-032-95999-3 (pbk)
ISBN: 978-1-003-58751-4 (ebk)

DOI: 10.1201/9781003587514

Typeset in Times New Roman
by codeMantra

Contents

Preface

The rapid digitalization of information has created new opportunities for cybercrime, necessitating advanced technological solutions for crime detection and analysis. Integrating machine learning methods such as text classification, clustering, and Latent Semantic Analysis, this book highlights the potential of artificial intelligence (AI)-driven approaches to improve public safety and address the limitations of traditional natural language processing (NLP) methods. The aim is to develop novel approaches for formalizing knowledge extraction and creating tools to enhance crime detection through structured fact representation based on the created Kazakh-Russian parallel corpus.

Chapters 1–3 collectively describe the challenges and methodologies involved in extracting and analyzing crime-related information from various textual formats using AI and NLP techniques. Chapter 4 discusses the concept of information extraction from text, examining language as a hierarchical system of interconnected elements. It explores how the meaning of text arises from the relationships between these semantic units. Chapters 5 and 6 focus on crime-related information extraction. Chapter 5 analyzes the relationship between the linguistic formalisms of web content and the real-world essence of socially significant events. It highlights methods like statistical, semantic, and machine learning-based techniques (e.g., LSA, clustering) to extract crime-related data, particularly from unstructured public sources. Chapter 6 develops a logical-linguistic model for fact extraction from textual corpora. Chapter 7 focuses on the characteristics of the Kazakh language that grow from its agglutinative nature. Chapter 8 describes the creation of a Kazakh-Russian parallel corpus of criminal texts and highlights the sentence alignment process between Kazakh and Russian in the corpus. Chapter 9 introduces a parallel corpus-based approach to crime-related event extraction, enabling the transfer of crime event extraction techniques across low-resource languages with minimal annotated data. The conclusion summarizes the methodologies for extracting crime-related information from multilingual texts, focusing on low-resource languages. It highlights the main findings of this book, including the creation of a Kazakh-Russian parallel corpus and advancements in automated crime data identification, and suggests directions for future research.

This book is highly relevant and will likely interest professionals and researchers working at the intersection of AI, NLP, and crime investigation. Specifically, it will be useful for NLP and AI researchers, linguists, computational linguistics experts, and cybersecurity professionals. We hope you will enjoy this book.

Orken Mamyrbayev
Nina Khairova
Waldemar Wójcik
Almaty, Umeo, Lublin 2025

About the authors

Orken Mamyrbayev was born in Kazakhstan in 1979. He is the Deputy General Director of Science and Head of the Laboratory of Computer Engineering of Intelligent Systems at the Institute of Information and Computational Technologies. In 2014, he obtained his PhD in Information Systems at the Kazakh National Technical University named after K.I. Satbayev. He was an Associate Professor in 2019 at the Institute of Information and Computational Technologies. He is a member of the dissertation council "Information Systems" at L.N. Gumilyov Eurasian National University in the specialties Computer Sciences and Information systems. His main research field of activity is related to machine learning, deep learning, and speech technologies. In total, he has published more than five books, over 120 papers, and authored several patents and copyright certificates for an intellectual property object in software. Currently, he manages two scientific projects, such as the development of an end-to-end automatic speech recognition system for agglutinative languages and information model and software tools for the system of automatic search and analysis of multilingual illegal web content based on the ontological approach.

Nina Khairova received her PhD degree in Information Technology from the Kharkiv National University of Radio Electronics, Ukraine. She conducted her postdoctoral studies in Computational Linguistics at the National Technical University "Kharkiv Polytechnic Institute" (NTU "KhPI") and Taras Shevchenko National University, Ukraine. Since 2013, she has held the position of Professor in the Intelligent Computer Systems Department at NTU "KhPI". Currently, she is a Visiting Professor in the Department of Computing Science at Umeå University, Sweden. Her main research interests include corpus linguistics, natural language processing, machine learning, and responsible artificial intelligence. She is the author of three books and has published more than 150 research articles. Her current research projects include "Information model and software tools for the system of automatic search and analysis of multilingual illegal web content based on the ontological approach" and "Building TRUST in social media: assessing the trustworthiness of public information".

Waldemar Wójcik was born in Poland in 1949. Currently retired. He was the longtime Director of the Institute of Electronics and Information Technology, former longtime Dean of the Faculty of Electrical Engineering and Computer Science at the Lublin University of Technology. He received Doctor Honoris Causa of five universities in Ukraine and Kazakhstan. He obtained his PhD in 1985 at the Lublin University of Technology, and DSc in 2002 at the Lviv Polytechnic National University, Ukraine. In 2009, he obtained a title of professor granted by the President of Poland. In his research, he mainly deals with process control, optoelectronics, digital data analysis, and also heat processes or solid state physics. Particular attention is paid to the use of optoelectronic technology in the monitoring and diagnostics of thermal processes. He is a member of Optoelectronics Section of the Committee of Electronics and Telecommunications of the Polish Academy of Sciences; Metrology Section of the Committee of Metrology and Scientific Equipment of the Polish Academy of Sciences; and many other scientific organizations of Poland as well as Europe and Asia. In total, he has published over 50 books, over 400 papers, and authored several patents. He is also a member of the editorial board of numerous international and national scientific and technical journals.

Chapter 1

Introduction

In recent decades, with the spread of networked computer technology, mobile communications, and the Internet, the information resources of modern society have been exposed to a growing number of threats that are fraught with economic damage and that increase the danger to national and global informational infrastructure. Both government and commercial systems are the subjects of such attacks. Increased criminal activity on global networks (in such forms as financial fraud, copyright infringement, distribution of child pornography, hacking, etc.) poses threats to the security of both individuals and society as a whole.

The more the Internet expands, the more online crimes are reported. Thanks to computer networks, violent extremism can spread globally at low cost and high speed. Thus, the openness of the global network makes it more vulnerable to criminal attacks.

At the same time, the openness and global reach of the Internet, a worldwide telecommunications network, create enormous potential opportunities for forensic and law enforcement professionals. Current text-processing technologies allow intelligence analysts and police to preemptively process computer network textual data by collecting, linking, and analyzing the "faint signals" or "digital footprints" of vast text arrays that are present on the Internet. In some cases, such analysis can help detect the potential of an illegal act before it takes place.

For this purpose, along with existing traditional ways of dealing with crimes in the field of security of circulation of computer information, the practical achievements of artificial intelligence and mathematical linguistics, related to the problems of natural language processing (NLP) should be used. At the same time, one of the main problems of determining the criminal relevance of Internet texts, along with the huge volume of the information under analysis (Meloy et al. 2012), remains the problem of weak "coloring" of criminal texts for the use of traditionally accepted approaches of classification, clustering, and extraction of NLP patterns.

Traditional language processing approaches used in the task of identifying crime-related information (CRI) and potentially terrorism-related texts are based on analyzing text style and recognizing the emotional component associated with the implicit intention of the text but do not take into account the topic and content of the text.

This publication examines the information-linguistic technology of automatic identification, extraction, search, and analysis of CRI in unstructured and semi-structured test arrays of various languages, focusing on textual content and factual extraction.

This chapter examines:

- the main problems in the field of existing technologies of searching for illegal information in texts;
- existing problems of formalization and automatic processing of the Kazakh language.

DOI: 10.1201/9781003587514-1

This chapter proposes:

- a logical-linguistic model of fact extraction from text corpora;
- implementation of this model for Kazakh, Russian, and English languages;
- information technology of identification of CRI in Kazakh-language text corpora;
- description of the created aligned parallel Kazakh-Russian corpus of crime-related texts.

Chapter 2

Major challenges of searching for crime-related information in a text

2.1 Current approaches to the formalization of crime-related information in unstructured texts

Most of the research related to the prevention of terrorist attacks has focused on analyzing the use of the Internet and social media by terrorists and terrorist organizations (Cohen et al. 2014; Cohn et al. 2001; Shyam Varan Nath 2006). For example, one of the research areas dedicated to the detection of "linguistic markers of violent extremism in the online environment" (Meloy et al. 2012) focuses specifically on identifying digital traces that are relevant to a potential "lone-wolf terrorist" (Meloy 2011); other studies look at potential types of online violence (Meloy et al. 2015). Areas of computer science, such as searching for illegal information in text data, detecting crime patterns, and assessing the risk of possible cybercrime, are becoming some of the most popular areas of NLP research. More and more researchers are focusing on the ways and forms of applying natural language processing (NLP) technologies within a wide range of activities relevant to preventing terrorist activity.

For example, to detect linguistic markers that are indicative of potential "warning" behavior (Meloy et al. 2012), it has been proposed to use lists of violent words whose preparation and retrieval are based on standard text processing approaches, such as lemmatization and Part of Speech tagging (POS tagging) as well as on the use of lexical databases like WordNet (Cohen et al. 2014). However, such linguistic markers, which are used as a supplement to standard text-processing algorithms, can identify potential signs of agreed, presumed radical violence. They cannot make automated decisions about any type of crime. In addition, if the individual steps of NLP are inaccurate, the accuracy of linguistic marker extraction will be greatly reduced, and the number of errors will increase.

Another area of NLP that is used in the task of highlighting crime-related information and potentially terrorism-related texts is the analysis of text style and the identification of the emotional component associated with the implicit expression of intent. Such an emotional component may include boasting, ideological statements, or admiration for terrorist leaders (Paul et al. 2013). Textual analysis of style, in this case, reveals patterns of phrases related to emotional motivations such as anger, humiliation, or shame. In this context, it should be emphasized that communication style does not depend on a particular topic or content. Adding to its analysis deeper psychological processing, the use of linguistic-psychology of speech activity and sociolinguistics allows not only to identify "preventive" criminal behavior but also to uncover, in some cases, corporate fraud (Meloy et al. 2014).

NLP classification and clustering techniques are used to analyze large volumes of heterogeneous texts whose themes are not known in advance. For example, clustering can highlight topics,

DOI: 10.1201/9781003587514-2

such as weapons, tactics, or targets (Paul et al. 2013). In this case, the additional use of speech recognition and machine translation technologies can significantly increase the amount of text available for analysis.

One form of classification is sentiment analysis. Various forms of online expression of opinion (e.g., reviews, personal opinions, ratings, and recommendations) have become major sources of information, both for companies hoping to sell *their* products and manage *their* reputation (Chen et al. 2004) and for the media, which determine public attitudes towards real-life events. For example, sentiment analysis is used by Shyam Varan Nath (2006) in the analysis of tweets to determine authors' views on certain areas of crime in real time. In addition, many studies that focus on crime pattern detection use time-varying data collection methods. Such studies, in addition to tweets, blogs, and social media, use media information to detect crime in each specific area (Bolla 2014).

NLP classification methods are fairly well-developed and fine-tuned. At the same time, *their* use in the analysis of the emotional component of a text or the identification of intent does not always yield good results. The main drawback of such approaches is the non-specificity of the identified patterns, when the identified patterns (even if they are clearly threatening), may not be related to threats, and *their* interpretation often depends on the cultural and individual characteristics of the person. Normally, text analysis and classification exclude indirect terminology that does not clearly refer to a weapon or violent act and does not include threatening vocabulary, i.e., terminology not strictly related to criminality.

In the articles and approaches discussed above, in the semantic analysis of the emotional component of a text, paragraphs that represent facts are usually removed and researchers focus on paragraphs in which the author expresses an opinion, using common classifiers, for instance, Naive Bayes, maximum entropy, or support vector machine.

2.2 The problems of crime-related textual information definition and identification

A significant contribution to the formation of scientific foundations of informatization of forensic activities at different times was made by such well-known scientists and criminalists as T.V. Averyanova (study of automatization of obtaining and use of information in forensic activities); L.E. Arotsker (definition of identification and non-identification methods of working with forensic textual information); A.V. Astakhova (possibilities of using computer expert systems in forensic research); D.D. Begov (problems of automation of forensic examinations, ways of creating technical systems for determination of emotional state of a person for forensic purposes); P.S. Belkin (philosophical theory of reflection as an epistemological basis of forensic science) and others.

Researchers have focused *their* research on four main areas: (1) exploring the possibility of using mathematical methods and computer technologies in forensic practice; (2) solving the problem of convenient forms of searching, storing, processing, and transferring forensic information; (3) determining the role and place of certain computer technologies in forensic information support; (4) studying and assessing typical difficulties of an organizational, legal, scientific, and psychological nature at the automation stage of particular types of forensic expertise.

Today, the modern intensive filling of information space and availability of information relevant for operational and official activities of law enforcement agencies forms several new challenges related to the possibility of search and automatic extraction of crime-related information. Although the activity of any law enforcement unit is still primarily aimed at detecting, preventing, and suppressing crimes and offenses, new directions and opportunities for this activity related to access to huge information flows have emerged.

In doing so, all information of interest to law enforcement agencies can be divided into two levels: the level of the individual, independent structural unit, whose interest is determined by a checklist of required information; and the macro or general level, which represents any information that has the characteristics of a criminal environment. It is macro-level information that will be the focus of most law enforcement agencies.

Searching for information from new sources is only one of the tasks involved in operational and official activities. Another important task is the retrospective search for latent patterns in unstructured arrays, such as the daily information of events in law enforcement agencies. This task consists of searching for events similar in some parameters (location, type, mechanism, participants, etc.) recorded in the daily reports or unconnected sources.

An indicative feature of crime-related information, which distinguishes it from ordinary information, is the concept of corpus delicti. Corpus delicti is a system of objective and subjective elements stipulated by the current legislation, which characterize a certain socially dangerous act – i.e., a specific crime. The interrelation of components that are the primary components of the system "corpus delicti" (object, objective side, subject, subjective side) is shown in Figure 2.1.

The information support of the criminalist's information-analytical system can only take into account the three elements of the offense: the object, the subject, and the objective side, as the subjective side does not carry the necessary semantic load.

The specific elements of the corpus delicti are determined by a checklist of relevant information for the specific law enforcement unit according to its jurisdiction. The formation of the checklist itself is based on the disposition of the law and falls under the jurisdiction of the unit.

When predicting crimes, identifying signs of hidden crimes, determining the relationship between the personal characteristics of criminals and the choice of the crime scene, as well as other analytical investigative work, the investigator (or another procedural person) needs to

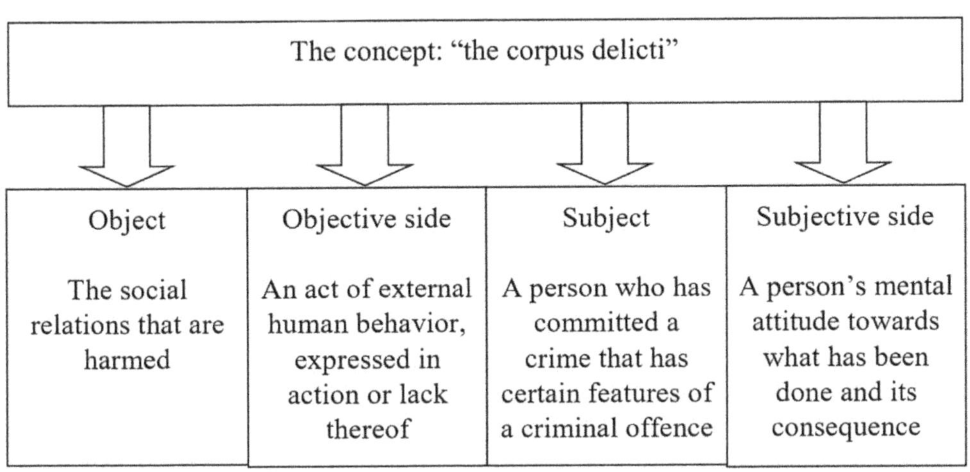

Figure 2.1 Structure of indicative indicators of crime-related information.

process a large number of electronic text documents, extracting crime-related information from them. These electronic texts can be electronic documents, such as explanatory notes, memos, reports, profiles of the persons involved in a crime, reports from the investigation, as well as electronic collections of Internet publications, Rich Site Summary (RSS) mailing lists, and social networks.

All such electronic documents are in the form of semi-structured textual information, by which we mean – a textual electronic document with a high degree of content variability, varying according to the specific situation. In general, these documents represent an accessible repository of forensic knowledge.

At the same time, the main quality of crime-related information lies in the content of information that contributes to the search for evidence and patterns inherent in the criminalistic aspects of criminal activity. In other words, the criminalistic characteristic of a crime, as a means of optimizing the investigation, should be a set of information that has not qualifying or procedural and preventive, but, namely, search and cognitive value (Westphal 2009).

In general, the information processes connected to investigating a crime, obtaining crime-related information as well as data and facts from arrays of electronic textual documents and electronic resources, can be represented as a scheme shown in Figure 2.2.

Actual CRI, which often has no causal link to the crime event but has potential forensic relevance, does not allow for the use of a pre-designed thesaurus of a known subject area when searching for it. Such information, on the one hand, is characterized by a lack of output

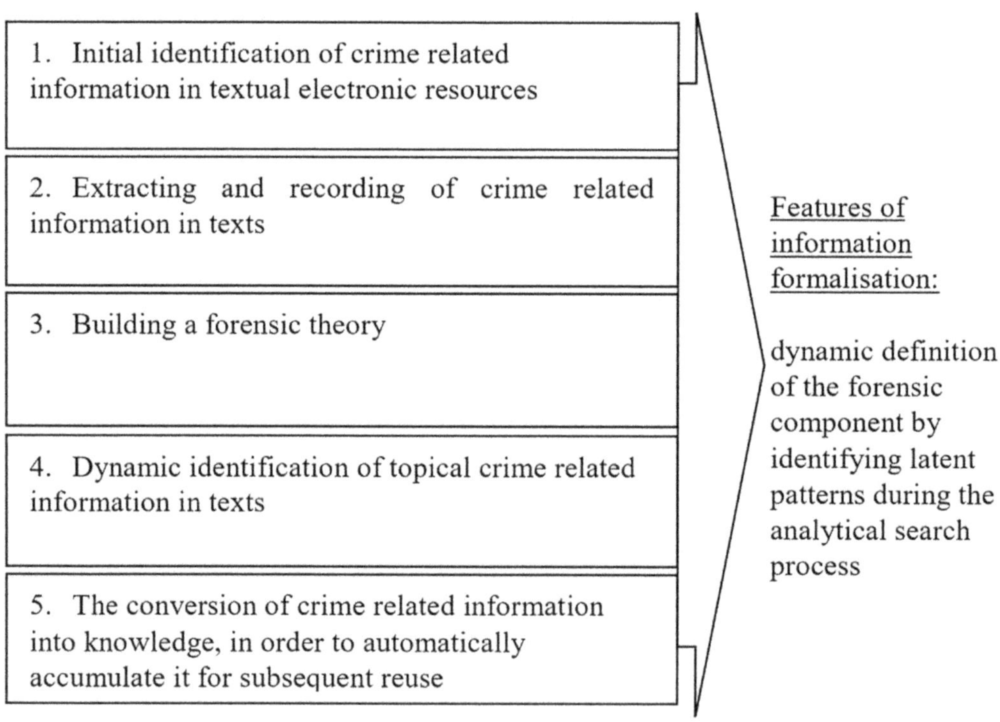

Figure 2.2 Outline of the information processes involved in obtaining crime-related information from electronic text resources.

attributes and, on the other hand, does not permit the use of only keywords describing criminal acts, which, being a kind of indicative attribute, usually have *their* own specifics.

For subsequent long-term use, the actual CRI needs to be transformed into knowledge by extracting new concepts, which are not always identifiers of criminality, as well as by carrying out *their* systematization. Thus, dynamic dissemination and accumulation of forensic knowledge need to be carried out through the processing of stream textual information of new documents and references.

2.3 Using IE techniques to extract crime-related information

In recent years, there has been a rapid increase in interest in the field of artificial intelligence and mathematical linguistics research, information extraction (IE), and related fact-finding or factual information retrieval (IR). The general goal of IE research is the possibility of extracting information from previously unstructured data. A more specific objective related to research specifically concerning crime-related texts is the possibility of obtaining facts from which logical reasoning can be conducted and conclusions about the criminal nature of the text can be drawn.

A fact, in general, is a recorded, classified event that has occurred. In computer science, a fact is explicitly represented technically as a triplet: subject → predicate → object. Subjects of facts are usually entities whose properties (temporal, spatial, qualitative, quantitative, etc.) are allocated additionally as attributes of the fact. In this case, a fact can be extracted from textual information (both semi-structured and unstructured) and can define both the properties of the entity and its relationship with other entities.

Typically, the first step of the fact extraction task is Named Entity Recognition, which includes identifying known entity names (for people and organizations), place names, temporal expressions, and some types of multiple expressions that use existing domain knowledge or information derived from other sentences. Typically, the recognition task involves assigning a unique identifier to extract the entity.

When identifying crime-related facts, the objective of entity recognition is to identify persons in the absence of any knowledge of a particular instance of the entities. For example, when processing the sentence "M. Smith participated in the organization of the meeting", entity recognition means understanding that the name "M. Smith" really refers to the person of interest. However, knowledge of some M. Smith referred to in the sentence might not necessarily have existed before the sentence was analyzed.

The next step in fact formation is the relationship extraction between the subjects defined by the fact.

At the same time, the greatest difficulties in extracting factual information from unstructured texts arise during the extraction of knowledge from open domains, as well as during the processing of "temporal" knowledge, which includes crime-related information. A particular difficulty lies in the assumption that the same fact can be expressed in different grammatical constructions and different words defining the entities and the relationships established between them.

Currently, the issue of fact extraction from texts with a broad thematic focus remains open at the time of the study. Existing general models and approaches depend directly on the level of specificity and structure of the text. Although there are quite a few methods to extract facts from structured text data (Crestan & Pantel 2010; Gatterbauer et al. 2007; Wong et al. 2009), a reliable technology to extract facts from semi-structured and unstructured text data is not yet on the market (Phillips & Riloff 2002; Jones et al. 2003; Agichtein & Gravano 2000).

- "The company management sold a part of share",
- "Management of Apple Inc. sold their share",
- "They marketed them".

} they may express the same fact

Figure 2.3 Example of presenting a single fact with different syntactic and lexical structures.

At the same time, the texts from social media, the media, and other Internet sources that interest us are presented precisely in an unstructured form; it is the facts extracted from them that should form the basis of crime-related information for subsequent analysis.

Current research in text mining is mainly based on statistical models using Supervised Learning (SL), Semi-Supervised Learning (SSL), and Open IE. The main difficulty of fact extraction in unspecified subject areas by SL and SSL methods is the need for a labeled training corpus (Mooney & Bunescu 2005). Open IE (Text Runner system) typically extracts only binary relationships from plain text and is not very comprehensive or accurate (Yahya et al. 2014).

In general, the use of statistical methods for IE and, in particular, for fact extraction has little effect. This is primarily due to the fact that statistical methods treat documents as an unordered "bag of words", which is well implemented in IR and text classification tasks, but cannot be used in fact extraction, where the processing unit is a sentence rather than a corpus of texts (Luckicgev 2009).

Another reason for the low efficiency of statistical methods of fact extraction is the inability of such methods to take into account the syntax and semantics of sentences and the homonymity, synonymy, and polysemy of natural language. At a time when the predicate, subject, and object of a fact may be represented by different words and even different parts of speech. For example, the English sentences "The company management sold a part of share", "Management of Apple Inc. sold *their* share", and "They marketed it" represent the same fact (Figure 2.3).

Based on our analysis, in this study, we propose to use the following to extract factual information from semi-structured and unstructured texts:

1 logical-linguistic models of fact extraction from semi-structured and unstructured texts;
2 formalization of grammatical ways of expressing the same fact in sentences;
3 a model of semantic proximity of short text fragments.

Chapter 3

Existing problems of knowledge extraction from semi-structured and unstructured text

3.1 Text-processing applications

Traditionally, the performance of extraction, processing, and storing of information is based on the formal description of the information. The efficiency of the information technology used depends on the degree of formalization and presentation of information, as well as the level of automation determined by the degree of human participation in the process of obtaining information.

The more accurate the formal presentation of information, the higher the possibility of its computer processing in the various information systems. According to the degree of formalizing and structuring, the following three types of information are distinguished:

- Structured data, usually represented by data in some fixed template structures. The data are facts and numerical, quantitative indicators characterizing them: names, dates of events, information about processes, places of action, etc.
- Semi-structured data, which has a certain level of organization. At the same time, the level of organization or structuring can be various, including for text information. For example, text dataset containing highly specialized text reports on breakdowns, survey results, etc., can be considered semi-structured. At the same time, there is a reasonable approach, according to which any syntactically literate and meaningful text is semi-structured due to syntactic and semantic coherence and organization.
- By semi-structured text information, we will understand multi-format files containing natural language texts. Such information contained in intranet and Internet networks cannot be successfully processed by analytical information processing information systems. Documents contain semi-structured text information, when, with a high degree of content variability, depending on the specific situation, they capture all the variety of details that correspond to the scope of the application. The content of full-text weakly formalized documents is significantly related to an arbitrary, changing, depending on the specific situation, structure.
- Unstructured information usually refers to various kinds of verbal information, in which verbal and communicative signals and methods are mostly used. Usually, verbal signals mean verbal wording (conversation), tone of voice, its timbre, sounds, and exclamations.

To date, the vast majority of information is presented in global and corporate networks in the form of semi-structured text information (Web pages, emails, and similar documents) (Figure 3.1).

DOI: 10.1201/9781003587514-3

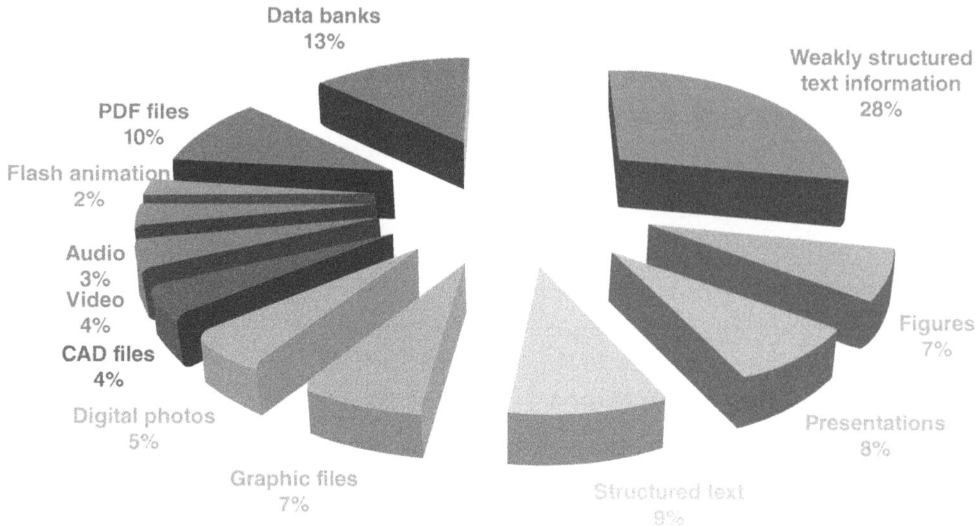

Figure 3.1 Structure of information flows of global and corporate networks.

At the same time, the explosive growth in the volume of full-text information continues not only in global networks (where the volume of unstructured information doubles every 18 months) but also in corporate (departmental) information systems.

A general information space, expressed by the knowledge base, is the intellectual capital of the intangible assets of a society or, in a narrow sense, an organization. Knowledge is the information needed to make decisions, i.e., true, reliable, and practice-tested information. At the same time, "new" knowledge for this industry is competitive in rapidly changing social and economic conditions. This kind of knowledge is mostly represented by the current non-formalized and weakly formalized information entering the system every day. Only in full-text information is it possible to identify soft aspects, allowing for multiple, fuzzy solutions and their various variants, as well as to achieve a deep understanding that reflects the essence of the phenomenon, the purpose and interrelation of its components, and the knowledge that is not contained in well-formalized data but has a major influence on making economically and socially essential decisions.

Extraction and identification of knowledge from semi-structured text information is a task that lies at the intersection of theories and methods of artificial intelligence (AI) and natural language processing (NLP) approaches.

To work with textual information, Text Mining technologies are used, which represent algorithms for identifying syntactic and semantic relationships and correlations in full-text information by extracting its specific elements and properties from the text. Text Mining tasks include:

- documents classification and clustering;
- information retrieval;
- thematic indexing;
- extraction of facts and concepts (event extraction (EE), argument mining);
- the development of thesaurus;

- building semantic networks;
- question answering;
- automatic text summarization.

Among the systems that implement most of the presented technologies, the most famous are: Intelligent Miner for Text (IBM), PolyAnalyst (Megaputer Intelligent), Text Miner (SAS), Semio Map (Semio Corp.), Oracl Text (Oracle), Knowledge Server (Autonomy), RetrievalWare (Convera), Galaktika-ZOOM (Galaktika Corporation), and InfoStream (ELVISTI Research Center).

IBM Corporation (www.ibm.com) has developed the Intelligent Miner for Text system [72], which is a set of utilities that implement Text Mining functions: language detection; automatic assignment of the text to some previously known category; splitting a large number of documents into groups similar in style, form and frequency characteristics of keywords; definition in documents of new concepts, such as proper names, titles, abbreviations, based on the analysis of a given dictionary; development of an abstract – annotations of the text.

Another PolyAnalyst system from Megaputer Intelligence (www.megaputer.com) can be used to automatically analyze numerical and text databases in order to identify previously unknown, non-trivial, useful, and understandable patterns. PolyAnalyst includes TextAnalyst, which allows for solving such Text Mining tasks as building a semantic network for large texts, preparing a text summary, searching for text, automatic classification, and clustering of texts.

The SAS system (www.sas.com) contains the SAS Text Miner component, which allows working with text documents of various formats from databases, file systems and the Web, as well as aggregate text information with structured data. Oracle (www.oracle.com) includes Text Mining technologies for searching documents with similar meanings, thematic analysis of texts in English, determining the key topic of a document, and automatic summarization.

The SemioMap system deals with indexing documents, clustering concepts, and visualizing link maps. During the indexing phase, the SemioMap server reads the unstructured text arrays, extracting key phrases (concepts) and creating an index from them. At the concept clustering stage, the SemioMap server detects links between the extracted phrases and builds from them, based on the analysis of joint occurrence, a lexical network ("concept map"). In the next stage, visualization of link maps is carried out, which provides quick navigation through key phrases and links between them. The main purpose of the Galaktika-ZOOM system is an intelligent search by keywords, taking into account morphology, as well as the formation of information portraits on specific aspects, with a focus on large information volumes. The system allows the formatting of an "image" of the problem – a multidimensional model in the form of a list of significant phrases. The InfoStream system supports real-time analytical work: building plot chains, digests, occurrence diagrams, and tables of relationships between concepts and media ratings.

Thus, Text Mining technologies are designed to process semi-structured text information. But the analysis of current trends shows that, from the point of view of their functionality, the Text Mining systems have nearly reached the limits of the possibility of practical implementation of the existing models and means of formalizing natural language text processing. Despite the declaration of "semantic processing" of texts, such systems effectively implement only statistical and probabilistic models and methods of Data Mining and the results of morphological and syntactic processing of texts, practically without considering (or weakly taking into account) their semantic component.

The further development of Text Mining methods in the direction of information and linguistic support of information systems is constrained not only by the lack of adequate models and methods of semantic analysis, semantic search, and semantic classification but also by the lack of a harmonious system of linguistic and information support. Thus, the insufficiency of ontologies and thesauruses of wide subject areas leads to the inability to consider the peculiarities of the semantic organization of texts of various thematic orientations.

3.2 Knowledge extraction from the textual information

One of the main problems in the development of intelligent information systems today is the choice of a knowledge representation model, which determines the architecture, capabilities, and advantages of the system. Knowledge about a certain subject area (software) is a set of information about the objects of this software, their significant properties, and binding relationships; processes running in this software, as well as methods for analyzing situations that arise in it, and methods for resolving problems associated with them.

Today, a number of basic models of knowledge representation and their modifications are known. This is the representation of knowledge using facts and inference rules, predicate calculus, neural networks, semantic networks, frames and some others.

Existing knowledge representation models can be combined into three large groups: declarative, procedural, and special (or combined) (Figure 3.2).

Each approach has its own advantages and disadvantages. Thus, one of the main disadvantages of the method of knowledge representation using inference rules is the significant time-consuming, and time expenditures for building an inference chain, which are also not always unambiguous. Systems are now increasingly using production rules, which are more memory efficient and faster than purely rule-based systems.

The knowledge representation, based on predicate logic, uses the mathematical apparatus of one of the sections of mythology representing symbolic logic. The main formalism of the representation of the predicate is "term", which establishes the correspondence of the sign to the described object and the predicate used to describe the relations of entities in the form of a relational formula containing the term.

The main advantage of neural networks, which were first proposed in the work of (McCulloch & Pitts 1943), is their high adaptability, as well as the ability to process incomplete information. At the same time, creating a learning algorithm, as well as designing a network

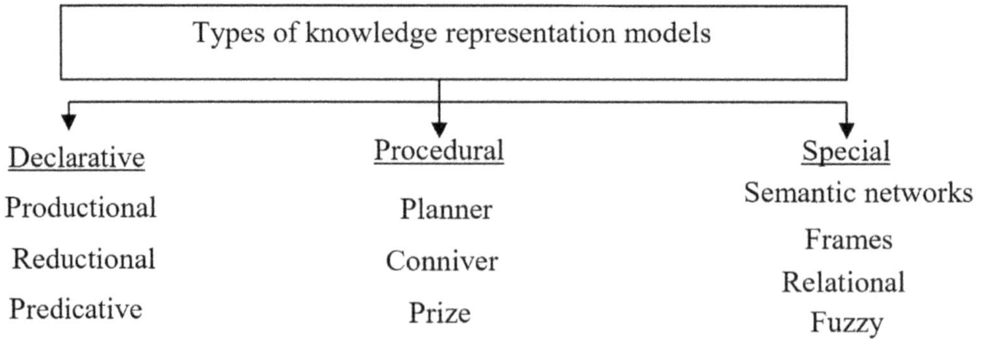

Figure 3.2 Scheme of the major types of knowledge representation models.

structure, is a creative task performed by highly qualified specialists for a specific task. Another significant drawback of neural networks is the subtle representation of knowledge: the images remembered by the network during learning are encoded in the form of the state of neurons, and the decision-making process cannot be represented in the form of a visual construction: IF – THEN.

The model of knowledge representation in the form of semantic networks consists of vertices corresponding to objects, concepts or actions, and arcs connecting them, describing the relations between objects. Such a model is universal and easily configurable and represents a fairly visual knowledge system. But since conclusions on semantic networks are realized through relations between elements, they contain a possible threat of contradictions.

The frame model of knowledge representation was proposed by Minsky, who defined it as follows:

> A frame is a data structure representing a stereotypical situation. Each frame corresponds to several types of information. Some of this information is about how the frame is used, some about what to expect, and some about what to do if the expectations are not confirmed.

The emergence of ontologies is primarily caused by the need to develop a format for representing Web information that allows automatic processing by software agents, for which it is necessary to translate a traditional Web representation into a semantic-level system. Therefore, one of the main directions of the Semantic Web today is represented by an ontological approach, which should be associated with research in the field of AI. In AI, an ontology is defined as a "specification of the conceptualization of a subject area", that is, it is a document or file that formally defines the relationship between terms.

Ontologies and information thesauruses represent a new way of representing and processing knowledge. Ontologies have their own processing means (logical inference) corresponding to the semantic tasks of information processing. Ontology is a formal specification taking place in some context of the subject area. Moreover, by conceptualization we mean, in addition to collecting concepts, the convergence of all information that refers to concepts – characteristics, relations, restrictions, axioms, and statements about concepts that are necessary to describe and solve problems in the selected subject area.

An ontology is a description of declarative knowledge implemented as classes connected by a hierarchy relationship. On a formal level, an ontology is a system that includes a set of concepts and a set of statements about these concepts, on the basis of which classes, objects, relationships, functions, and theories can be created (Hitzler et al. 2010).

Individual cases of ontology are the thesaurus, which includes the most important repository for representing word values, with a limited number of relations between terms, and taxonomy with clearly specified types of such relations.

Thesauruses are used today by almost all applications that work with a natural language: information extraction, information search, question-answer systems, machine translation, many medical information applications, etc.

The most used and well-known today is the WordNet online thesaurus (WordNet, Miller et al. 1990), which represents a hierarchically organized lexical database. WordNet was designed for English, but today it is being expanded for German, Portuguese, Finnish, and some other languages. The thesaurus includes about 100,000 nouns, 10,000 verbs, as well as adjectives and adverbs, each of which has a definition and ontological links. In WordNet, values are defined

Table 3.1 Interconceptual Relations of the WordNet Thesaurus

Relation	*Definition*	*Example*
Hypernym (superordinate)	From concept to superordinate	Breakfast1→meal1
Hyponym (subordinate)	From concept to subtypes	Meal1→lunch1
Member meronym	From groups to their members	Faculty2→professor1
Has-instance	From concepts to concept instances	Composer1→Bach
Instance	From instances to their concepts	Austen1→author1
Member holonym (Member-of)	From members to their groups	Copilot1→crew1
Part meronym (has-part)	From wholes to parts	Table2→leg3
Part holonym (part-of)	From parts to wholes	Course7→meal1
Antonym	Semantic opposition between lemmas	Leader1→follower1

using synsets or a set of synonyms. This is a set of close synonyms, simple words to which the meaning or concept is attributed (concept), and a gloss is added (Jurafsky & Martin 2008).

In each of its meanings, the word WordNet has a hierarchy. For example, bass subClassOF Class (singer), singer subClassOF Class (musician), musician subClassOF Class (performer), performer subClassOF Class (human), human subClassOF Class (physical entity), physical entity subClassOF Class (entity). In addition to the hierarchy relationship, WordNet includes the relationships shown in Table 3.1.

Another important thesaurus is the MeSH (MEdical Subject Headings thesaurus from the National Library of Medicine) (US National Library of Medicine), which currently includes two hundred thousand entities corresponding to many headings, between which the relations of synonymy and hierarchy (hypernyms) are established.

Each heading includes a plurality of synonyms provided with a definition, which are represented similarly to WordNet synsets. The Thesaurus representation is used to provide synonyms, a separate term (entry terms). The Hypernym Hierarchy representation is similar to WordNet. The MeSH thesaurus is used to index journal articles in the National Library of Medicine (MEDLINE/PubMed) bibliographic database of 12 million journal articles, each with 10–12 MeSH terms manually defined.

Thus, the use of ontologies (and its subspecies of thesaurus and taxonomy) for knowledge representation is the most modern and in demand, which is due to the technical possibility of its use both as a component of the Semantic Web and as constituent parts of various NLP systems (machine translation, question-answer systems, information retrieval, automatic summarization, etc.) (Nirenburg & Raskin 2004).

Any modern knowledge representation language defines some specification of the subject area and requires an explicit definition of concepts – the basic concepts of this subject area and connections between concepts – relations and interactions of basic concepts for the representation and exchange of knowledge about this subject area. The main relations used by almost all modern thesauri/ontologies are the relations of hypernymy and meronymy.

3.3 Unsolved tasks and existing problems of the NLP applications

The task of developing a linguistic processor is a convergence of tasks from many disciplines: applied, computer, structural, mathematical and theoretical linguistics, AI, information technology, and mathematical modeling. Thanks to their interaction, NLP has been developing at an ever-accelerating pace in recent years. This, not least, is due to the rapidly developing Internet, its saturation with natural language texts, and the increasing need for their automatic processing.

The current level of NLP application implementations can be divided into three large categories: areas in which there are commercial products and systems; areas in the implementation of which working algorithms are involved; and the problems of the linguistic processor practically not solved today (Figure 3.3).

For example, there are currently a sufficient number of commercial applications for defining spam in a user-received text stream in e-mail. And although these applications continue to make enough erroneous decisions, they are included in modern email applications.

Similarly, speech synthesis systems are quite commercialized, with successfully developed applications, like the Speech Application Language Tags (SALT) specification (Jurafsky & Martin 2008).

At the same time, today there is a large group of text processing tasks in which sufficient progress has been made, but they have not yet been fully solved. These tasks include information extraction systems that include Opinion Mining tasks. Such systems are used, including in marketing research, to extract positive or negative information about a particular product or service on the Web.

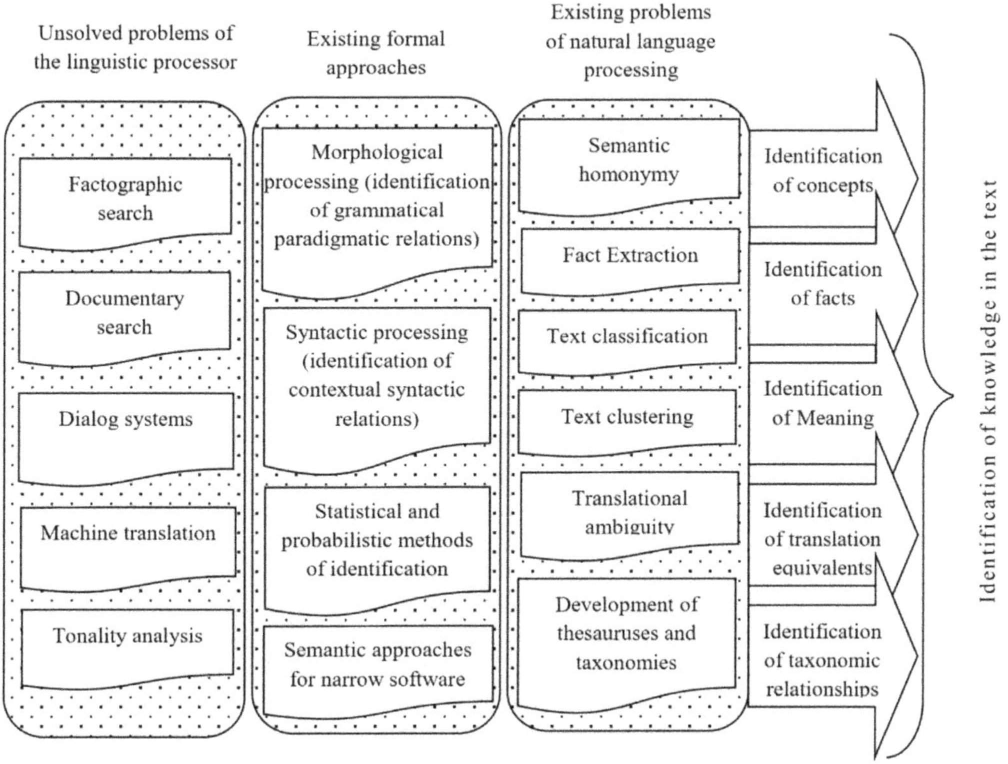

Figure 3.3 Structural classification of unsolved tasks and existing problems of the NLP applications.

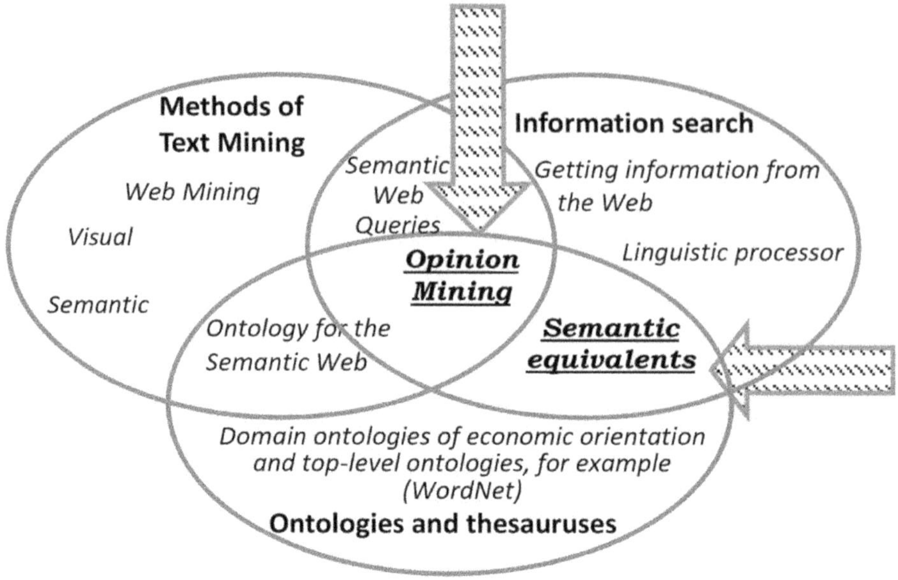

Figure 3.4 Opinion Mining methods in the general scheme of tasks of processing semi-structured text information.

Opinion Mining methods, which allow classifying texts by sentiment, have appeared relatively recently, and largely use the approaches of Text Mining and information retrieval (Kobayashi et al. 2007) (Figure 3.4).

Another important application of a linguistic processor belongs to the same group of tasks – machine translation, which implies a fully automatic translator. In automatically received translations, despite the recent progress in the development of parsing technology, there are still a sufficient number of errors, in particular when using it on the Web.

The last, third, area of the tasks of the linguistic processor is practically unsolved today. So, question-and-answer systems that are used to automatically answer questions of any kind have real algorithms only for the formulation of the simplest, factual questions. Simple but general questions are still a difficult problem.

Similarly, the question-answer systems used in the intelligent interface of modern Automated Information Systems (AIS) are significantly behind the level of practical demand and belong to the third group of practically unsolved tasks of the linguistic processor.

Another, practically unsolved area of the linguistic processor is paraphrasing. In order to make a decision that the sentence "13 soldiers lost their lives" has the same meaning as the sentence "part of the army was killed", the paraphrasing system must have powerful semantic analysis tools that practically do not exist today.

Another task that adds problems of semantic generalization to the difficulties of paraphrasing is automatic summarization. The system of automatic summarization, which receives text information on the existing financial problems in Portugal, Greek debt obligations and Italian debt, at the output should conclude that all this is like the European debt crisis. Currently, there are still only quasi-referencing systems on the market, using mostly statistical-positional approaches, and there are practically no algorithms for "true" semantic generalization.

The greatest complexity and the least number of solutions are dialogue systems that can answer questions and interpret the existing situation. These are systems for which only primary variants of algorithms exist.

The analysis shows that despite the fact that work towards automation of NLP has been going on for more than 50 years and intensified in recent years, when huge full-text information arrays have been accumulated, and linguistic technologies are moving from the means involved in the development of formal language models into a production factor, at the moment it is possible to distinguish a clearly defined class linguistic processor applications that are not solved or only partially solved (for narrow subject areas).

Two main (fundamental) reasons for the inability to quickly solve the problem of automatic processing of natural language texts can be distinguished:

- task of developing a linguistic processor relates to complex problems related to uncertainty;
- almost all existing problems of text processing today are associated with the problem of semantic analysis and the need to formalize an understanding of the meaning of text semi-structured information.

Uncertainty or ambiguity in text processing can be identified at the grapheme, morphological, syntactic, and semantic levels of the language system.

For example, the selection of lexemes at the stage of grapheme text analysis, taking into account the hyphen, can have two options (Manning et al. 2008):

the	New	York-New	Haven	Railroad	or	the	New York	-	New Haven	Railroad

Homonymy is one of the challenges of developing a language processor application. For example, when performing an information search, for a query about "bat care", a double semantics is possible: a bat or a baseball game. A similar problem often manifests itself in machine translation.

Another problem is the presence of idioms in the language and the existence of names of special concepts of subject areas that have a spelling similar to the usual common words of natural language. For example, in biology, gene names consist of words that often look like ordinary English words (F-O-R).

In addition, the complexity of the tasks of the linguistic processor and ambiguity have significantly increased due to the appearance of texts in global information networks. The number of non-standard texts present in user Web content has significantly increased. These are, for example, the presence of lowercase letters, and the use of words that have the same pronunciation, such as 2 and too, to or U and you, as well as the need to analyze neologisms.

To date, to solve problems related to automatic processing of text information, mainly statistical and probabilistic models are used with the addition of some linguistic data, usually morphological and (or) syntactic information (Jurafsky & Martin 2008). So, in machine translation, the approach is used, according to which the French word "maison" is compared to the English word "house" with a fairly high degree of probability, and the word "avocate" is associated with the phrase "the general avocado" with a fairly low degree of probability. This very often does not lead to the right decision.

The main statistical theories and methods used today to solve problems of a linguistic processor (extraction and identification of knowledge, information search, spell checking, text classification, and Opinion Mining):

- Viterbi algorithms;
- naive Bayesian algorithms;
- use of N grams for linguistic modeling;
- statistical parsing;
- inverted index, TF-IDF, vector models.

At the same time, to solve the problems of NLP, it is necessary to have linguistic knowledge about the world and be able to formalize the association of this knowledge. To do this, the tasks related to the development of NLP should be approached from the point of view of system analysis, considering the language as a hierarchical system that is difficult to formalize, in which, in order to formalize the semantics, it is necessary to model the functions of the human intellect for understanding and identifying knowledge in natural language texts.

3.4 The methods of factual knowledge extraction

One of the main applications of NLP is information search, which, based on the results of the issuance, can be divided into a documentary search – this is the process of searching for a document, in arrays of primary or secondary documents, and factual search is the process of finding facts that meet an information request. Fact (from Latin Factum – "made, accomplished") is knowledge, the reliability of which has been proven, in the usual sense of the word – a synonym for the concepts of "truth", "event", and "result". Fact – knowledge in the form of a statement, the reliability of which is strictly established. However, in practice, in the field of information technology, factual information is usually interpreted in a slightly different way – as specific information or data, regardless of whether it is actual or predictable. The main thing is that this information reports on some subject area, and not on documents dedicated to this area.

Factual information can be divided into well-structured and unstructured. Well-structured information (the so-called parametric information) includes, first of all, quantitative information, as well as qualitative (verbally expressed) information that has a well-regulated form: equipment parameters and their values (for example, the dimensions of mechanisms and devices), the name and addresses of organizations and institutions, etc. Usually, this information is drawn up (or can be easily drawn up) as questionnaires, tables, etc.

Unstructured factual information includes information presented by various unregulated verbal constructions given in natural language (Baeza-Yates & Ribeiro-Neto 1999).

Facographic analysis algorithms depend on the degree of structuring of the requested information of a specific document. By the degree of structuring, document data can be divided, similar to the general classification of the degree of formalization of information (see Section 3.1), as follows: tabular data displayed as facts: for example, characteristics of objects, geographic features, etc.; arrays of homogeneous semi-structured text documents, usually describing a specific subject area: bibliographic reference books, geological, botanical or zoological catalogs, etc. Algorithms and methods working with such texts take into account information on the laws of the text structure of this array of homogeneous documents (for example, general syntactic or semantic constructs), as well as on hypertext markup of processed documents (if any) (Baeza-Yates 1996); the third type of documents includes documents of arbitrary semi-structured type.

The main efforts of the developers of fact search engines are aimed precisely at well-structured facts, the extraction of which, obviously, is easier to automate. At the same time, almost all production and economic information circulating in the field of material production and management belongs to this type. This explains the fact that, first of all, the main efforts of the developers were directed at the creation of data retrieval systems that work with such information.

Thus, to extract the facts presented in documents of the first and second types, there are sufficiently reliable algorithms. The problem of extracting facts from arbitrary natural language texts still does not have any general solution (Baeza-Yates & Ribeiro-Neto 1999). One of the approaches to extracting facts from texts of the third group is to use ontologies or thesauruses of the subject area. With this approach, the existence of any fact is determined within the framework of a given ontology. But this kind of approach, again, limits the analyzed full-text documents to a narrow subject area of ontology.

At proper time, the development of methods and models for extracting factographic information was greatly influenced by a series of conferences on message understanding (MUC), held from 1987 to 1997 with the support of the American DARPA Agency (Defense Advanced Research Projects Agency) and contributing to the ordering of information on factographic search systems.

But it was only in the last few years that systems began to appear that included elements of this kind of search. For example, almost the only Russian search engine in the Commonwealth of Independent States (CIS) in test mode nigma.ru. Its main extraction resource is semi-structured wikipedia.org as the largest database of texts of a similar structure. Ask.com and answers.com (Answers. Asking a question on WikiAnswers) are also factographic search systems. They search documents and most often use a link to the wikipedia.org resource as an answer to more general questions.

Some of the latest developments in fact retrieval are GoogleSquared and WolframAlpha. These systems search for facts with the greatest accuracy. GoogleSquared appeared in 2009 but was closed for further development in September 2011. GoogleSquared collects information based on a user query and presents it as an interactive table. Google squared has databases that describe the associations of objects with features that act as column headers of the table for the requested object.

The WolframAlpha system, like Google squared, provides information structured according to the request. In addition, since this system was developed as a system of any mathematical calculations, it can give an answer to a quantitative request. For example, what is the diameter of the trachea of a child aged 5 years, 42 feet tall, and weighing 45 pounds? And although the main resource of WolframAlpha is wikipedia.org, it can analyze graphic files, tables, and documents (About Wolfram|Alpha's knowledge base covers an immense range of areas).

In the general case, fact retrieval systems work according to the following algorithm:

1 named entities recognition;
2 building template elements;
3 building template links;
4 coreference.

The NER is based on the analysis of proper names existing in the system database and recognized at the grapheme analysis stage. This is justified because the basis of the fact search object is individuals, companies, organizations, and their location.

The second stage – building template elements – is an intelligent development of an array of context-sensitive semantic-syntactic templates of sentences of the type:

<Person> [stolen – VV of passive voice] (Subordinate circumstance) <by the Organization>.

Qualitative construction of template elements involves the definition of possible entity names that may occur in texts under different names. In addition, attributes of dimensions, nationalities, etc., can be included in templates.

The task of constructing template links is aimed at recognizing in the text a set of possible relations between template elements developed at the previous stage. These may be kinship or subordination relationships between individuals, relationships between companies, or geographical names. This stage of identifying relationships between entities is one of the central tasks of extracting knowledge from texts.

The last stage, which is the most difficult task of coreference, that is, the division of meaningful text expressions into classes of semantic equivalence, is practically not solved in modern fact retrieval systems.

A typical modern system using factual search elements includes the phases of parsing the input text into words, lexical and morphological parsing, and some components of basic syntactic analysis for a given subject area. If the system is aimed at recognizing proper names, the phases of syntax and analysis associated with the subject area are optional, but in applications aimed at extracting information about events and relationships between entities, they are almost always present (Smrž & Mrnuštik 2011).

In general, the operation of fact extraction systems based on this technology is characterized by high accuracy based on general and reliable rules, but low completeness, since there are many not implemented in templates, rare and less reliable rules. In addition, such systems continue to focus on highly specialized and well-structured texts.

The development of methods and algorithms for extracting facts from dynamically changing semi-structured text flows, not limited to certain subject areas, requires accurate modeling of human cognitive activity to understand and identify facts, as well as the presence of powerful means of both syntactic and semantic analysis of texts that take into account semantic equivalence and multilingualism.

3.5 Knowledge identification in the semi-structured text

Modern information systems developed to solve various application problems are increasingly based on the use of knowledge bases. According to the European Guide to good Practice in Knowledge Management (European Guide to good Practice in Knowledge Management – Part 1: *Knowledge Management Framework CWA 14924-1*), whatever knowledge presentation model is used (logical, network, production, frame (see Section 3.2), the first and main stage of the knowledge life cycle is the identification of knowledge.

There are two classes of knowledge extraction sources that can be used by intelligent information systems. The first is the knowledge of experts, specialists in this subject area, and the second is text information flows represented by weakly formalized text information that dynamically varies in space and time. Note that the text itself is a universal means of representing, accumulating, and transferring knowledge in human society.

By semi-structured text information, we mean text electronic documents that have a high degree of variability in content that varies depending on the specific situation. These are electronic journals, corporate documents, mailing lists, correspondence, and other Web content of computer networks representing an accessible repository of knowledge.

From the point of view of pragmatics, any knowledge makes sense only when it is identified, that is, recognized, structured, and somehow ordered. By the identification of knowledge of semi-structured text information, we will mean the extraction of knowledge from the texts of the natural language (that is, the totality of information about objects of the subject area and their relationship) and their comparison with some standard, which is an intellectual image of understanding, that is, identification by some essential, general and specific features and properties with some known system class or object.

The first studies on the identification of knowledge in natural language texts took place within the framework of the creation of formalisms for describing the semantics of words in 1963–1966 (Katz & Fodor 1964). Later, Ch. Fillmore and, independently of him, Yu.D. Apresyan propose to use predicative ways of describing the semantics of lexical units in sentences. The principle of using extralinguistic knowledge as a guiding factor in the process of language processing of sentences was developed by Wilks (1975, 1979), and further developed by Schenck, who uses the word as a unit of analysis (Schank 1972). Melchuk proposes one of the most developed models of natural language – the "Meaning-Text" model, in which semantics was considered at the level of a morpheme and a word.

The number of proposed approaches and solutions to the problem of modeling the understanding of NL is constantly growing. At the same time, despite the abundance of currently available works, it is not necessary to talk about removing the problem. None of the proposed methodologies has been implemented in broad and extensible subject areas. The limitations of existing approaches are concentrated mainly around the condition of the subject dependence of automatic text processing systems.

To date, there are quite a few systems of grammatical identification (identification of grammatical paradigmatic relations) of linguistic units of various levels of the language system (Melchuk 2000), and quite a lot of formal models of the semantic classification of document texts, words, less often phrases.

In the commercial text classification systems and search engines of the global Internet presented on the market, statistical probabilistic methods based on linguistic data are used in the vast majority of cases. The main feature of such methods is the availability of a high-quality mathematical model that allows developing relatively simple algorithms: Markov models, Naive Bayesian Method, Fisher's method, distance-based methods, Machine Leaning, etc. The main disadvantage of this approach is the impossibility of taking into account the semantic load of the text of the collection, which often leads to the irrelevance of the identification results. Statistical and probabilistic approaches, although they can be used on various changing software, give a fairly low completeness and accuracy of output, with a high degree of noise (completeness and accuracy for documentation systems below 0.7; for hypertext $\approx$ 0.85).

The semantic methods and models for classifying words and collocations used to automate the construction of ontologies and thesaurus are based on lexical-grammatical, latent-semantic methods, and methods for highlighting semantic words based on Wiki-texts and explanatory dictionaries (Table 3.2).

For the semantic classification of semi-structured text information, mainly association rules, decision trees, neural networks, vector space models (vector space model, VSM) are used, which are used by such global and commercial projects as SearchMonkey (Yahoo), RichSnippets (Google), BingPowerset AskNet (JSC "Intel Service"), RCO (Russian Context Optimizer, Odeon-AST), Integrum Galaktika-ZOOM (Corporation "Galaktika"), Convera (Convera AG Schweiz) (Blondel et al. 2004; Vishal & Lehal 2009).

Table 3.2 Comparative Analysis of Methods of Identification of Linguistic Element

Identification methods	*Linguistic unit*	*Implementation*	*Implementation disadvantages*
Grammatical methods of identification	Word collocation	Grammatical paradigmatic relations	Practically solved tasks
Statistical identification methods			
Markov models, naive Bayes method, Fisher's method, etc.	Word, collocation unmarked text and marked text	Definition of synonyms, construction of thesauruses for specified collections Search portals (Google, Yahoo, Rambler, HotBox, etc.)	High noise level Completeness and accuracy for documentation systems below 0.7, for hypertext ≈ 0.85
Semantic identification methods			
Lexical and grammatical (Highlighting phrase patterns based on corpus texts, using regular expressions), latent-semantic indexing Distance method, highlighting chains of semantically close words based on Wiki texts and explanatory dictionaries	Word, collocation Word	Experimental systems for the development of thesauri (selection of taxa, hyponyms) Global projects SearchMonkey (Yahoo), RichSnippets (Google), BingPowerset.	Only for narrow subject areas requires "manual adjustment"
Associative rules, decision trees, neural networks, the use of thesauruses and ontologies (RDF triplets, measuring similarity of concepts in WordNet), vector semantic models using semantic classes and roles (vector space model, VSM)	Semi-structured text information (source text documents)	Commercial projects: AskNet (JSC "Intel Service"), RCO (Russian Context Optimizer, Odeon-AST), Integrum Galaktika-ZOOM (Corporation "Galaktika"), Convera (Convera AG Schweiz)	the need for Semantic Web (software ontologies); the need for hypertext; the presence of a "manual classification scheme"; each Natural Language requires a separate development

Almost all these projects require "manual adjustment" of the classification scheme for each narrow subject area of analysis (for example, taxonomy development), have a high cost, and do not include (for the most part) Ukrainian and Russian languages.

Another disadvantage of such semantic approaches is the need to develop special methods and algorithms for each specific analyzed natural language. In this regard, the implementation of existing approaches to semantic identification in multilingual systems is very complex and time-consuming work.

Another direction of semantic identification of text and hypertext documents is the use of thesauri and linguistic ontologies of subject areas (RDF triplets, synsets in WordNet). The ideology included in the concept of the Semantic Web, in contrast to statistical approaches, which takes into account the semantic content of texts, does not allow the processing of most texts presented in computer networks, since most of the textual information presented in the form of simple HTML pages or text documents of other formats does not include a semantic description of content in XML, RDF, OWL, etc.

Thus, most of the currently existing models and methods for identifying knowledge of semi-structured text information flows either do not allow automating classification procedures or give a high noise level and low accuracy in their practical implementation (Figure 3.5). This is due to the fact that, until now, the development of systems for automatic processing of texts in natural language took place without the use of semantic analysis or with its minimal use.

The analysis shows that only the use of formalization means based on the semantic proximity of linguistic units of different levels of the language hierarchical system allows to identify and extract knowledge that is actually used in the work of intelligent information systems.

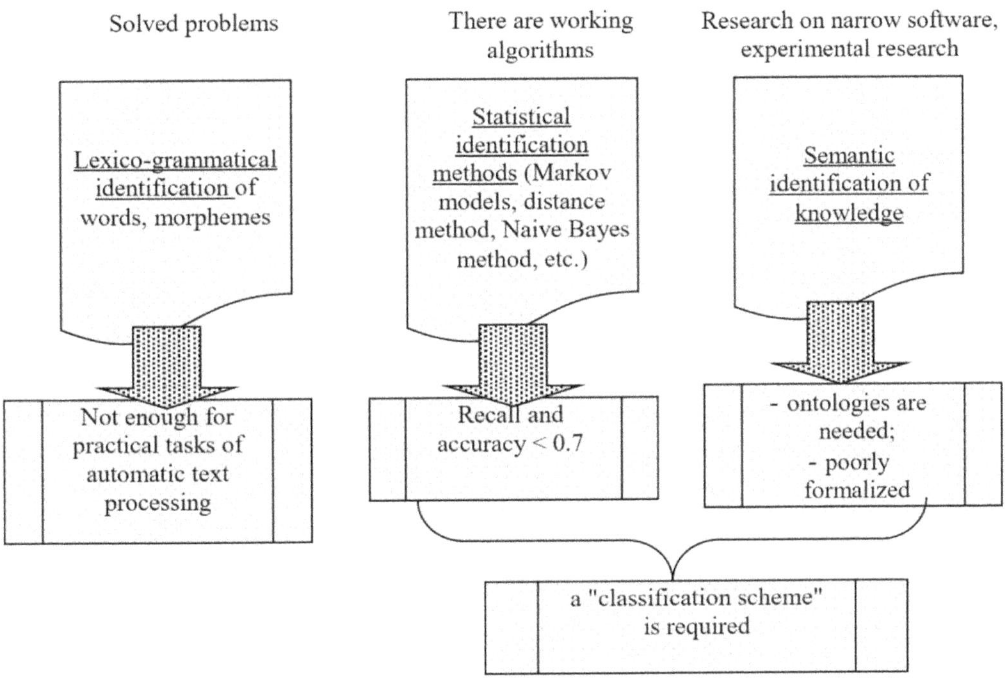

Figure 3.5 Existing approaches to the task of identifying knowledge in semi-structured text.

In addition, the further development of Text Mining methods in the direction of knowledge extraction and identification is constrained not only by the lack of adequate models and methods for semantic analysis, semantic search, and semantic classification but also by the lack of a coherent system of linguistic support. The insufficiency of ontologies and thesauruses of wide subject areas leads to the inability to take into account the peculiarities of the semantic organization of texts even on a specific topic.

The analysis shows that large results and areas of serious applications of intellectualization of models and methods of NLP have not yet been observed: the existing achievements use mainly fairly simple means that provide sometimes useful functions with a minimum of intelligence. More complex tools are used, as a rule, only in experimental systems and in narrow subject areas.

Chapter 4

Concept of information extraction from text

4.1 Natural language as a comprehensive poorly formalized system

Traditionally, linguistics has considered natural language (NL) as a system, meaning an integral entity with properties that are not limited to the properties of interconnected subsystems included in this formation. A language system is a set of language elements of any NL that are in a relationship and related to each other. It forms a certain unity and integrity.

However, the modern development of computational linguistics, associated with the development of natural language processing (NLP) models and methods, shows the necessity and possibility of approaching NL from the point of view of a complex weakly formalizable system. This approach is traditionally used in system analysis when modeling complex technical systems.

A complex system is currently understood as a system, the knowledge (study) of which requires the joint involvement of different types of models, many theories, and in some cases, many scientific disciplines (organization of interdisciplinary research). In order to be able to talk about language as a complex system within the framework of the tasks solved by computational linguistics, we will consider the accepted aspects of the complexity of the system in the application to the NL:

- structural complexity;
- complexity of functioning;
- difficulty in choosing behavior;
- complexity of development.

The structural complexity of the language system has been proven by the current possibility of distinguishing various kinds of structural language subsystems. For example, traditionally structural linguistics considers NL as an interaction of a semiotic system (considering NL as a sign system), a grammatical system (studying grammatical relations – word formation, inflection, syntax), a lexicographic system and a knowledge system (studying concepts and relations between them).

Language, having functional complexity, is a multifunctional phenomenon. Three well-known basic functions of the language are communicative, thought-forming, and cognitive (Jakobson & Verbal Categories 1990), modern linguistics complements cognitive, emotional-expressive, metalinguistic, ideological, and others.

The complexity of behavior and the complexity of development are associated with evolution and progress in the language, subject in their development to the general laws of dialectics. In

DOI: 10.1201/9781003587514-4

connection with the sharp modern development of society, thinking and language reflecting this development are developing intensively. The complexity of language development is expressed, for example, by the dual understanding of this term by modern linguistics: as the transition of a language unit from one state to another (for example, the development of a suffix from an independent word) and as the process of adapting the language to the growing needs of communication. At the same time, reflecting the complexity of behavior, many language changes do not form a constant ascending line associated with the development of the language but have a more complex trajectory. For example, the transformation of Indo-European "e", "o" into "a" in Old Indian, the fall of nasal and reduced vowels in many Slavic languages, the movement of consonants in Germanic languages, etc.

The consideration of language as a system involves the interconnection and mutual agreement of its parts. Many linguists believe that parts of the system are correlated in the form of a hierarchy of levels. Units of each level – phonological, morphological, lexical, syntactic – have a set of inherent properties and qualities that distinguish them from units of other levels, on the one hand, and connect them with units of other levels, on the other.

Considering the language system as complex and poorly formalized, we will speak of NL as a set of language systems structured in the form of a complex semiotic hierarchical system, in which the semantic content of higher-level units is not completely reducible to the semantic content of their constituent units more low-level, that is, the meaning of higher-level units cannot always be "calculated" on the basis of information about the meaning of lower-level units and information about the relationships between these units.

Language is a system of elements of different levels and a set of relations between these elements that form the structure. For the task of automatic processing of textual information, today it makes sense to process only the top five elements of a sign language system: a document, a superphrasal unity, a sentence, a phrase, and a word.

The core of any level of the sign language system is the limit, indivisible units, and the relations connecting them. The paradigmatic relations passing vertically in the language represent all the relations of the division of the upper-level unit into lower-level elements. At each individual language level, paradigmatics is a grouping of units of this level by their differential features. In this case, the paradigmatic relations do not depend on the specific environment of the elements of the system but show the connection or dependence of elements within the system. For example, if the inflectional categories of a language are used as the basis of classification, then the paradigmatic relations of a word form its inflectional forms.

Of particular interest to the tasks of automatic processing of text information, development of applications of a NL processor or systems involving automatic processing of NL texts today are structural models of the levels of the language system using meaningful, that is, thematic or semantic, classification features.

The semantic field of features can be defined as a series of paradigmatically related elements of a sign system of one level (words, phrases, sentences, etc.) that have a common integral semantic feature (semantic relationship with an upper-level element – a text) and differ in at least one differential feature, forming a certain hierarchical structure.

It is proposed to develop a conceptual (semantic) classification of significant units of a language to use a decomposition of the value of a text into semantic components of these units. Since each sign sense element of a language consists of the sense components of the sign elements of a lower hierarchy level, the values assigned to the sign units of the lower hierarchy level will be determined based on their comparison with the value of the entire context of what is said, that is, with the meaning of the associated text of the elements of the upper level of the sign hierarchical system of the language.

We use the well-known example of Yu.D. Apresyan. The sentence: "Each pastry chef knows how to fry brushwood on a gas stove" contains four multi-valued words that have common elements of meaning -semes, which allow them to be combined into semantically correct text. Defining a semantically correct text (document, super-phrasal unity, sentence) as a text to which some meaning can be attributed, that is, it can be interpreted in some model of knowledge about the world (or in some sign system of a higher level of hierarchy). By seme (from the Greek sέma – sign) we mean the minimum limit unit of value.

Thus, in order to determine the semantic paradigmatic relations between linguistic units of different levels of a complex linguistic system, it is necessary to develop a system of conceptual classification of significant units of language using decomposition of the meaning of a text. This decomposition allows us to break down the elements of the text into semantic components of the language units located below at the next level of the hierarchy.

4.2 The identification of the meaning of elements in a complex hierarchical language system

Let's introduce a lexicon, or a set of linguistic units *T*. A language unit is an element of a language system that has various functions and meanings. Sets of basic language units form the "levels" of a complex hierarchical language system (for example, phonemes – phonemic level, morphemes – morphemic level). As defined in Section 4.1, we will consider linguistic semantic units *t*, starting from the sign level of the word and moving to higher levels of the language system, the analysis of which leads to the practical result of NLP.

The space of linguistic semantic units Θ is defined as a set of linguistic units of the lexicon *T*, on which grammatical rules define relations between units that act as restrictions for correct syntactic structures.

To determine the distance $\beta(t',t'')$ between two linguistic units t' and t'', we will use a measure of semantic proximity $f(t',t'')$:

$$\beta(t',t'') = 1/f(t',t'') \tag{1}$$

The measure of semantic proximity *f* is formally defined by relation (2) through the corresponding definitions of the glossaries x_1 and x_2 as the cardinalities of the sets formed by the set-theoretic intersection and union of the sets of definition terms:

$$f(t',t'') = \frac{|X_1 \cap X_2|}{|X_1 \cap X_2|} \tag{2}$$

Here, $X_1 \cap X_2$ are the general terms of the definitions, and $X_1 \cap X_2$ are all the terms of the definitions X_1 and X_2. Under the term in this context, we mean the concept of a glossary in its canonical form.

Since in order to determine the semantic proximity between concepts, we will use several dictionaries in which there are permissible different definitions of the same linguistic semantic units, it is more convenient to rewrite the distances between two linguistic units in the form:

$$f(t',t'') = \frac{\sum_{i=1}^{n_1} \frac{\sum_{j=1}^{n_2} f(x_{1i}, x_{2j})}{n_2}}{n_1} \tag{3}$$

where n_1 is the number of definitions of the first term taken from the processed glossaries; n_2 is the number of definitions of the second term taken from the processed glossaries; x_{1i} is the *i*th definition of the first term; x_{2j} is the *j*th definition of the second term.

Let *d* be a coherent text including linguistic semantic units $t \in \Theta$. The concept of "coherent text" as an object of linguistic science allows for many definitions and interpretations, which are due to the complexity and multidimensionality of approaches to the study of the object. We will understand a coherent text as a complete informational and structural whole, semantically and syntactically uniting a sequence of linguistic units into a single fragment with a semantic connection. A connected text is an integral object of a sign semantic unit of the upper level of a hierarchical language system. A connected text can be represented by a statement (a realized sentence), an inter-phrase unity (a number of statements in a single fragment), a paragraph, a chapter, a section, a document, etc.

The hierarchy of relations between the elements of a coherent text of a multilevel language system is visually represented by the corresponding set-theoretic structure. Let *D* be a graph of a finite set of connected texts $\{D_1, D_2, \ldots, D_m\}$, belonging to the space of the studied connected texts Ω (Jungnickel 2008). Here is the text $D_i \in \Omega$, $i = 1, \ldots, m$. At the same time, the text D_i of a higher level of the hierarchy of the language system can be formally defined through the elements $D_i^j\ (D_i^j \subset D_i, j = 1, 2, \ldots n)$ of the connected text of the previous level of the hierarchy (superphrasal unity is defined through a phrase, the connected text of a document is through superphrasal units, etc.):

$$D_i = \cup_{j=1}^{n} D_i^j;\ \cap_{j=1}^{n} D_1^j = \phi \tag{4}$$

In the considered space Ω, the vertex D_i of the graph *D* will be the parent for the vertices of the set $\{D_i^1, D_i^2, \ldots, D_i^n\}$. Then, the distance between two connected texts can be defined as the length of the path between the corresponding contexts $\alpha^{`}(D_i, D_j)$, determined by the number of mismatched leaves of the vertices D_i and D_j, and the shortest path between two elements of the connected text is defined as follows:

$$\alpha_{\min}(D_i, D_j) = \{\alpha D_i, D_j \text{ such that } \forall \alpha^{`}(D_i, D_j)\alpha^{`}(D_i, D_j) \geq \alpha(D_i, D_j)\} \tag{5}$$

Let $(t, d) \in (\Theta, \Omega)$ be a pair of one linguistic semantic unit and one element of a connected text, where Θ is the space of linguistic units of the considered lexicon *T*, and Ω is the space of the considered connected texts.

If we consider all possible pairs of the Cartesian product $\Theta^*\Omega$, then we can construct a mapping F: $(\Theta^*\Omega) \rightarrow \vartheta$, where ϑ is the space of semantic fields of connected texts. The scheme

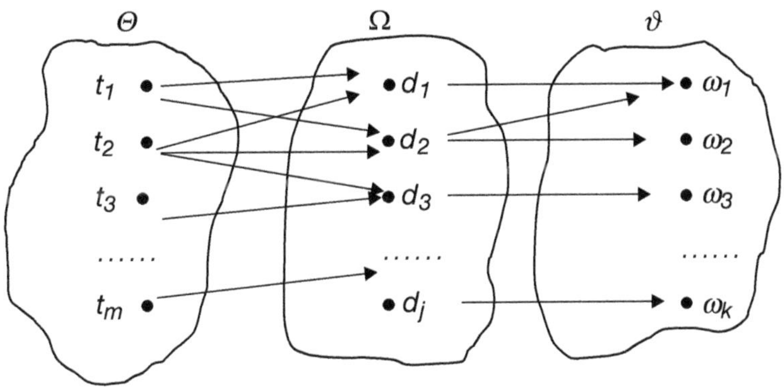

Figure 4.1 Space mapping scheme $(\Theta^*\Omega) \rightarrow \vartheta$.

of the appearance of the space of semantic fields from the considered connected texts and the attracted linguistic semantic units is shown in Figure 4.1.

Thus, by choosing a linguistic semantic unit t and a connected text d, which includes this linguistic unit, we determine the meaning of the connected text element ω through the mapping F.

For example:

F (spring, "I made a spring towards a boat") = jumping by a person.
F (spring, "He was in the spring of his years") = period of a person's life.
F (spring, "I was in my five and twentieth spring") = period of a person's life.

Let us introduce a mapping G such that $G(\Theta^*\Omega) \rightarrow Z$. Here Z is the space of concepts expressed by signs of linguistic semantic units. By uniquely defining the pair *(d, t)*, we attribute one concept to a linguistic semantic unit through the mapping G.

For example:

G ("evening attire may consist of a small black dress", outfit) = clothes;
G ("the team was issued a work order," a work order) = an order;
G ("a detachment was sent to guard the border", detachment) = unit.

The mapping G is a single-valued mapping: for each pair $(d, t) \in (\Omega, \Theta)$ only one concept of a linguistic semantic unit is defined, that is, in a connected text, a linguistic unit expresses only one meaning or one concept.

Let $t \in \Theta$ be the linguistic unit under consideration, and $D_1, D_2, \ldots, D_m$ be the list of analyzed text elements associated with the given linguistic unit. Then, the expression takes place $\forall(t, D_i)\ \exists\,!\, h \in Z \,/\, F^{-1}(t, D_i) = h$.

We will say that two connected texts are contextually related and write $(t', d') \sim (t'', d'')$, unless $G(t', d') = G(t'', d'')$. By contextual connectivity, we mean some commonality in a given context, that is, the display of some single semantic field (some single meaning or theme) in a certain situation of the language environment or speech communication. We will say that two linguistic units are related in one sense (or in one of its significative meanings) and write $(t_i, d_i) \sim (t_j, d_j)$, if only $F(t_i, d_i) = F(t_j, d_j)$.

For example:

F ("application", "the most Internet applications for the Web are XML-applications") = "software";
F ("application", "application for admission to a university") = "application";
F ("software", "using commercial computer-based software") = "software";
F ("application", "the most Internet applications for the Web are XML-applications") = F ("software", "using commercial computer-based software").

It can be shown that the relation ~ established between the linguistic semantic units t and the elements of a connected text d expresses equivalence and factorizes the space of linguistic semantic units Θ and connected texts Ω under study, dividing them into equivalence classes. To do this, it suffices to show that the relation ~ is reflexive, transitive, and symmetric.

The relation $(t_i, d_i) \sim (t_j, d_j)$ is a reflexive relation. One linguistic unit in its one significative meaning is connected with itself because

$$(t_i, d_i) \sim (t_i, d_i) \leftrightarrow F(t_i, d_i) = F(t_i, d_i) \tag{6}$$

The relation $(t_i, d_i) \sim (t_j, d_j)$ is a symmetrical relation: if one linguistic unit in one of its significative meanings is connected with another (in one of its meanings), then the second linguistic unit is connected with the first one in the meanings mentioned above:

$$(t_i, d_i) \sim (t_j, d_j) \leftrightarrow F(t_i, d_i) = F(t_j, d_j) \equiv F(t_j, d_j) = F(t_i, d_i) \leftrightarrow (t_j, d_j) \sim (t_i, d_i) \tag{7}$$

The relation ~ is a transitive relation: if one linguistic unit defines the same significative meaning as the second one and the second linguistic unit has the same significative meaning as the third one, then the first linguistic unit in one of its significative meanings is connected with the third one:

$$(t_i, d_i) \sim (t_j, d_j) u (t_j, d_j) \sim (t_k, d_k) \times F(t_i, d_i) = F(t_j, d_j \text{ and } F(t_j, d_j) = F(t_k, d_k) \Rightarrow F(t_i, d_i) = F(t_k, d_k) \leftrightarrow (t_j, d_j) \sim (t_k, d_k) \tag{8}$$

For example:

("application", "the most Internet applications for the Web are XML-applications") ~ ("software", "using commercial computer-based software") and *("software", "using commercial computer-based software") ~ ("program", "everything done on a computer is done by using a program") ↔ F("application", "the most Internet applications for the Web are XML-applications") = F("software", "using commercial computer-based software") = F("program", "everything done on a computer is done by using a program") = "software".*

This equivalence relation allows organizing various pairs of linguistic units and connected texts, including these units (t, d) into equivalence classes that define the same significative meaning, thereby factoring the space of concepts expressed by signs of linguistic semantic units, $(\Omega, \Theta) \rightarrow Z$.)

$$[(t_j, d_j)] = \{(t_i, d_i) \in (\Omega, \Theta) / (t_i, d_i) \sim (t_j, d_j)\} \equiv \cdot \{(t_j, d_j) \in (\Omega \times \Theta) / F(t_i, d_i) = F(t_j, d_j)\} \tag{9}$$

The equivalence relation ~ makes F a one-to-one mapping in which two linguistic units have the same significative value if they belong to the same class. In each such class, one representative linguistic unit can be distinguished, representing the value from this equivalence class.

4.3 The major categories of the model

The value attributed to the sign units of the lower level of the hierarchy is determined by intellect based on their comparison with the value of the entire context of what is said, that is, with the meaning of the connected text of the elements of the upper level of the sign hierarchical system of the language (see Sections 4.1 and 4.2).

To identify semantic paradigmatic relations of the elements of the five upper levels of the sign language system (coherent text, super-phrasal unity, sentence, phrase, word), we introduce functions of understanding the semantic unit and coherent text. Perceiving the semantic unit t determined by the sign of the language system, intelligence correlates it with a certain concept or concept of ρ, which represents the significative meaning of the semantic linguistic unit. The significative meaning is a reflection of the properties of an object in the human mind, occurring through a sign, according to the definition of *G*. Frege: "A linguistic sign is a material carrier of the concept of an object".

By concept, we will understand the information that the semantic unit t carries about all kinds of denotations, that is, the totality of judgments about any object, expressing its essence and relating it to objects of a certain class according to general and specific characteristics.

We will assume that the concept ρ is uniquely determined by a sign semantic unit. Understanding of the semantic unit by the intellect denotes a component of his thinking, a psychological state that determines the correct perception or interpretation of this sign, that is, the establishment of a connection between the disclosed new properties of the object of knowledge with the already known ones. This is the so-called actual articulation, which involves the allocation of the topic and the rhema of the utterance.

By the topic of utterance of semantic units at any level of the language system, we mean the basis of the utterance, a part of the message already known from the situation or the previous context. Whereas, by the rhema of the utterance, we will understand the core of the utterance, new information about the subject or phenomenon for the sake of which the utterance is built.

We will call the function $\rho = f(t)$ f correspondence of the sign semantic unit t ($t \in T$) to the concept ρ the function of the signification of the semantic unit (conceptualization). Here, T is the set of all sign units of a given level of the language system, which in turn is a unit of the next hierarchical level of the language system. For example, T is a set of words, phrases, document text sentences, full-text database documents, site texts, etc.

Function f describes the process of converting a sign semantic unit (keyword, text, sentence, etc.) into a set of judgments about some denotatum η, that is, converting it into a concept or notion. The denotatum η is understood as a subject or object representing the denoted, knowledge about non-linguistic reality.

If the intellect considered the set of sign semantic units of a given level of the language system T, then the set of all values of the function f, that is, the set of all concepts generated by elements from the set T will be denoted by θ. Thus, the function f maps the set T to the set θ. In this case, the set θ is less than or equal to the set T ($\theta \leq T$). It may turn out that the variety of concepts is less than the variety of signs; then one concept corresponding to one denotation can be

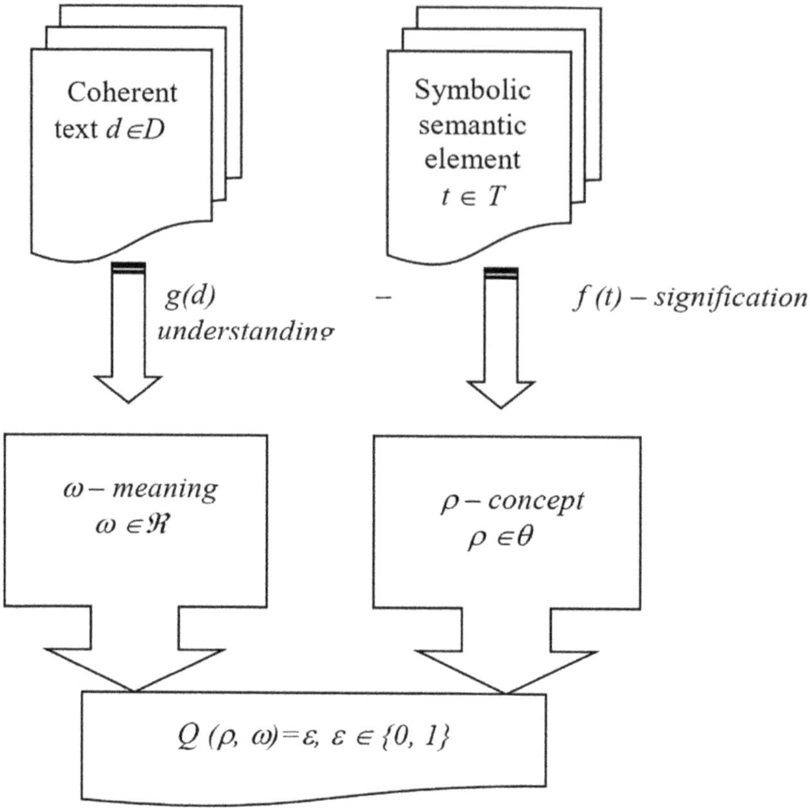

Figure 4.2 Implementation of the comparator identification method in the concept correlation model.

expressed by different signs. For example, in this case, the synonymy of the signs may appear. Two signs are called synonymous (synonyms) if they correspond to one denotation, that is, such elements t_1 and t_2 ($t_1 \in T$ u $t_2 \in T$) are possible that correspond to one concept.

Synonymy of signs can be considered at the level of words and phrases, whereas for sentences, super-phrasal units, or documents defined by us as a coherent text, we can talk about the identity (equivalence) of an insightful understanding of the meaning (Duncker 1936). Further, under the connected text $d(d \in D)$, we will understand the sign semantic unit representing the integral object of the upper level of the hierarchical language system (Figure 4.2). Here, D represents a set of sentences, super-phrasal units, site documents, a full-text database of a linguistic element repository.

Analyzing the content of a coherent text d from the set under consideration and understanding it, the intellect usually forms in its mind some insightful meaning ω, which is the main meaning of the text. According to the definition of the explanatory dictionary: meaning is the ideal content, idea, essence, purpose, ultimate goal (value) of something, the integral content of any statement, which is not reduced to the meanings of its constituent parts and elements, but itself determines these values.

We will assume that the meaning of ω is uniquely determined by the coherent text that generated it. Such a statement is proved by a possible reflection, that is, by the reaction of the intellect to a coherent text (see Section 4.2).

The function $\omega = g(d)$ of the dependence of the meaning of a coherent text on the sign semantic unit that defines it will be called the function of understanding a coherent text. The set of values of the function g, that is, the set of all meanings displayed by connected texts from the set D, will be denoted by R. The function g maps the set D to the set R.

The same insightful meaning can be contained in different connected texts. There are cases when lexically and syntactically different connected texts (sentences, documents, etc.) have the same meaning or contain the same knowledge. We will assume that connected texts d_1 and d_2 are identical in meaning if, as a result of their insightful understanding by the intellect, through understanding the essential relations and structure of the situation, a certain problem is unambiguously solved, or the "subject" of the presentation is determined. In a narrowly specialized sense, the concept of "subject" is defined as the main theme of a coherent text, the identification of which makes it possible to speak about understanding the meaning of a coherent text.

4.4 The model of correlation between a linguistic element sign and its concept

The signification function of a semantic unit $\rho = f(t)$ describes the process of transforming a sign semantic unit t into a set of judgments about some denotation η, that is, converting it into a concept of ρ. The function of understanding a connected text $\omega = g(d)$ shows the dependence of the meaning of a connected text on the symbolic unit that defines it.

Using the intelligent method of comparator identification of objects, it is possible to verify the existence of some semantic (semantic) relation Q, connecting the concept ρ and meaning ω, which shows the presence of some integral semantic feature. If the relation Q is fulfilled or the elements ρ and ω then the relation is assigned the value 1, and if it is not fulfilled, then the value 0 is assigned. Thus, in the process of work, the intellect implements the predicate $\varepsilon = Q(\omega, \rho)$ (Figure 4.2).

The predicate $Q(\rho, \omega)$ characterizes the work of intelligence to distinguish common elements of meaning, common properties mapped by intelligence in signs of the nearest levels of the hierarchy of the language system. The choice of $Q(\rho, \omega)$, $\varepsilon \in \{0, 1\}$ is completely determined by the concept of the sign of the semantic element $\rho = f(t)$ and the meaning of the connected text $\omega = g(d)$. Let's define $Q(\rho, \omega)$ as a conceptual and semantic predicate that implements the work of the intellect in comparing (corresponding) the concept of signification and the meaning of a connected text.

The predicate $P(t, d)$ characterizes the operation of the system that performs intellectual and semantic processing of significant elements of the sign system, which responds to signals t_i and d_j with the answer $\{0,1\}$.

The predicate $L(t_i, d_j)$ implemented on the Cartesian product of sets $T * D$ is called context-signed since it sets the relationship between the signs of the two nearest levels of the hierarchical language system. The set D represents some clearly defined set of connected texts, including elements of the upper level of the language system, to be analyzed.

The set T represents a certain, clearly defined set of sign units of a given level of the language system, allocated a priori by the intellect or extracted by the stages of the linguistic processor. The set of sign units T is included as constituent elements in connected texts of the set of elements of the upper level of the language system D. Therefore, when the intellect perceives a pair of elements (t_i,d_j), it establishes whether the semantic sign unit of the lower level of the hierarchical language system corresponds to the connected text of the upper level of the sign language system, sequentially analyzing all possible pairs of the Cartesian product $T * D$.

If $L(t_i,d_j) = 1$, then this means that the semantic sign unit t_i from the set T uniquely corresponds to the connected text being processed $d_j \in D$. If $L(t_i,d_j) = 0$, then t_i does not correspond to the connected text d_j.

Thus, predicates L and Q, functions f and g, and variables t, d, ρ, ω are related by dependence:

$$L\left(t_i, d_j\right) = Q(\rho,\omega) = Q\left(f\left(t\right), g\left(d\right)\right) = \varepsilon \tag{10}$$

The conceptual model of the task of intellectual identification of semantic paradigmatic relations of language units consists in the basic definition of paradigmatic relations as the relations of entry of lower-level units into upper-level units. The implementation of this model in the language of finite predicate logic allows the transition from subjective relations between the meaning of a connected text (super-phrasal unity, document, etc.) and the concept of the sign of the language system to objective comparison of the sign of the linguistic semantic element and the sign of the upper level of the language system (connected text).

The conceptual sign predicate P under consideration satisfies the existence postulate: the predicate $P(t_i,d_j)$ really exists if and only if, upon repeated iteration of any pair (t, d) of the Cartesian product $T * D$, the intellect will always respond with the same answer as the first time.

Thus, the conceptual sign predicate $P(t_i, d_j)$ reflects the relations between the elements of each pair t_i, d_j:

$$P(t_i, d_j) = \varepsilon, \text{где } t_i \in T, d_j \in D, \varepsilon = \{0,1\} \tag{11}$$

Definition 1. We will say that two sign semantic units t_v and t_w have a common integral semantic feature within the system under study $(t_v, t_w \in T)$ if and only if for $\forall\, d$:

$$P\left(t_v, d\right) = P\left(t_w, d\right) \tag{12}$$

In this case, we can say that two symbolic semantic units are identical in relation to the subject matter of the connected text element, and write $t_v \sim t_w$.

Definition 2. We will say that two connected text units d_v and d_w map a single referent within the studied system $(d_v, d_w \in D)$ if, and only if, for $\forall\, t$:

$$P\left(t, d_v\right) = P\left(t, d_w\right) \tag{13}$$

In this case, we can say that two units of a connected text are identical in relation to the significative meaning of a sign semantic element, and write $d_v \sim d_w$.

Having considered all possible pairs on the Cartesian product $T * D$, we obtain a mapping Ω of the set of the considered sign semantic units T to the set of units of the connected text D. The mapping Ω can be represented as a bipartite graph, the upper set of vertices of which is the set T, the lower set of vertices is the set D. The arcs of this graph will show the truth of the conceptual sign predicate $P(t_i, d_j) = 1$. Inverse mapping Ω^{-1} of the set of units of a connected text D to the set of sign semantic units considered T.

Let us show that the relation $t_v \sim t_w$ is valid if and only if $\Omega(t_v)=\Omega(t_w)$. Assume that $t_v \sim t_w$, but $\Omega(t_v) \neq \Omega(t_w)$. Then, there exists such that $d_k \in \Omega(t_v)$ and $d_k \notin \Omega(t_w)$. But, then $\exists\, d_k$, for which is executed: $P(t_v, d_k)=1$ and $P(t_w, d_k)=0$, that is $\overline{t_v \sim t_w}$. Conversely, $\Omega(t_v) = \Omega(t_w)$ and $\overline{t_v \sim t_w}$. For all $d_k \in \Omega(t)$, we have $P(t_v, d_k) = P(t_w, d_k)=1$, and for all $d_k \notin \Omega(t)$, we have $P(t_v, d_k) = P(t_w, d_k) = 0$, that is $t_v \sim t_w$, which contradicts the statement tasks. Thus, our assumption is proved.

Similarly, it is proved that the relation between units of a connected text $d_v \sim d_w$ is true if and only if $\Omega\,(t_v)^{-1}=\Omega^{-1}(t_w)$.

It can be shown that the identity relation ~ between the connected text units d_v and d_w under consideration is reflexive, symmetric, and transitive.

Statement. The relation $d_v \sim d_w$ between the considered units of connected text is reflexive, symmetric, and transitive.

Proof. Reflexivity – since $\Omega(d_V) = \Omega(d_v)$, then according to the considered lemma $d_v \sim d_v$.

Symmetry. If $d_v \sim d_w$, then according to the lemma $\Omega(t_v)=\Omega(t_w)$. But, this relation has the property of symmetry, that is, if $\Omega(t_v)=\Omega(t_w)$, then $\Omega(t_w)=\Omega(t_v)$. Hence, according to the lemma, it follows that $d_v \sim d_{ww}$.

Transitivity. If $d_v \sim d_w$ and $d_w \sim d_{ww}$, then $d_v \sim d_{ww}$. According to the lemma, from $d_v \sim d_w$ follows $\Omega(d_v)=\Omega(d_w)$, and from $d_w \sim d_{ww}$ follows $\Omega(d_w)=\Omega(d_{ww})$, then we get $\Omega(d_v)=\Omega(d_{ww})$, from which, according to lemma, in turn, follows $d_v \sim d_{ww}$.

Using the inverse mapping Ω^{-1}, we similarly prove that the identity relation $t_v \sim t_w^k$ between the sign semantic units of the language system is reflexive, symmetrical, and transitive.

Itskov et al. (1992) show that, since the relation ~ is reflexive, transitive, and symmetric, it factorizes the sets T and D, splitting them into equivalence classes.

On the Cartesian square $D * D$ of the universe, we introduce the predicate of the correspondence of the elements of a connected text to the significative value of the sign semantic element:

$$G_1\left(d_v, d_w\right) = \forall t \in T\ \left(P\left(d_v, t\right) \sim P\left(d_w, t\right)\right) \tag{14}$$

On the Cartesian square $T * T$ of the universe, we introduce the predicate of integral semantic features of the semantic elements of the hierarchical sign system of the language:

$$G_2\left(t_v, t_w\right) = \forall d \in D\ \left(P\left(t_v, d\right) \sim P\left(t_w^k, d\right)\right) \tag{15}$$

The predicates G_1 and G_2, defined by expressions (14) and (15), are reflexive, transitive, and symmetric, which means that they are equivalence predicates and are uniquely determined by the predicate P.

The predicates $G_1(d_v, d_w)$ (14) can be used to objectively define the mapping in two any elements of the connected text (sentences, super-phrasal unity, documents) d_v and d_w, belonging to set D, of one insight value (i.e., to the mapping of some knowledge in the human mind). If $G_1(d_v, d_w)=1$, then for any sign semantic element t of the set T: $P(d_v, t) = P(d_w, t)$. Thus, if the same semantic linguistic element is included in different elements of a connected text, then in both texts it will have the same significative meaning. Otherwise, if $G_1(d_v, d_W) = 0$, then there is a linguistic semantic element $t_k \in$ T, for which $P(d_V, t_k) \neq P(d_w, t^k)$. In this case, the significative meaning (concept) of the same semantic linguistic unit will be different in different connected texts; therefore, they will belong to different natural-thematic groups.

The predicate $G_2(t_v, t_w)$ (15) can be used to objectively reveal the existence of integral semantic features for any two sign semantic elements of the hierarchical sign system of a language that belongs to the set T. Indeed if $G_2(t_v, t_w)=1$, then $P(t_v, d) = P(t_w, d)$ for any connected text unit $d \in D$. This means that the sign semantic units t_v and t_w are either simultaneously included in the semantic content of units of a higher level or at the same time they are not elements of the semantic content of units of the next level of the hierarchy of the language system. That is, sign semantic units (for example, words or phrases) t_v and t_w either have one or more common integral semantic features or do not have such features.

If $G_2(t_v, t_w) = 0$, then there is an element of the connected text $d \in D$, for which $P(t_v, d) \neq P(t_w, d)$. That is, either the semantic content of a connected text d includes elements of the meaning of the sign language unit t_v and does not include the meaning expressed by the sign semantic unit t_w, or, conversely, the semantic content of a connected text d includes the elements of meaning expressed by the sign language unit t_w and does not include the meaning expressed by sign language unit t_v. In both cases, the sign semantic units t_v and t_w will have different semantic features.

Chapter 5

Relationship between the linguistic formalisms of web content texts and the real essence of the socially significant event

5.1 Generation of structured machine-readable information from unstructured texts

To date, the problem of extracting information and facts from unstructured texts has not been conclusively solved. Existing models and algorithms for fact extraction depend on the degree of structuring of the analyzed document. Similar to the general classification of the degree of information formalization, we can divide textual documents according to the degree of structuring into (1) well-structured texts, often represented by tabular data; (2) semi-structured textual documents describing a particular domain (e.g., patents, references, reports), and (3) unstructured texts of any subject area (e.g., web media texts) (Sint et al. 2009).

Sufficiently reliable algorithms exist to extract facts presented in structured text documents (Crestan & Pantel 2010; Gatterbauer et al. 2007; Wong et al. 2009). At the same time, despite the continuous growth of interest in research focused on finding ways to identify and extract facts from text corpora and web content, at present, there is no general reliable method for extracting structured information from unstructured heterogeneous texts (Phillips & Riloff 2002; Jones et al. 2003). The growing interest in this area of research is primarily due to the huge amount of textual information in corporate and Internet networks, presented in unstructured and semi-structured forms (according to some sources, such information is more than 85%). In addition, the growing interest in text-based identification and fact generation is due to the increasing use of such structured information.

For example, fact extraction from unstructured texts can be a serious additional source for creating ontologies based on web content knowledge. Recent Open IE approaches extract fact as a triplet Subject -> Predicate -> Object, where Object and Subject are usually represented by nouns or nominal phrases, whereas Predicate is mostly expressed by a verb. This approach corresponds to the RDF graph shown in Figure 5.1, which structurally represents some fragment of knowledge.

Today there are two main approaches to extracting information from unstructured texts: IE and Open IE. Both of these approaches allow the processing of a huge volume of texts containing relatively little factual information. At the same time, IE techniques can be seen as a special kind of IR, where a query to a database is formulated in advance. However, the result of IE is structured data describing facts from a set of documents, whereas the result of IR is a set of links to documents matching the query.

The first IE systems were mainly domain-specific and based on knowledge gained through a pre-development process. An example of this approach is one of the first IE systems dealing with Latin American terrorism texts, which used predefined morphosemantic patterns (Etzioni

DOI: 10.1201/9781003587514-5

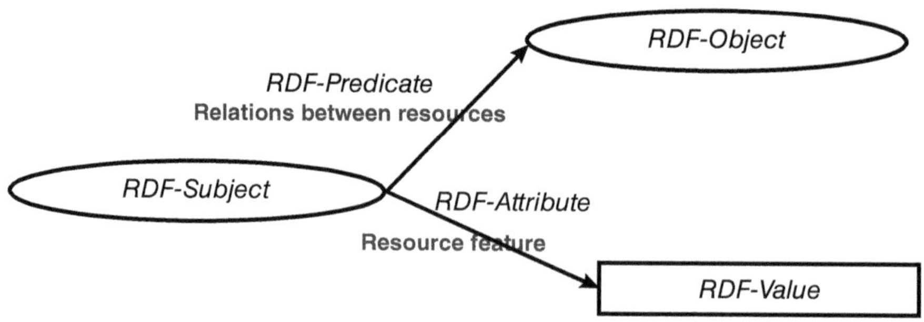

Figure 5.1 RDF triplet representation, corresponding to the concept of fact in Open IE models.

et al. 2008). Modern IE systems also use a predefined set of rules to identify the information that defines a particular fact (Fader et al. 2011). Most IE systems extract and present information in the form of tuples of two objects, with a predefined type of relationship between them (Duc-Thuan & Bagheri 2016) Thus, IE approaches aimed at creating predefined knowledge structures do not allow working with arbitrary web content of unlimited knowledge, where the target relationships cannot be predefined.

IE technologies typically use statistical methods as well as supervised and unsupervised machine learning (ML) techniques (Shinzato & Sekine 2013). Additionally, domain-specific object recognition methods (faces, company names, etc.) are based on traditional Named Entity Recognition (NER) approaches; syntactic parser and semantic tagging are used (Liyuan et al. 2017; Wang et al. 2018).

A new knowledge extraction paradigm, Open IE (Etzioni et al. 2008), introduced in 2007, allows to identify an unlimited number of relationships and is therefore domain-independent. Open IE includes a wide range of tasks: (1) identifying and tracking entities, (2) identifying relationships and attributes of those entities, and (3) defining and characterizing events.

Most Open IE applications include NLP tools such as Part-of-Speech (POS)-tagging as well as dependency parsing (Gamallo et al. 2012; Akbik & Loser 2012). In addition, these applications use lexical restrictions (Fader et al. 2011) or semantic annotations (Angeli et al. 2015) to limit the number of possible specific relationships (Gashteovsk et al. 2017).

The main reasons for the inefficiency of statistical methods in Open IE tasks are the following. First of all, the statistical approach used in IR, classification, or text clustering tasks treats the document as an unordered "bag of words" (Mooney & Bunescu 2005). The knowledge associated with grammar and semantics is largely lost.

The second reason for not using the bag-of-words approach in Open IE tasks is due to the obvious need to extract facts from sentences rather than full text (Nivre et al. 2016). This approach is related to the previously mentioned representation of fact in the form of a triplet: Subject → Relation → Object. In this approach, knowledge about the objects/subjects of the domain, their properties, and relations is a set of information expressed in isolated sentences.

The third reason for the low efficiency of using statistical methods in Open IE tasks is related to synonymy and ambiguity of language units, which leads to hidden facts in the text (Agichtein & Gravano 2000). One such problem is the resolution of co-referencing, where the same entities or actions are represented by different words (sometimes, different parts of speech).

Today the problem of automatic fact extraction is being studied for all languages and has a high level of implementation not only for English texts but also for many others.

For example, there was an experiment (Gamallo & Garcia 2015) for assessing the adequacy of using factual density and informativeness of 50 randomly selected Spanish documents in the CommonCrawl corpus. In a recent study (Khairova et al. 2017), the density of simple and complex facts was considered as characteristic for measuring the quality of articles in the Russian Wikipedia. This paper (Tseng et al. 2014) presented the first Open IE system capable of extracting triplets of facts from arbitrary Chinese texts.

However, despite the results achieved, today there are no multi-lingual standard Open IE methodologies and approaches (Gamallo & Garcia 2015), particularly for languages with limited linguistic resources, such as the Kazakh language.

5.2 Gnoseological aspects of the identification of semantic, lexical, and grammatical benchmarks of criminality

Crime investigation is a dynamic system whose primary function is to effectively counter criminal activity. Such investigation can be considered a type of cognitive activity, which has specific features. Criminal procedural legislation of the Republic of Kazakhstan defines the forms, means, and terms of activity carried out by bodies of pre-trial investigation and inquiry during the investigation of crimes. The content of this activity consists of the processes of detection, recording, seizure, storage, and use of information relevant to the event under investigation and the establishment of the truth in the case. These processes are called informational and form a gnoseological series in cognitive activity: Fact → Reflection → Information → Knowledge.

Terabytes of basic textual information about cognitive activity are stored in Kazakhstan's information networks, being updated daily. All information resources used by law enforcement agencies can be divided into two types: internal and external.

The internal information resources of government and law enforcement agencies are characterized by large arrays of data that are presented in the form of various text files: unstructured data produced in the process of administrative, operative-investigative, investigative, analytical, and other activities.

However, in addition to internal information resources, operational units often need data such as information on conflicts (criminal, economic, political, domestic, religious, family, etc.); data about acts with signs of illegality (illegal industrial and commercial activities, seizure of movable and immovable property); robberies, fraud, fires with signs of arson, mass fights, mass protests, and other violations of public order. Such data is mostly contained in various textual arrays, not pre-defined as the basis of operative investigative activities, and does not represent well-defined criminal information. These can be, for example, social networks, directories, catalogues, and forums, which can contain data on the persons involved in a criminal case and nevertheless have no criminal connotation. They can also be advertisements that contain information on fraudsters and illegal economic activities in the field of production and finance but which are no different from ordinary consumer advertisements.

In general, an external resource consists partially of a set of files similar to an internal resource, but usually in web-based formats. External sources include in particular: the media; data from various institutions, organizations, and enterprises (file cabinets, archives, libraries, electronic files); data from other government agencies; the Internet with all its resources; and corporate networks and social networks.

Thus, a feature of the crime-related event extraction (CREE) is the fact that the criminal meaning of some data sets will only be determined by the metadata set. The metadata set is generated by processing an array of certain crime-related texts and texts of any other domain containing some semantic/lexical or/and grammatical identifiers of criminality.

Therefore, structurally, all information of some interest to law enforcement and other interested public bodies can be represented at two levels:

- the individual organizational unit level, which is defined by a checklist of required information;
- the macro or general level, which includes any information with indications of a criminal environment.

Global intelligence agencies have found that, at the macro level or in open sources of information, a considerable amount of knowledge of interest to government and law enforcement agencies can be contained. However, in order to extract the necessary information from unstructured data and analyze it, it is necessary to have a special toolkit, which is based on a certain information-linguistic technology.

One of the best-known technologies is Text Mining, which is the algorithm-based identification of unknown relationships and correlations in existing textual data. At the same time, currently, available traditional Text Mining approaches [abstracting, machine translation (MT), classification, clustering, dialogue systems, thematic indexing, taxonomy and thesaurus support, creation tools, and keyword searching] do not allow obtaining linguistic markers of crime-related event (CRE).

The analysis of CRE provided in additional external sources of information open to law enforcement agencies should include the following necessary steps:

1 Identification of sources containing crime-related information;
2 Investigating the feasibility of extracting such information and structuring it, based on algorithms tailored to the subject area (software).

Generally, when identifying the part of the general information space of interest to law enforcement agencies, it is primarily necessary to highlight information about a crime or its potentiality. Usually, the formation of a checklist of the necessary information is done from the disposition of the rule of law falling under the jurisdiction of a particular unit. From the point of view of informatics, the disposition is a filter for the objective side of the crime. At the same time, when analyzing textual information found in sources external to law enforcement agencies, it is usually not possible to identify and formalize such a checklist of the necessary information.

Obtaining crime-related data is a non-trivial text-processing procedure, depending on the depth of analysis and the objectives of the specialist or automated analytical system that performs the analysis.

The following existing developments can form the basis of the approach that is being developed for identifying the linguistic markers of CRE:

- text classification using statistical criteria to construct rules for assigning documents to specific categories;
- clustering based on the attributes of the documents carried out without the identification of specific categories and using linguistic and mathematical methods with the possible use of taxonomy and ontology, providing effective coverage of large amounts of data;

- design semantic networks of descriptors (keyword and phrases) of the document during searching;
- fact extraction – extracting facts from text to improve classification, retrieval, and clustering.

In fact, doing these tasks in the presented sequence is the process of comprehending textual information in order to identify new knowledge.

5.3 The method for semantic CRE benchmarks identification in a text corpus

Corpora of criminally related texts should, along with morphological markup, contain elements of semantic annotation. Semantic annotation is important not only for future language research, questions of lexical compatibility, and the development of a semantic dictionary of criminally related terminology but also for highlighting the linguistic identifiers of CRE.

There are several basic approaches to domain-specific semantic text processing:

1 manual (intelligent) assignment of some attributes to an object, and the processing of exactly those attributes;
2 the use of frequency dictionaries;
3 latent semantic analysis (LSA) method.

The first approach, involving much manual (intellectual) labor, can include semantic tagging, manual cataloguing, the use of ontologies, and the concept of Web 3.0. This creates a knowledge base representing RDF triplets, either manually created or automatically derived from processed texts.

The second approach, which allows processing semantics and finding common semantic elements in texts, is based on the use of frequency dictionaries. In order to take into account different sizes/volumes of corpora, the relative frequency of words in a corpus (instances per million words) is usually taken into account. Dictionaries can be created on the basis of existing corpora classified according to different topics. For example, the word "shotgun" may occur many times more frequently in a corpus of news texts related to criminal information than in a corpus of news texts related to economics. However, when it comes to the narrow specialization of a particular domain, the use of dictionaries tends to have a less significant effect.

The third approach uses statistical computing, machine, and deep learning methods, which are based on the hypothesis that closely related words occur in similar contexts, and closely related texts contain semantically similar words. Co-occurrence information can be formally represented as a matrix or as a set of vectors in the multidimensional vector space model (VSM). The vector space model has a number of basic advantages over the standard Boolean model. First of all, VSM is a simple model based on linear algebra; in addition, this approach allows calculating the continuous degree of similarity between terms and documents.

In our study, a vector model of a document describing a trained corpus dataset is used as input to the LSA method. It does not take into account the order of words in the document and their morphological forms but only the number of occurrences of a particular lemma in the text. In this approach, the rows of the term-document matrix correspond to lemmas (where T is the total number of words or lemmas in the corpus) and the columns correspond to the texts of our corpus, where D is the total number of texts or documents.

Such a matrix can be an incidence matrix; its cells contain zeros and ones: 1 if the word is in the document and 0 if the term is not in the document. In a more complex case, the cells of the matrix can contain the number of occurrences of a term in a document, represented by a term weight that takes into account the frequency of use of each term in each document and the occurrence of the term in all documents (Tf-idf). In order to compare the semantics of two documents, the degree of similarity of the two table columns or the cosine similarity of the vectors in the vector model of the document must be determined:

$$Tf - idf\left(t,d,D\right) = tf\left(t,d\right)\times idf\left(t,D\right) \tag{16}$$

where *Tf* is the frequency of the term; *idf* is the inverted frequency of the documents, calculated as the quotient of the number of texts in which the term occurs divided by the total number of texts in the corpus; *t* is the term analyzed; *d* is the text in which the term is found; and *D* is the total number of texts in the corpus.

In our study, we use the positive pointwise mutual information value as the vector value. The pointwise mutual information (PMI) metric has been proposed as a probabilistic measure of how often events *x* and *y* occur simultaneously, compared to how they would occur if they were completely independent. PMI between two events is defined as the probability that the two events occur together, divided by the product of the probabilities of the two independent events, taking the logarithm of that division.

Applying this formula to verify that the context vectors match, we define PMI between the target word *w* and the context word *c* as the logarithm of the probability of the two words appearing together at the same time, divided by the probability of each of the two words appearing separately:

$$\text{PMI}\left(w,c\right) = \log_2 \frac{P\left(w,c\right)}{P\left(w\right)P\left(c\right)} \tag{17}$$

The range of PMI values is from minus infinity to plus infinity. But since negative values indicate that words (target and context) appear together less often than they would appear even if they were completely independent, only positive PMI values are considered, and all negative values are replaced by zero.

$$\text{PPMI}\left(w,c\right) = \begin{cases} \text{PMI}\left(w,c\right), \text{ if PMI}\left(w,c\right) > 0 \\ 0, \text{ otherwise} \end{cases} \tag{18}$$

In order to take into account, the problem of rare words, i.e., words which did not occur in the created corpora and hence the probability of co-occurrence of these words is zero, Laplace smoothing is used. The idea of Laplace smoothing is as follows: we assume that each word appeared in the text two times more than it actually did, i.e., initially when forming the vector, we add two to the frequency of occurrence of each word.

5.4 Semantic similarity of the crime-related colocations

Words describing criminal acts are specific, and they are often the indicative trait by which documents are selected for further analytical processing. A specialist understands words, such as stabbing, signs of violence, gunshot wounds, explosives, drugs, car theft, acquisition of property, arson, theft of money, etc. Sometimes, however, it is interesting to identify less familiar but more effective combinations of words to search for criminally related information, such as "screw hodgepodge". For professional law enforcement officials, both common and professional word combinations evoke associations with a particular type of crime, and therefore, their presence in a text requires at least an in-depth examination of that text.

In this regard, at the first stage of processing the array of criminally related texts, it is necessary to identify the noun phrases or collocations used as objects or characteristics of these objects, which are defined through the mutual informational influence of words in a sentence. Within the semantic-syntactic approach, collocations (stable word combinations) are considered syntactically related, lexically defined elements of grammatical structures, which are characterized by semantic, syntactic, and distributive regularity.

When collocations are extracted, we consider sentences that have syntactically and semantically related words that are close to each other and their position in the sentence. For example, a noun group can only be formed from related words while it is not possible to have a break in the phrase.

When solving the problems of semantic analysis of semi-structured and unstructured texts, we are interested not only in identifying collocations but also in searching for synonymous collocations denoting concepts that are similar in meaning.

Recently, the number of studies related to the semantic similarity of different-level text elements (words, phrases, collocations, short text fragments of different lengths) has been steadily increasing. This is connected, first of all, with expanding the boundaries of using semantically similar text fragments in various NLP applications. The second reason for the growing interest in the identification of semantically similar elements in texts is the daily publication of billions of small text messages in social networks, each consisting of 30–40 words, while the traditional popular algorithms, such as Tf-idf, for example, do not work on texts of such small size (De Boom et al. 2016). For texts of such length, new algorithms, different from statistical algorithms, are often required.

At the same time, there are a sufficient number of methods for searching for semantically related words, but there are no reliable algorithms for identifying semantically related sentences or word combinations (collocations), and this is primarily due to the difficulty of formalizing the meaning of a short text fragment.

Approaches to determining the semantic proximity of short text fragments:

- using a bilingual corpus (Wu & Zhou 2003),
- aligning two sentence fragments to extract small phrases with the same meaning (Pasca & Dienes 2005),
- Using MT to obtain several translations of the same phrase (Barzilay et al. 2001),
- Using LSA (Han et al. 2013) and others.

However, these approaches are not universal for all languages and subject areas and do not yet allow us to obtain sufficiently high rates of accuracy and precision in searching for semantically related collocations in a text.

In our study, we use logical-linguistic equations to search for semantically similar collocations and then distinguish their criminal meaning. The equations are a conjunction of the morphological and semantic characteristics of the words that make up the collocations (Khairova et al. 2018). In order to correctly identify the grammatical characteristics of words in a sentence, Stanford POS-tagger and Stanford Universal Dependencies (UD) parser are used. Additionally, the WordNet synset library is used to find synonyms for words in the extracted collocations.

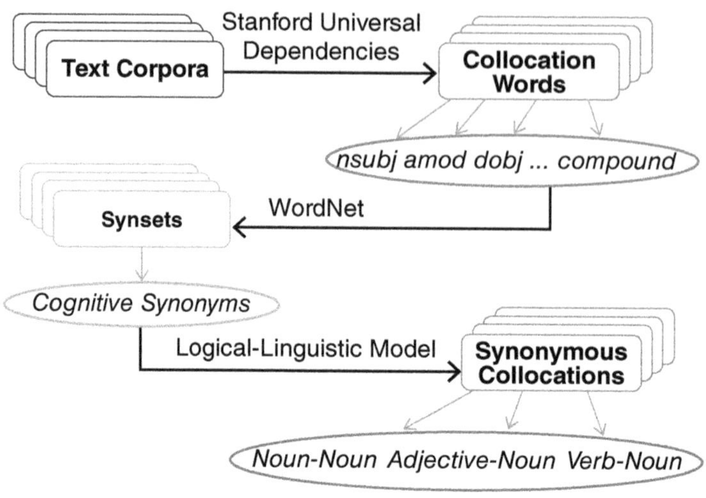

Figure 5.2 Structural diagram of the technology for semantically related collocations searching.

Figure 5.2 shows a block diagram of the technology for searching semantically related collocations, which includes several steps. In the first step, POS tagging and a UD parser are used to mark up the processed texts correctly. The main reason for using the UD parser is that its tree structures correspond to the natural organization of the concepts of the subject, object, clausal phrase, noun determiner, noun modifier, etc. (Nivre et al. 2016). Therefore, the syntactic relations defined by the UD parser between the words in a sentence can express the semantic characteristics of collocations.

We use six types of UD parser syntax labels to identify relationships between two nouns, verb, and noun, and noun and adjective*: compound, nmod, nmod:possobj*, obj (*dobj*), *amod* и *nsubj*.

In the next stage, we use the developed logical-linguistic model (Khairova et al. 2018) to formalize semantically similar text fragments through the conjunction of grammatical and semantic characteristics of collocations. Semantic-grammatical characteristics determine the role of words in substantive, attributive, and verbal collocations.

In the model, the set of grammatical and semantic characteristics of collocation words is defined by two subject variables a^i and c^i. In all three types of collocations, possible grammatical and semantic characteristics for the main collocation word are defined by predicate $P(x)$, and possible grammatical and semantic characteristics for the dependent collocation word are defined by predicate $P(y)$.

The binary predicate $P(x,y)$ describes a binary relation determined on the Cartesian product $P(x)\bullet P(y)$ and defines the correlation of semantic and grammatical information of the first x and second y collocation words:

$$P(x,y)=\left(x^{NSubAg}\vee x^{NSubOfAg}\vee x^{VTr}\right)\left(y^{NObjAtt}\vee y^{NObjPac}\vee y^{AAtt}\vee y^{APr}\right) \quad (19)$$

Using this equation, we define the predicate of semantic equivalence between two two-word collocations as:

$$P(x_1,y_1)\times P(x_2,y_2)=\gamma_i(x_1,y_1,x_2,y_2)*P(x_1,y_1)*P(x_2,y_2) \quad (20)$$

where

× means the semantic similarity of two collocations,

* Cartesian product,

and predicate γ_i excludes collocations between which semantic equivalence cannot be identified. The predicate values for the three main types of collocations are shown in Table 5.1.

In the next step, we use WordNet to extract synonyms for the words included in the specified collocation types. For each collocation type (substantive, attributive, and verbal), a WordNet synset is searched. If a synonymous word is found, the correspondence between the grammatical and semantic characteristics of the collocations for the potential synonymous word combination is checked using the developed logical-linguistic equations. Table 5.2 shows examples of identified synonymous collocations.

Table 5.1 Predicates of Semantic Proximity of Substantive, Attributive, and Verbal Collocations

Collocation type	*Predicate* γ_i	*Example of semantically related word combinations*
Attributive (adjective-noun)	$\gamma_1(x_1,y_1,x_2,y_2) = y_1^{AAtt} x_1^{NSubAg} \wedge$ $\wedge x_2^{NSubAg} y_2^{APr_1}{}^{AAtt}{}_1{}^{NSubAg}$ $\wedge y_2^{AAtt} x_2^{NSubAg} \vee$ $\vee x_1^{NSubAg} y_1^{APr_2}{}^{NSubAg}{}_2{}^{APr}$	*Guaranteed outcome ~ assured result*
Substantive (noun-noun)	$\gamma_2(x_1,y_1,x_2,y_2) = x_1^{NSubOfAg} y_1^{NObjAtt} \wedge$ $\wedge y_2^{NObjAtt} x_2^{NSubAg} \vee$ $x_1^{NSubOfAg} y_1^{NObjAtt} x_2^{NSubOfAg} y_2^{NObjAtt} \vee$ $\vee y_1^{NObjAtt} x_1^{NSubAg} y_2^{NObjAtt} x_2^{NSubAg}$	Access control ~ admission monitoring
Verbal (verb-noun)	$\gamma_3(x_1,y_1,x_2,y_2) = x_1^{VTr} y_1^{NObjPac} \wedge$ $\wedge x_2^{VTr} y_2^{NObjPac}$	Receive commands ~ obtain instructions

Table 5.2 Examples of Synonymous Collocations Found in the Corpus of English Texts

Collocations	*Tags of syntactic relations*	*Synonymous collocations*	*Tags of syntactic relations*	*Collocation types*
History of land	*nmod:of*	*Nation's story*	*nmod:poss*	*Substantive*
Soul power	compound	Ability of person	nmod:of	Substantive
Spectacular progression	amod	Outstanding advance	amod	Attributive
Restoration is incompetent	nsubj:cop	Restitution is incapable	nsubj:cop	Attributive
Qualify place	dobj	Modify position	dobj	Verbal
Preservefire	dobj	Maintain flame	dobj	Verbal

Chapter 6

Logical-linguistic model of fact extraction from a text corpus

6.1 Basic mathematical tools for fact extraction model for unstructured texts

Knowledge about some subject area is a set of information about the objects/subjects of this subject area, their essential properties, binding relationships, and facts describing the actions or properties of these objects/subjects. That is, a particular fact must include a pointer to an action agent, to an attribute or predicate of that object, and give a specific value to that attribute. Such a fact makes it possible to extract concepts from semi-structured textual sources of information and to represent the relationships between them in a structured form. The resulting structure represents facts, both in the form of fairly simple concepts – keywords, personas, organizations, place names – and in a more complex form, such as the name of a persona with its job title and occupation.

In texts with crime-related information, data about the constituent elements of a crime can be presented as semi-structured facts, which semantically unite the subject-area participators and their relationships into a triple *subject-attribute-value (or subject-relation-object)*.

On the basis of the available grammatical types of Kazakh, Russian, and English sentences, we distinguish four types of structured fact (Figure 6.1). The first type, subj-fact, is expressed by a simple grammatical sentence, including an action, called a verb, and a subject of the action called a noun.

The second similar type, *obj-fact*, is also expressed by the simplest smallest grammatical form of a sentence, including a verb and a noun. The noun in this type identifies the object of the action, that is, the object or person to whom the action is directed.

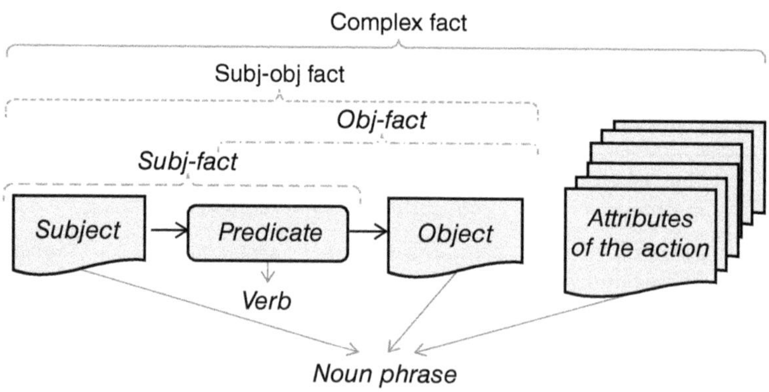

Figure 6.1 Structural diagram of formalizing the four semantic fact types in an unstructured text.

DOI: 10.1201/9781003587514-6

The third type of fact we distinguish, the *subj-obj* fact, is expressed by a simple sentence, including an action (verb) and two nouns (*subject* and *object* of the action).

And the fourth type of fact, *complex fact*, is expressed by a simple sentence consisting of a verb naming an action and several nouns (or personal pronouns). In this case, one of the nouns refers to the subject of the action, the second noun refers to the object of the action, and the remaining nouns define the attributes of the named action. These may be attributes of time, place, instrument, duration of action, and so on.

In general, fact extraction from semi-structured textual information involves the following steps:

- Entity Extraction or Named Entity Recognition – extraction of words or phrases that are important for describing text meaning (lists of subject area terms, personalities, organizations, place names, etc.);
- Feature Association Extraction – examination of relationships between extracted concepts;
- Event and Fact Extraction – extraction of entities, recognition of facts and actions.

The second processing step, which represents the extraction of relations between entities, remains the central and, to date, not fully solved task of obtaining factual information. The semantic case grammar is proposed to identify such semantic relations. For this purpose, a strict model linking the information contained in the definition of semantic roles with the elements of the surface structure of natural language sentences is developed. This approach is considered within the case grammar and is based on the concept of deep cases introduced by Fillmore (1977). Fillmore distinguished a proposition (or the main sense of a sentence), including the predicate, expressed in the surface structure often by a verb, and participators (participants in a given action), expressed more often by nouns or noun groups, which are linked to the predicate by certain deep cases.

Since a semi-structured fact is usually expressed by various unstructured constructions of natural language, in order to identify it, it is necessary to extract some predicate represented by certain verbs and to identify the participators of the relation or action represented by the given predicate from the sentence.

In the proposed model, semantic functions that explicitly define relations between morphological and semantic categories of sentence participators are used to set semantic relations. Such relations of morphological and semantic attributes of the action participants can be described by means of finite predicate algebra (FPA).

In the role of basic FPA elements, we use predicates 0 and 1, and predicates x_i^a of recognizing the element a by a variable $x_i, i = \overline{1, m}, a \in A_i$, where

$$x_i^a = \begin{cases} 1, \text{if } x_i = a, \\ 0, \text{if } x_i \neq a. \end{cases} \quad (21)$$

Disjunction and conjunction of predicates are used as basic operations in the disjunctive-conjunctive algebra of predicates. Any predicate $P(x_1, x_2, ..., x_m)$ in this algebra can be written as a formula in the form of its disjunctive normal form:

$$P(x_1, x_2, ..., x_m) = \vee_{(a_1, a_2, ..., a_m) \in P} x_1^{a_1} x_2^{a_2} \ldots x_m^{a_m}. \quad (22)$$

Using FPA as the basic mathematical apparatus, we introduce the universe of elements U, reflecting the specifics of the given subject area. In the studied SA of semi-structured and unstructured texts, the universum U includes all possible characteristics of language system objects: lexemes, collocations, grammatical, semantic characteristics of words, syntactic characteristics of word combinations and sentences, etc.

A finite subset of grammatical and semantic characteristics of the participators of the sentence $M = \{m_1, \ldots, m_n\}$, where n is the number of the given characteristics is formed from the elements of the universum. The relation between characteristics can be represented as $m_i \bullet m_j \bullet \ldots \bullet m_k$, where $m_i, m_j, \ldots, m_k \in M$ and the sign • – denotes that these characteristics correspond to a noun that performs a particular semantic function.

The set of all n-ary predicates given on the universum U, on which the operations of disjunction, conjunction and negation are defined, is called the algebra of n-ary predicates on U. Thus, the operations of disjunction, conjunction, and negation are basic to the algebra of predicates. The predicate algebra at any value of n is a kind of Boolean algebra; all basic identities of Boolean algebra are fulfilled in it.

A predicate system S is introduced on the set M such that any predicate $P(q_m) \in S$ equals 1 on the set of nouns with grammatical-semantic information corresponding to a particular semantic function, and equals 0 otherwise. A predicate P given on U is any function $\varepsilon = P(x_1, x_2, \ldots, x_n)$, mapping the set U to the set = $\Sigma = \{0,1\}$. The variables $x_1, x_2, \ldots, x_n$ are called subject variables, and their values are subjects.

The multi-d predicate $P(x_1, \ldots X_n)$ defines the semantic role of the action participant through predicate variables of the grammatical and semantic characteristics of the sentence word:

$$P(x_1,\ldots,x_n) \rightarrow P(x_1) \wedge \ldots \wedge P(x_n) \tag{23}$$

Predicate $P(x_1,\ldots,x_n) = 1$, if the word under analysis, performing some semantic function, has certain morphological and semantic characteristics of the language. Obviously, the relations of grammatical characteristics described by the equation are independent from the particular word.

In practice, a subset of the agreed morphological, syntactic, and semantic features of the action participants is not the same as the Cartesian product of the set of all features. On this basis, we can define the predicate on the Cartesian product $S \times S$:

$$P(x_1,\ldots,x_n) = \gamma_k(x_1,\ldots,x_n) \times P_1(x_1) \times \ldots \times P_n(x_n), \tag{24}$$

where $k \in [1, h]$, h – the number of participants and action attributes considered in the model. Predicate $\gamma_k(x_1,\ldots,x_n) = 1$, if the conjunction of grammatical characteristics of sentence words shows some semantic role of participants (*subject, object*) or action attributes; and $\gamma_k(x_1,\ldots,x_n = 0)$ otherwise. Thus, if the relations between grammatical characteristics of sentence words do not express any constitutive element of a fact, they are excluded from formula (24) by the predicate $\gamma_k(x_1,\ldots,x_n)$.

Thus, the semantic functions of participants and action attributes are explicitly expressed by the relation of grammatical characteristics of the surface structure of natural languages. However, due to the existing differences in grammar and sometimes semantics, it is possible for each specific language to have a specific implementation of the model (Khairova et al. 2020a).

Due to the fact that in different natural languages the deep semantic relationships are expressed by different surface features and structures, it is obvious that this logical-linguistic model has to be implemented separately for different natural languages. The number and composition of semantic roles and, consequently, the subject variables allocated in the description of a language may vary significantly in each implementation of the model, depending on the tasks of description, the language and its level of detail.

We consider the implementation of our Open IE logical-linguistic model for English (Khairova et al. 2016), Russian (Khairova et al. 2017), and Kazakh (Khairova et al. 2020b).

6.2 A logical-linguistic model for fact extraction from semi-structured Russian texts

For both Kazakh and Russian, the semantic roles or functions of sentence participants are determined, for the most part, by grammatical cases. To formally define the semantic cases of the Russian language, let us distinguish a quite clearly formed set of semantic-grammatical features, using an irreducible set of three variables:

- X – a feature of animate nature (with values x^{O} – predicate variable describing a semantic feature of animate, $x^{\text{н}}$ – predicate variable describing a semantic feature of inanimate);
- Y – an element of the semantic meaning of a noun ($y^{\text{м}}$ – mechanism, $y^{\text{с}}$ – proper name, $y^{\text{и}}$ – instrument, $y^{\text{ч}}$ – body part, $y^{\text{т}}$ – plane/point, $y^{\text{о}}$ – volumetric space, $y^{\text{в}}$ – definite time, $y^{\text{п}}$ – period, $y^{\text{ц}}$ – destination);
- Z – a grammatical case of a noun ($z^{\text{и}}$, $z^{\text{р}}$, $z^{\text{д}}$, $z^{\text{в}}$, $z^{\text{т}}$, $z^{\text{п}}$ – are predicate variables describing properties of nouns to have one or another grammatical case).

The area of variation of the introduced variables is formally defined as follows:

$$
\begin{aligned}
& x^{\text{О}} \vee x^{\text{Н}} = 1 \\
& z^{\text{и}} \vee z^{\text{Р}} \vee z^{\text{д}} \vee z^{\text{В}} \vee z^{\text{Т}} \vee z^{\text{П}} = 1 \\
& y^{\text{М}} \vee y^{\text{С}} \vee y^{\text{и}} \vee y^{\text{ч}} \vee y^{\text{Т}} \vee y^{\text{О}} \vee y^{\text{В}} \vee y^{\text{П}} \vee y^{\text{ц}} = 1
\end{aligned}
\tag{25}
$$

The semantic function of a noun – the participant of a sentence – is described by the predicate $P(x, y, z) = 1$, linking the semantic meaning elements of the noun x and y with its grammatical meanings z. Then, using the conjunction of predicates, one can write:

$$P(x, y, z) \rightarrow P(x) \bullet P(y) \bullet P(z) \tag{26}$$

where • – conjunction.

Since the possibility of coordinating grammatical and semantic information does not depend on which word form it belongs to, on the Cartesian square of the set $S * S$, we can define a predicate $\gamma\ (x_n, y_n, z_n)$, which takes value 1 if the morphosemantic information of word form n makes some semantic case of the lexeme and value 0 otherwise.

Thus, the relationship of the morphosemantic features of the nouns of a sentence expressing the semantic cases required by the valency of the verb can be given by the formula:

$$P(x_n) * P(y_n) * P(z_n) = g_k(x_n, y_n, z_n)\ P(x_n) \bullet P(y_n) \bullet P(z_n) \tag{27}$$

Almost never a subset of the concordant morphosemantic information expressing semantic cases coincides with the Cartesian product on the set of morphological and semantic features. Those morphosemantic features that do not form a semantic case of the noun in their concordance must be excluded from formula (27) by multipliers $\gamma_k(x_n, y_n, z_n)$, $k \in [1;m]$, where m is the number of semantic cases taken into account in the system. Predicate γ_k takes value 1 if morphosemantic information of word form n makes some semantic the function of the lexeme and value 0 otherwise.

The semantic function *Agent*, representing the *subject* of the action, usually identifies the initiator of the action, the person or object having the potentiality to perform the action, and it is expressed by the predicate:

$$\gamma_A(x_n, y_n, z_n) = x_n^o z_n^u \vee z^{и} x_n^H y_n^M \vee z^{и} x_n^o y_n^c \tag{28}$$

The semantic function *Patient*, defining the *object* on which the action is directly carried out, is expressed by the predicate:

$$\gamma_O(x_n, y_n, z_n) = z^e x_n^H \vee z^e x_n^o \tag{29}$$

The semantic function *Instrument*, which identifies the immediate cause of the action that plays a role in the process, is expressed by the predicate:

$$\gamma_{и}(x_n, y_n, z_n) = z_n^m x_n^H y_n^u \vee z_n^m x_n^H y_{п}^{ч} \tag{30}$$

The semantic function of the *Locative*, which expresses the characteristics of the location, and spatial orientation of an action or state, is expressed by the predicate:

$$\gamma_{д}(x_n, y_n, z_n) = z^{П} x_n{}^H y_n{}^T \vee z^{П} x_n{}^H y_n{}^M \vee z^{П} x_n{}^H y_{п}{}^{ч} \vee z^{П} x_n{}^H y_n{}^O \tag{31}$$

The set of possible connections between the grammatical and semantic information of the semantic case noun *Temporalis* is given by the predicate $\gamma_{Т}(x_{п}, y_{п}, z_{п})$:

$$\gamma_T(x_n, y_n, z_n) = z^B x_n{}^H y_n{}^B \vee z^{П} x_n{}^H y_n{}^{П} \tag{32}$$

The application of this model allows an investigator (or another procedural official) to extract the facts of a particular criminal case from the vast information flows of full-text information processed in the course of operational activities (summaries, explanatory notes/ memos, reports, newspaper and Internet publications, verbal portraits of the persons involved, etc.). In the vast majority of cases, such facts include information on the persons involved in a crime, information on the target of the crime, and information on the mechanism and method of committing the crime.

Thus, the following semantic functions, expressed by the aforementioned predicates, are used when extracting from unstructured textual information the facts of the date, the location of the subject, and the object of some illegal act:

Agent – the semantic function representing the subject of the action, usually the initiator of the action (in our case: the person/subject of the illegal action);

Patient – a function that defines the spheres and products of human activity (in this case: information about the object of encroachment);

Temporalis – a temporal characteristic of an event that allows determining a date (in our case: the date of birth of a person or of some illegal act);

Locative – a function describing the location, position, or state of an object or subject, defines the location (in our example, the birthplace of a person or some criminal event).

Figure 6.2 shows a structural diagram of the identification of a fact related to a criminal event.

Table 6.1 shows the semantic functions corresponding to the facts of the criminal act and personal identification and defines their corresponding predicates (formula (28–32)) that describe the relationship between the morphological and semantic categories of the noun participants of these facts.

6.3 A logical-linguistic model for fact extraction from semi-structured English texts

For the formalization of the semantic functions of English sentences and their explicit representation by means of surface structure, the following syntactic and morphological categories have been identified and described:

$$\begin{aligned}
&z^{to} \vee z^{by} \vee z^{with} \vee z^{about} \vee z^{of} \vee z^{on} \vee z^{at} \vee z^{in} \vee z^{out} = 1 \\
&y^{ap} \vee y^{aps} \vee y^{out} = 1 \\
&x^{f} \vee x^{l} \vee x^{kos} = 1 \\
&m^{is} \vee m^{are} \vee m^{havb} \vee m^{hasb} \vee m^{hadb} \vee m^{was} \vee m^{were} \vee m^{out} = 1 \\
&p^{III} \vee p^{ed} \vee p^{I} \vee p^{ing} \vee p^{II} = 1 \\
&f^{can} \vee f^{may} \vee f^{must} \vee f^{should} \vee f^{could} \vee f^{need} \vee f^{might} \vee f^{would} \vee f^{out} = 1 \\
&n^{not} \vee n^{out} = 1
\end{aligned} \qquad (33)$$

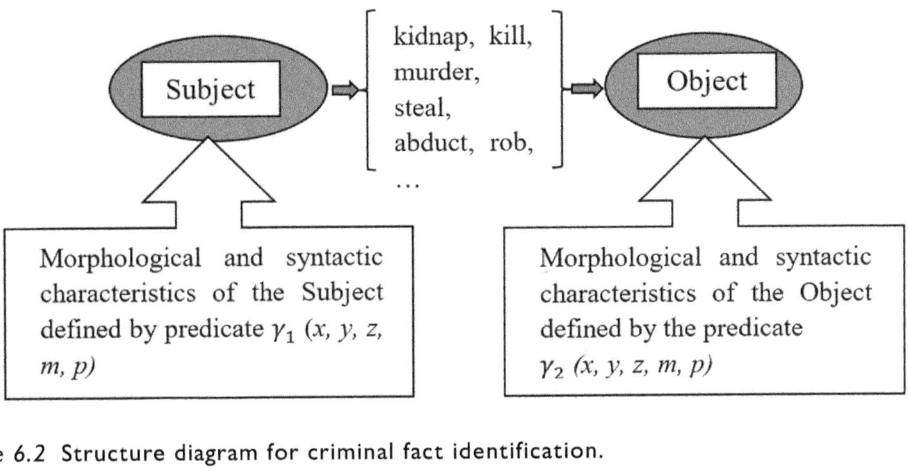

Figure 6.2 Structure diagram for criminal fact identification.

Table 6.1 Formal Structure of the Facts of the Criminal Act and Personal Identification

Action defined by a verb	*Basic semantic functions*	*Predicates that implement semantic functions*
To be born, kidnap, abduct, murder, kill, steal, rob, defraud, cheat, robbery, etc.	Temporalis (*whenacted*) Locative (*whereacted*) Patient (*toactsmth*) Agent (*tobeactedbysmth*) Instrument (*bysmth*)	$\gamma_T(x_n, y_n, z_n)$ – formula 32 $\gamma_Л(x_n, y_n, z_n)$ – formula 31 $\gamma_O(x_n, y_n, z_n)$ – formula 29 $\gamma_A(x_n, y_n, z_n)$ – formula 28 $\gamma_И(x_n, y_n, z_n)$ – formula 30

where the following categories of predicate variables have been used:

- the predicate variable *z* characterizes the presence of a preposition to, *by, with, about, of, on, at, in* after the triplet predicate, or its absence – *out*;
- the predicate variable *y* describes the presence or absence of an apostrophe at the end of the word that determines the possessive case of the *subject* of the triplet – *ap, aps, out*;
- the predicate variable *x* characterizes the location of the noun defining the entity: before a personal verb – *f*, after a personal verb – *l*, or after an indirect complement – *kos*;
- the predicate variable *m* characterizes the presence of any form of the verb *to be* – *is, are, havb, hasb, hadb, was, were* or its absence *out*;
- the predicate variable *f* characterizes the presence of a modal verb in a simple sentence – *can, may, must, should, could, need, might, would* or its absence – *out*;
- predicate variable *n* characterizes the presence of – *not* or absence – *out* in a negative sentence;
- predicate variable *p* characterizes the form of the main verb of the sentence: the first, second/third and fourth forms of a regular verb – *I, II, III, ing*; and the third form of an irregular main verb – *ed*.

The semantic relations of action participants in the English simple sentence are determined by P_k, predicates, linking the categories of the presence of a preposition after the predicate; the existence of an apostrophe defining a possessive case; the position of the noun in the sentence; the presence of negation; the presence of a modal verb; and presence of the verb *to be* and the main verb form:

$$P\left(x, y, z, m, p, n, f\right) \rightarrow P\left(x\right) \wedge P\left(y\right) \wedge P\left(z\right) \wedge P\left(m\right) \wedge P\left(p\right) \wedge P\left(n\right) \wedge P\left(f\right) \tag{34}$$

We can write predicates P_k (x, y, z, m, p, n, f), explicitly defining the relations of the predicate variables $x, y, z, m, p, n,$ and f for each semantic function:

$$\begin{aligned} P_k\left(x, y, z, m, p, n, f\right) &= \gamma_k(x, y, z, m, p, n, f) \wedge P\left(x\right) \wedge P\left(y\right) \wedge P\left(z\right) \wedge P\left(m\right) \wedge \\ &\wedge P\left(p\right) \wedge P\left(n\right) \wedge P\left(f\right) \end{aligned} \tag{35}$$

where the predicate γ_k (x, y, z, m, p, n, f) takes the value 1 or 0.

Almost never a subset of the concordant grammatical and semantic categories of a word, which is an element of a fact coincides with the Cartesian product on the set of features. Grammatical categories that in their conjunction do not form semantic relations of triplet concepts, and, consequently, semantic cases of a participant of some fact, are excluded from formula (35) by the multiplier γ_k (x, y, z, m, p, n, f), $k \in [1; h]$, where *h* is the number of action participants taken into account in the system of types of semantic cases or semantic functions.

According to the resulting model of fact extraction from English sentences; the semantic relation determining the subject of action in fact types such as *subj-fact, subj-obj fact*, and *complex fact* can be explicitly defined through the following logical-linguistic equation:

$$\begin{aligned} \gamma_1\left(z, y, x, m, p, f, n\right) = y^{out} \\ \left(f^{can} \vee f^{may} \vee f^{must} \vee f^{should} \vee f^{could} \vee f^{need} \vee f^{might} \vee f^{would} \vee f^{out}\right) \\ \left(n^{not} \vee n^{out}\right)\left(p^{I} \vee p^{ed} \vee p^{III}\right) x^{f} m^{out} \vee \\ \left(x^{I}\left(m^{is} \vee m^{are} \vee m^{havb} \vee m^{hasb} \vee m^{hadb} \vee m^{was} \vee m^{were} \vee m^{be} \vee m^{out}\right) z^{by}\right) \end{aligned} \tag{36}$$

The *object of action* is the second most important argument of the verb (action) after the *subject of action*. We define the grammatical characteristics of the *object of action* in *obj-fact, subj-obj fact*, and *complex fact* of English sentences by the following logical-linguistic equation:

$$\begin{aligned}&\gamma_2(z,y,x,m,p,f,n)=\\&y^{out}\left(n^{not}\vee n^{out}\right)\left(f^{can}\vee f^{may}\vee f^{must}\vee f^{should}\vee f^{could}\vee f^{need}\vee f^{might}\vee f^{would}\vee f^{out}\right)\\&\left(z^{out}x^{1}m^{out}\right)\left(p^{I}\vee p^{ed}\vee p^{III}\right)\vee x^{f}\left(z^{out}\vee z^{by}\right)\\&\left(m^{is}\vee m^{are}\vee m^{havb}\vee m^{hasb}\vee m^{hadb}\vee m^{was}\vee m^{were}\vee m^{be}\vee m^{out}\right)\left(p^{ed}\vee p^{III}\right)\end{aligned}\tag{37}$$

Similarly, action attributes, such as time, place, type of action, belonging to *subject* or *object* of action, an instrument of action, and others, are defined using logical-linguistic equations. For example, we can define the semantic function of the time of action as a disjunction of the following grammatical attributes:

$$\begin{aligned}\gamma_3(z,y,x,m,p,f,n)=&\left(z^{on}x^{\text{kos}}y^{out}\vee z^{in}x^{\text{kos}}y^{out}\vee z^{at}x^{\text{kos}}\right)\\&\left(p^{III}\vee p^{ed}\vee p^{I}\vee p^{ing}\vee p^{II}\right)\\&\left(m^{is}\vee m^{are}\vee m^{havb}\vee m^{hasb}\vee m^{hadb}\vee m^{was}\vee m^{were}\vee m^{out}\right)\\&\left(n^{not}\vee n^{out}\right)\\&\left(f^{can}\vee f^{may}\vee f^{must}\vee f^{should}\vee f^{could}\vee f^{need}\vee f^{would}\vee f^{out}\right)\end{aligned}\tag{38}$$

We use both Part-of-Speech (POS)-tagging and syntactic Parser to identify correctly the grammatical and semantic categories of words during the processing of English sentences of a corpus of texts. The choice of Universal Dependencies (UD) parser as the syntactic parser is grounded on its ability to correctly analyze syntactic verb groups, subordinating sentences, and multi-word phrases for a large group of languages. The UD parser represents an extension of the Stanford Dependencies (SD) parser, based on grammatical relations explicitly defined in many linguistic corpora and representing relations clustered around the concepts of a subject, an object, a clausal indirect object, a definition, a noun modifier, etc. (Nivre et al. 2016). The verb is the structural center of the grammar of the syntactic dependency trees and all other words of the sentence directly or indirectly depend on the verb.

Syntactic relations linking words to each other in a sentence and which are defined by the parser often express some semantic content. Similar to the structural scheme of the fact triplet

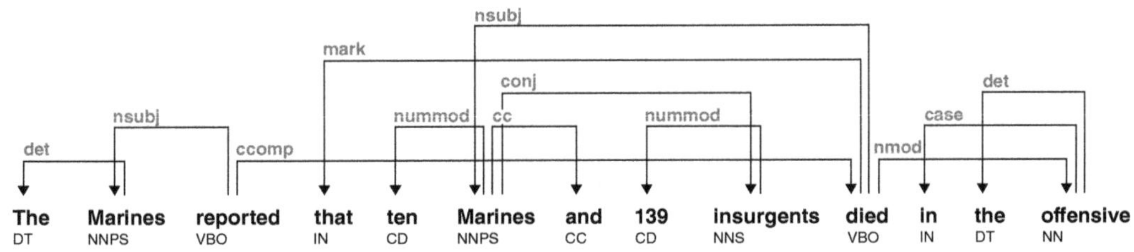

Figure 6.3 Graphical representation of the UD parser for the sentence *The Marines reported that ten Marines and 139 insurgents died in the offensive*, obtained using DependenSee.

(*subject→predicate→object*) in the dependency grammar, the verb is the central element and all participants in the action (participants) depend on it directly or indirectly. For example, Figure 6.3 shows a graphical representation of the UD for the sentence *The Marines reported that ten Marines and 139 insurgents died in the offensive*, obtained using the special UD parser visualization tool, DependenSee.

For our analysis, we use 7 of 40 grammatical relations between words in English sentences, which include UD version 1. For example, in order to identify *subj-fact*, we distinguish three types of dependencies: *nsubj, nsubjpass*, and *csubj*. The label <*nsubj*> shows the syntactic dependency of a *subject* on the verb labeled <*Root*>. The tag <*csubj*> shows the clausal syntactic *subject* of the sentence and the tag <*nsubjpass*> shows the relation between the verb labeled <*Root*> and the *subject* in the English passive voice sentence.

In order to define an *obj_fact* fact we allocate four types of UD parser dependencies: *obj, iobj, dobj*, and *ccomp*. The tag < *obj* > indicates an entity that is affected or whose state is changed or moved. The labels <*iobj*>, <*dobj*>, and <*ccomp*> are used to indicate more precise types of object dependencies on verbs.

Table 6.2 shows an example of the result of the automatic extraction of facts from English texts, based on the developed logical-linguistic model of fact extraction, POS tagging, and UD parser.

6.4 Formalization for grammatical ways of encouragement to act in the English language

There are five main ways to express the same meaning in a short piece of text: (1) using different types of vocabulary for the same meaning; (2) replacing word order; (3) using different types of grammar; (4) replacing text with definitions; (5) combining sentences. The most used is the first method, which is usually implemented through the use of multiple synonyms (synsets).

Thesauri or dictionaries of subject area synonyms are used to determine the identity of facts conveyed by different sentences. For English, the thesaurus of the English conceptual system WordNet is used as a dictionary of synonyms of broad fields of knowledge. Although in the synonymic rows (synsets) of the thesaurus, concepts are linked by various paradigmatic and syntagmatic relations (hypo-hyperonymy, holonymy-meronymy relations, etc.), the basic lexical relation of WordNet is the synonymy relation, and the main logical relation is the hierarchical subordination of words (Pedersen et al. 2004). Moreover, WordNet relationships link concepts rather than words.

Although words often have many synonyms, the synonyms may differ from each other quite significantly in meaning. Consequently, the existence of multiple pairs of synonyms in sentences may lead to a change in the meaning of the fact being expressed, i.e., simply put, a different fact.

The meaning of a fact is most fully retained when the word order in a sentence is changed, or when the grammatical construction is changed. A word order change is the easiest way to express the same meaning (fact) because the words included in the sentence remain unchanged. However, this method is not very easy to apply to English, where the word order in a sentence is rigidly defined by the grammar of the language.

Despite the seeming difficulty of using different grammar to express the same fact, this method seems to be simpler than changing the vocabulary. In addition, changing the grammar rarely changes the meaning of a fact, whereas errors in changing the vocabulary may lead to a distortion of the meaning of a fact.

Table 6.2 A Fragment of the Result of the Automatic Extraction from English Sentences

Sentence №	*Predicate, verb*	*Action subject*	*Type of relations*						*Root*
			nsubj	*iobj*	*Advcl*	*dobj*	*ccomp (object)*	*xcomp (object)*	
1	Consisted	War	nsubj		Fighting				Root
2	Lasted, took	War, majority	nsubj			Place			Root
3	Focused	Insurgents	nsubj		Featured, ambushing				Root
3	Featured	Fighting	nsubj			Warfare			
4	Killed	Iraqis	nsubjpass					Many	Root
5	Saw	Anbar	nsubj			Fighting			Root
6	Occupied	It	nsubjpass						Root
7	Killed	Iraqis	nsubjpass						
7	Began	Violence	nsubj						Root
8	Relinquished	Army	nsubj			Command			Root
10	Occurred	Fighting	nsubj						Root
11	Struggled	Sides	nsubj					Secure	
11	Secure					Valley			
11	Escalated	Violence	nsubj		Struggled				Root
12	Became, turned	Qaeda	nsubj			Capital		Group	Root
13	Issued	Corps	nsubj		Declaring	Report			Root
13	Lost	Province	nsubjpass						
14	Become	What	nsubj					Awakening	
14	Form						Become		

We consider different grammatical constructions of the representation of the same urging fact using lexical synonyms of the expression of the predicate and the participants of the action (*subject* and *object*). The choice to study the fact of the urge to action is based on the wide possibility of using urge-action sentences in criminally related texts.

In our study, we formalize the most common grammatical constructions of urging to action in English, such as the imperative, gerund sentences, sentences with modal verbs, and the passive voice.

To analyze the syntactic structure of a sentence, we used a parser that represents the process of mapping the linear sequence of natural language tokens with its formal grammar. The result is a syntactic parse tree. We use the UD parser of the English language, which is based on the dependencies representing cross-lingual correspondences of the most familiar concepts to the user and the existing standards of annotating.

The resulting formal schemes of grammatical constructions are regular expressions that use POS tagging as an alphabet.

The resulting formal schema of a grammatical model that uses modal verbs will look as follows:

$$TO - VB - [JJ^*] - NN^* - NN \mid NNS1 - MD - VB - [JJ^*] - NN \mid NNS2 \qquad (39)$$

where MD = {should, have to, need to, must, may} a modal verb which is used to express the imperative,

VB – main verb in the first form,

$NN \mid NNS2$ – direct object

$NN \mid NNS1$ = {user, customer, operator, worker, employer, manipulator, handler, manager} – *subject* of an action,

NN^* – indirect object of the infinitive of purpose,

$TO\text{-}VB$ – infinitive of purpose.

Examples of sentences that fit this pattern are shown in Table 6.3.

A formal diagram of a grammatical model of the imperative would be the following expression:

$$\left(V1\ obj\ V_{purpose} object_{purpose}!\right) \qquad (40)$$

where $V1$ – the verb in the first form, which takes first place in the sentence,

obj – a secondary part of a sentence, representing the object to which the action is directed or with which the action is connected,

Table 6.3 Examples of Sentences, Parsed Using the Formal Model (39)

TO-VB	*NN**	*NN|NNS¹*	*MD*	*VB*	*NN|NNS²*
To add	2 pin contact at center of connector	User	Should	Update	Figures and text 95 mm to 25 mm
To reproduce	(No) part of this material	User	Have to	Give	He written permission of the copyright owner
To use	The power cable	User	Must	Switch on	Power and fan module

$V_{purpose}$ – first form verb indicating the infinitive of the purpose,
$object_{purpose}$ – indirect object of the infinitive of purpose.
The sentences presented in Table 6.4 would correspond to this scheme.

In addition to the above ways to urge action, a certain degree of inducement in English can be expressed by the active and passive forms of the gerund sentence.

The formal scheme of a sentence using a gerund is as follows:

$$VBG-\left[JJ*\right]-NN|NNS1-VB-NN|NNS2 \tag{41}$$

where *VBG* – infinitive,
NN | NNS1 – direct object,
VB – the sense verb of the first form (in some cases with the ending s),
NN | NNS2 – indirect object of the infinitive of purpose.
The sentences shown in Table 6.5 will correspond to this scheme.
A formal scheme for a passive voice inducement sentence would look as follows:

$$\left[JJ*\right]-NN|NNS1-VB-VBD|VBN-RP-VBG-\left[JJ*\right]-NN|NNS2 \tag{42}$$

where *NN | NNS1* – indirect object of the infinitive of purpose,
VB-VBD | VBN-RP – a grammatical structure consisting of an auxiliary verb *to be (am, is, are, were, have been)*, a verb in the third irregular form or a verb with the ending *-ed*, and a preposition forming the instrumental case *by* or *with*,
VBG-[JJ]-NN | NNS2* – a gerund grammatical structure that includes a dynamic or derivative verb, with the ending ing.
The sentences shown in Table 6.6 will correspond to this scheme.

Table 6.4 Examples of Sentences, Parsed Using the Formal Model (3.20)

VV	*NN|NNS¹*	*TO-VV*	*NN|NNS²*
Update	Figures and text from 95 mm to 25 mm	To add	2-pin connector contact center
Give	The written permission of the copyright owner	To reproduce	(No) part of this material
Switch on	Power and fan module	To use	The power cable

Table 6.5 Examples of Sentences, Parsed Using the Formal Model (41)

VBG	*NN|NNS¹*	*VB*	*NN|NNS²*
Updating	Figures and text 95 mm to 25 mm	Add	Two pin contact at center of connector
Giving	The written permission of the copyright owner	Reproduce	(No) part of this material
The switching-on	Power and fan module	Use	The power cable

Table 6.6 Examples of Sentences, Parsed Using the Formal Model (42)

NN|NNS[1]	*VB-VBD|VBN*	*RP-VBG*	*NN|NNS*[2]
2 pin contact at center of connector	Is added	With updating	Figures and text 95 mm to 25 mm
No part of this material	May be reproduced	Without giving	The written permission of the copyright owner
The power cable	Is used	With the switching-on	Power and fan module

Chapter 7

The identification of crime-related information in the Kazakh-language text corpora

7.1 Analysis of existing problems in the formalization of the Kazakh language

The Kazakh language belongs to the Kipchak branch of the Turkic group of the Altai language family. Nogai and Karakalpak languages are the closest to it. In total, about 12 million people in the world speak Kazakh, of which 8 million are in Kazakhstan, 2 million in other Commonwealth of Independent States (CIS) countries, and 1.5 million in China. In addition, this language is widespread in Mongolia, Afghanistan, Pakistan, Iran, Turkey, and Germany. Since 1991, Kazakh has been the state language of the Republic of Kazakhstan. If we analyze the Kazakh language from the point of view of the possibility of its formalization and automatic processing, it is possible to distinguish its main features as follows.

First of all, the Kazakh language clearly has a strict word order: the subject is in the first place, then the direct object and the predicate complete the sentence. In addition, the clear order requires that the modifier must come before the noun or pronoun in question and that the time and place must usually come before the subject or before the direct object, but not after the predicate.

Besides, Kazakh is an agglutinative language, where a word usually consists of a stem and a number of morphemes following it, each of which has a specific meaning. For example, *отырғанмын, киындықтарға*.

A special role for factual information extraction is given by the predicate, which indicates the action that is described by a phrase or sentence. In Kazakh, the predicate can be expressed by a verb, noun, adjective, participle, and auxiliary words (*бар*; *жоқ*; *көп*; *керек*, and others). However, in the vast majority of cases, the predicate in Kazakh is expressed by a verb. In connection with the special role of the verb in the representation of the occurring fact in a Kazakh sentence, let us consider the possibility of its formal description more closely.

Verbs in the Kazakh language are characterized by two types of word formation. A verb can be formed: (1) synthetically (by affixation), forming derivative verb stems; (2) analytically, forming compound and complex verbs.

More than 80 verb-forming affixes of Kazakh verbs are determined during synthetic word formation. Along with phonetic variants, their number is about two hundred, and the affixes of the voice are not taken into account. In the syntactic method of verb formation, the first component is responsible for the semantic meaning, and the auxiliary verb completely loses its original lexical meaning and turns into a grammatical format carrier.

DOI: 10.1201/9781003587514-7

In modern Kazakh, there are two groups of verbs generated by the syntactic method of word formation:

- complex verb stems consisting of a name, or sound-simplifying word, plus an auxiliary verb;
- compound verb stems consisting of a verb in a verbal participle form plus an auxiliary verb;
- the developed table of the main word-forming verb affixes allows us to classify them according to the type of formation (Appendix A).

The verb form is a semantic characteristic of the main meaning of a verb. In Kazakh, the verbal form is expressed analytically. The verb form is expressed by a special auxiliary verb, which is combined with the main verb in one of the verbal participles forms.

The perfective form is formed by the combination of the main verb in the form of a participle ending in -n, used with special auxiliary verbs: *бол, бітір, біт, кет, қой, жібер, шық, шығ, сал, таста, қал*. The imperfective verb is formed by the combination of the main verb in the form of a participle ending in –п (-ып, -іп) with special functional auxiliary verbs: *отыр, жат, тұр, жат, жүр, бер* (with participle ending–a [-е, -й]).

Besides, in many cases, auxiliary verbs specify the type of action. The table (Appendix B) shows the auxiliary verbs in the Kazakh language, which give a detailed characteristic of the action.

Another grammatical category of word formation of a Kazakh verb, recognizable by its semantics, morphology, and syntactic functions, is the voice. The voice is formed by adding affixes that express the relationship between the action and the subject or object to the verbal stems. In the Kazakh language, there are five voices divided according to their grammatical formation, semantic meaning, and syntactic functions: the reflexive, passive, reciprocal, causative, and main voices. The first four, however, are formed with affixes (Appendix C).

All other grammatical meanings (mood, tense, person, etc.) are given by the relevant morphological formants (Appendix D).

For example, the conjugation of verbs in Kazakh, as well as in other Turkic languages, is formalized by predicate affixes. That is, any part of speech that acts as a predicate in a sentence may take personal endings that determine the subject of the action. Figure 7.1 shows the structure of verb formation in the personal form. The personal endings of verbs are divided into predicative and possessive. Figure 7.2 shows the scheme of formation of predicative and possessive verb endings.

The Kazakh verb mood includes such grammatical categories as tense, person, and number. In modern Kazakh, there are five moods: imperative, indicative, optative, conditional, and nominative. The infinitive is the most popular mood. It contains grammatical forms of the verb expressing temporal relations. In this case, the category of time is formally expressed morphologically and syntactically. Morphologically, the category of time is formed by adding personal endings to participle and verbal participle forms; in turn, syntactically, the form of time is formed by combining verbal names with appropriate auxiliary verbs.

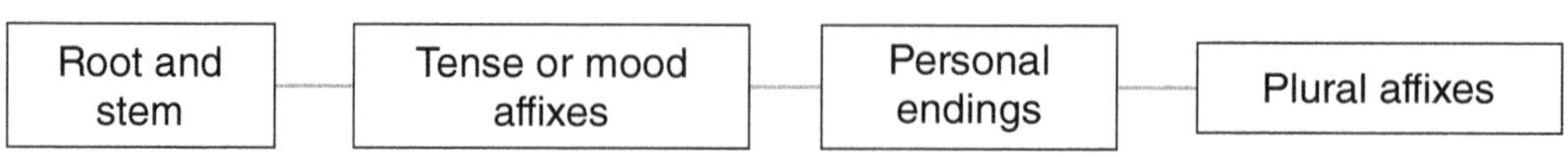

Figure 7.1 Scheme of formation of the personal form of a Kazakh verb.

Personal flexions of verbs

Predicatives are added to:	Possessive affixes are used in:
- Participles; - Verbs with suffix мак (-мек) - Auxiliary verbs in compound forms and form with them the category of time	- The conditional mood; - The recently past tense; - Descriptive form of the optative.

Predictive Personal flexions		
(not added to the recently past (final) tense; conditional forms that take possessive affixes of the 1st and 2nd persons singular and plural) flexions	Person, Number	Examples
-сың , -сыз -сін, -сіз	2, singular.	аласын, аласыз айт-а-сың айт-а-сыз бара-сың келе-сін
-сыңдар, *-сыздар, сіндер, сіздер*	2, plural.	айт-а-сың-дар айт-а-сыз-дар
-мын, -мін, -пын, -пін, -бын, -бін	1, singular.	айт-а-мын быры-мын келе-мін
-мыз (міз, -пыз, -піз, -быз, біз)	1, plural.	айт-а-мыз, бара-мыз
-ды	3, singular.	айт-а-ды
-ды	3, plural.	айт-а-ды
Possessive Personal flexions		
-ң -ңыз –ңіз *-сың, -сің*	2, singular.	сент қайт-са-ң, сіз қайт-са-ң-ыз, ал-а-сың, бер-е-сің
-дар, -сындар, *-сіндер, -сыздар,-сіздер*	2, plural.	сендер қайт-са-ң-дар, сіздер қайт-са-ң-ыз-дар, жина-са-ң-дар
-м	1, singular.	мен қайт-са-м, сана-са-м, терле-се-м
-қ, -к	1, plural.	біз қайт-са-қ, жаз са-қ
	3, singular.	ол қайт-са, барса, келсе
	3, plural.	олар қайт-са, таб-а-ды

Figure 7.2 Scheme of formation of predicative and possessive endings.

To determine the logical-linguistic equation of the formal action in the Kazakh phrase, we are based on the hypothesis that a fact is a real event, an action that really happened or will happen. On this basis, we determine the indicative mood of verbs and do not take into account imperative, optative, and conditional moods that exist in the Kazakh language.

The specific form of the verb *тұйық рай* (indefinite mood) is not an infinitive but acts as the name or the name of the action. It is formed by adding the affix – *у*. to the verb stem. For example, *тапсыр-у*, *шақыр-у*.

The indefinite verb form is lexically closer to nouns – it is not conjugated, but declined, taking possessive affixes: *у-дың*, *-у-ды*, *-у-га*, *-у-дан*, *-у-да*, *-у-мен*, *-у*, *-у-ім*, *-у-ің*, *-у-і*,

-у-і-міз, -у-і-ңіз, -у-дің, -у-ге, -у-ді, -у-де, -у-ден (уы, уым, уымыз, у-ың, у-ы-ңыз). Verbs of the indefinite form make an genitive-possessive construction, requiring a personal pronoun or a noun in the genitive case in front of them.

Many verbs in indefinite form transform into verbal nouns *(жаз-у (письмо), ойла-у* (thinking)). Then, by the word-formation chain, derivative nouns are often formed from verbal names with the help of affix *–шы (жаз-у-шы* (writer), *сайла-у-шы* (voter)).

In the logical-linguistic model that we have created (Section 5.2), nouns, which, in the point of view of semantics, act as subject, object, and attributes of action, have a special meaning. In Kazakh, compared to Russian, the boundaries between parts of speech are slightly blurred: nouns can be modifiers, subjects, direct objects, or predicates in a sentence.

In the syntactic relation of two adjectives, the first is always the modifier of the second noun or pronoun. The noun that acts as the modifier (the first component) may be formed by the affix of the genitive or the affix of belonging. Nouns change by number, case, and person, and they also take possessive affixes. There are two types of declension: simple and possessive. Figure 7.3 shows a structural diagram of the simple declension of nouns.

In the possessive declension, nouns contain an indication of the owner, the belonging of the object to someone/something, which is expressed by attaching affixes of belonging to the word stem. The possessive form indicates both the object of possession and the name of the owner. Table 7.1 shows the peculiarities of affix formation of the possessive case in Kazakh.

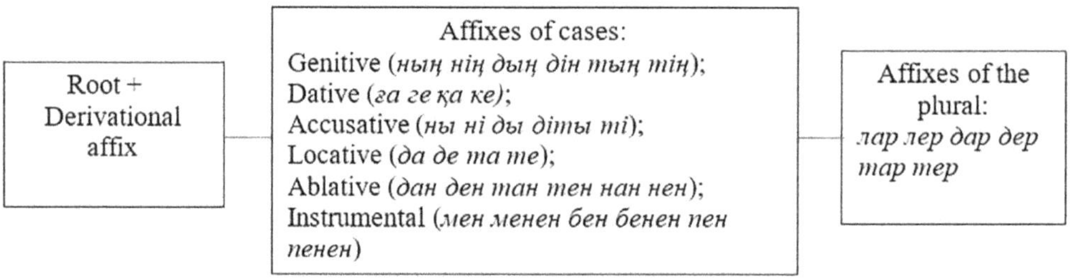

Figure 7.3 Structural diagram of simple noun declension.

Table 7.1 Affix Formation of the Kazakh Possessive Case

The owner's name is in the singular		
Person	*Affix*	*Examples*
1	м, ым, ім	ана-м, ка л ам-ым, д әптер-ім
2	ң, ың, ің	ана-ң, қа л ам-ың, д әптер-ің
3	сы, ы, і, сі	ана-сы, қа л ам-ы, д әптер-і
The name of the owner and the object of possession are in the plural		
1	ымыз, іміз	қа л ам д ар-ымыз, д әптер л ер-іміз
2	ыңыз, ныз, іңіз, ңіз	қа л ам д ар-ыңыз, д әптер л ер-іңіз
3	ы і	қа л ам д ар-ы, д әптер л ер-і

Table 7.2 Case Affixes of Singular and Plural Possessive Declension

Cases	*1 person*	*2 person*	*3 person*
Genitive	ның, нің	ның, нің	ның, нің
Dative	а, е	а, е	на, не
Accusative	ды, ді	ды, ді	н
Locative	да, де	да, де	нда, нде
Ablative	нан, нен	на н, нен	нан, нен
Instrumental	мен, менен	мен, менен	мен, менен

Table 7.2 shows the case affixes of the singular and plural possessive declension of the Kazakh language.

7.2 Implementation of the Open IE model for the Kazakh language

In contrast to Russian or English, Kazakh, as mentioned earlier, is an agglutinative language. This means that a word is constructed of morphemes, each of which has a certain morphological or semantic meaning (see Section 4.1). Such word formation is opposite to the inflective language, where each morpheme has several inseparable meanings simultaneously (e.g., case, gender, number, etc.), and also to the analytic language, in which there are almost no inflections.

Adapting the developed model of fact extraction from semi-structured texts to the Kazakh language, we introduced a rather clearly defined irreducible set M of ten grammatical and semantic features, which affect the semantic role of participators of the Kazakh sentence (Fillmore 1971, 1985). Most of these features are morphological or semantic characteristics expressed with the help of affixes. These are characteristics such as the position of the analyzed word in the phrase; the presence of the auxiliary verb in the phrase; the grammatical case of the analyzed noun; plural and person suffixes; affixes of a predetermined action, and other morphological and semantic characteristics.

A large number of predicate variables in the Kazakh language model is primarily due to the agglutinative nature of this language, where each grammatical feature is expressed by a specific affix, as well as the need to identify not only action participants and their attributes but also the types of actions themselves in the Kazakh language.

The predicate $P_x(x)$ determines the location of the analyzed word in the phrase. The choice of the word location in a sentence is predetermined by the strict word order in the Kazakh phrase, where the subject comes first, then the object, and the predicate closes the sentence, with the modifier always in front of the noun or pronoun in question:

$$P_x\left(x\right) = x^1 \vee x^2 \vee x^3 \vee x^{-1} \vee x^{-2} \vee x^{-3} \vee x^0 \qquad (43)$$

where 1, 2, 3, −1, −2, −3 show the word shift in the phrase, "minus" indicates the beginning of the countdown from the end of the phrase; 0 shows any other word position except the first three and last three words in the sentence.

The predicate $P_f(f)$ determines whether there is an auxiliary verb in the phrase:

$$P_f\left(f\right) = f^{aux} \vee f^0 \qquad (44)$$

where *aux* shows the presence of any verb from the list of 35 auxiliary verbs of the Kazakh language in the analyzed phrase [ал, бар, біт, бітір, бол, ғой, де, деген, дейтін, деп, е, еді, екен, емес, ер, ет, жазда, жат, жатыр, жет, жібер, жүр, кел, келеді, кет, кір, көр, қал, қой, сал, отыр, түс, тұр, шығ, шығар].

The $P_z(z)$ predicate identifies seven grammatical cases of the Kazakh language: nominative, genitive, dative-directive, accusative, locative, instrumental, and ablative:

$$P_z(z) = z^{Nom} \vee z^{Gen} \vee z^{Dat} \vee z^{Acc} \vee z^{Ela} \vee z^{Ins} \vee z^{Abl} \tag{45}$$

where *Nom* – nominative (атау септік); *Gen* – genitive (ілік септік), defined with a list of case affixes [*ның, нің, дың, дің, тың, тің*]; *Dat* – dative (барыс септік) defined with a list of case affixes [*ға, ге, қа, ке, а, е, на, не*]; *Acc* – accusative (табыс септік), defined with a list of case affixes [*ны, н, ні, ды, ді, ты, ті*]; *Loc* – locative (жатыс септік), defined with a list of case affixes [*да, де, нда, нде, та, те*]; *Abl* – ablative (шығыс септік), defined with a list of case affixes [*дан, ден, тан, тен, нан, нен*]; *Ins* – instrumental (көмектес септік), defined with a list of case affixes [мен, менен, бен, бенен, пен, пенен].

Because there are two types of noun declension in Kazakh: simple (without reference to the owner) and possessive (with reference to the owner), we introduce the predicate $P_a(a)$, which defines two possible types of declension of Kazakh nouns:

$$P_a(a) = a^{NSim} \vee a^{NPos} \tag{46}$$

where *NSim* – the noun simple declension, and *NPos* – the noun possessive declension, determined by the presence of affixes [*м, ым, ім, ң, ың,ің, сы, ы, і, сі, ымыз, іміз, ыңыз, ныз, іңіз, ңіз, ы, і*]. The suffixes of the simple declension correspond to the suffixes of the appropriate cases defined by formula (45).

The $P_n(n)$ predicate identifies the specifics of negation in a Kazakh sentence:

$$P_n(n) = n^{me} \vee n^{emes} \vee n^{joq} \vee n^{0} \tag{47}$$

where *me* – the sign of a negative sentence, which is represented by the presence of a particle from the list [*ma, me, ba, be, pa, pe*], *emes* and *joq* – the sign of a negative sentence, which is represented by the presence of *"emes"* and *"joq"* in the sentence, respectively; 0 shows the absence of any sign of negation in the sentence.

The $P_c(c)$ predicate determines the presence or absence of multiple suffixes:

$$P_c(c) = c^{tar} \vee c^{ter} \vee c^{dar} \vee c^{der} \vee c^{lar} \vee c^{ler} \vee c^{0} \tag{48}$$

where 0 indicates that the word is used in the singular, i.e., the word has no plural affix, and the values *tar, ter, dar, der, lar,* and *ler* show the presence of plural affixes *tar, ter, dar, der, lar,* and *ler,* respectively.

The predicate $P_y(y)$ identifies the sign of a word-forming affix of a particular part of speech – verb, participle, and noun:

$$P_y(y) = y^{Parp} \vee y^{Vpas} \vee y^{VaP} \vee y^{UnFu} \vee y^{FuCo} \vee y^{VAd} \vee y^{OAd} \vee y^{Psuf} \vee y^{Usuf} \vee y^{Part} \vee y^{NoV} \vee y^{NoN} \vee y^{VCom} \vee y^{NDer} \vee y^{y} \vee y^{0} \tag{49}$$

where:

- *0* defines the verb stem in its natural form, in the second person singular of the future tense of the imperative when used with the word "you";
- *y* determines the sign of the affix of the infinitive form;
- *Vad, Oad, VaP* – signs of the verbal participles: *Vad* defines signs of verbal participles with the help of the affixes [*п, ып, іп*]; *Oad* defines verbal participles with [*а, е, й, и*], *VaP* defines verbal participles with [*ға, ғалы, ге, гелі, гі, ғы, ке, келі, қа, қалы, қі, қон, қы*];
- *FuCo, UnF* signs of the future indicative tense: *FuCo* determines the list of verb affixes of the future indicative tense [*ар, ер, ыр, ір*], *UnFu* determines affixes of the indefinite future tense [*мақ, мек, пақ, пеқ, бақ, бек, пақшы, мақшы, мекшы, пеқшы, бақшы, бекшы*, пақші, *мақші, мекші, пеқші, бақші, бекші*];
- *Part, ParP* signs of participle word formation: *Part* defines affixes of participle word formation from the list [*ған, ген, қан, кен, қон, ға, ге, қа, ке*], *ParP* defines affixes of participle word formation from the list [*атын, етін, йтын, йтін*];
- *Vpas* defines 20 special word-formation affixes of the verb [*ді, дік, діқ, дім, дің, ды, дык, дық, дым*, дың, қ, *ті, тік*, тім, *тің, ты, тык, тық, тым, тың*];
- *Psuf* determines 189 productive affixes of verb word formation, including voice affixes (Appendix C);
- Usuf identifies 65 unproductive affixes of verb formation [азы, ақта, ал, ала, аңғыра, аура, бала, бе, беле, би, бі, бы, дала, ди, ді, ды, екте, ел, еңгіре, еуре, жи, жіре, жыра, зы, і, ін, ірей, іс, іт, қи, лі, лы, ма, мала, меле, ми, мсіре, мсыра, ңра, ңре, палапеле, пи, пі, пы, ра, ре, си, сіре, сый, сыра, т, ти, ті, ты, усіре, усыра, ши, ші, шы, ы, ын, ыра, ырай, ыс, ыт] (Appendix A);

The four values *NoN, NoV, Ncom, and Nder* of the predicate variable y determine the sign of a token belonging to a noun via lists of specific affixes:

- *NoN* – determines the presence of the affix of noun formation [*гай, гей, гер, ги, гой, дас, дес, дік, дық, кер, кес, қай, қар, қи, қой, қор, лас, лес, лік, лық, ман, паз, пана, сақ, тас, тес, тік, тық, хана, ша, шақ, ше, шек, ші, шік, шы, шық*];
- *NoV* – determines the presence of the affix of the verbal noun formation [*ақ, ба, бе, ғақ, ғаш, гек, гі, гіш, ғы, ғыш, дақ, дек, ек, ік, ім, іс, іш, к, кі, кіш, қ, қаш, қы, қыш, лақ, лек, м, ма, мақ, ме, мек, па, пақ, пе, пек, с, тақ, тек, уік, уық, ш, ық, ым, ыс, ыш*];
- *Ncom* – determines the presence of a compound affix of noun formation [*герлік, гіштік, ғыштық, дастық, дестік, ділік, дылық, кеәтік, қорлық, ластық, лестік, лілік, лылық, паздық, сақтық, сіздік, сыздық, тастық, тестік, тілік, тылық, шақтық, шілдік, шілік, шылдық, шылық*];
- *Nder* – determines the presence of an affix of expressive evaluation (diminutive and derogatory connotations) of noun formation [*жан, ке, қан, сымақ, тай, ш, ша, шақ, ше, шік, шық*].

The $P_d(d)$ predicate determines the presence of subjunctive action:

$$P_d\left(d\right) = d^{shi} \vee d^0 \qquad (50)$$

where the value of the predicate variable *shi* determines the presence of subjunctive suffixes *ші* or *шы* in the analyzed word, and the value 0 determines the absence of subjunctive suffixes.

Predicate $P_m(m)$ determines the presence of a personal predicate or possessive ending of a verb or verbal forms:

$$P_m(m) = m^{PrFl} \vee m^{PoFl} \vee m^0 \tag{51}$$

PrFl (personal predicative flexion) – determines the presence of personal predicate endings of participles, main verbs, and auxiliary verbs [*біз, бін, быз, бын, ды, міз, мін, мыз, мын, піз, пің, пыз, пын, сіз, сіздер, сіндер, сің, сыз, сыздар, сың, сыңдар, ті, ты*];

PoFl (personal possessive flexion) – determines the presence of the personal possessive ending of some verb forms [*дар, йік, йін, йық, йын, іздар, к, қ, м, ндар, ң, ңдер, ңіз, ңіздер, ңыз, сіздер, сің, сіңдер, сыздар, сың, сыңдар, ыздар*];

0 – determines the absence of a verb personal ending.

The predicate $P_b(b)$ determines the presence of some additional semantics or meaning of the verb that is analyzed:

$$P_b(b) = b^{se} \vee b^{mic} \vee b^0 \tag{52}$$

where *mic* shows the presupposition of the action, defined through the presence of suffixes [мыс, міс]; *se* shows the existence of the conditional mood, defined by suffixes [*са, се*].

Table 7.3 presents the predicate variables and their areas of variation that were previously defined in the logical-linguistic model of the Open IE of the Kazakh language.

The resulting equations (43)–(52) allow us to transform the predicate of consistency of grammatical and semantic features of words that are elements of the fact in the Kazakh language to the following form:

$$P() = \gamma_k \times P_x x \times P_y y \times P_z z \times P_f f \times P_m m \times P_n n \times P_a a \times P_b b \times P_c c \times P_d d \tag{53}$$

The predicate of the action initiator or *subject* of the fact is defined by γ_{1K}:

$$\gamma_{1K} = \left(x^1 \vee x^2 \vee x^3\right) z^{Nom} \left(c^{tar} \vee c^{ter} \vee c^{dar} \vee c^{der} \vee c^{lar} \vee c^{ler} \vee c^0\right) \tag{54}$$

The semantic role of the object of the fact in a Kazakh phrase, i.e., the person or object to which the action is directed, is determined by $\gamma 2K$:

$$\gamma_{2K} = \left(x^0 \vee x^2 \vee x^3\right)\left(z^{Gen} \vee Z^{Acc}\right)\left(y^{NoV} \vee y^{NoN} \vee y^{VCom} \vee y^{NDer} \vee y^0\right)| \left(c^{tar} \vee c^{ter} \vee c^{dar} \vee c^{der} \vee c^{lar} \vee c^{ler} \vee c^0\right) a^{NSim} \tag{55}$$

The formalization of the logical-linguistic equation of the predicate in the Kazakh phrase is based on the identification of the fact. According to the "New Encyclopedia of Philosophy", a fact is a real, concrete single event or a result of an action that has happened or will happen. Thus, the equation of the triplet action predicate takes into account only the indicative inclination of the Kazakh language, leaving the imperative, optative, and conditional inclinations beyond the boundaries of the study.

Table 7.3 The Predicate Variables and Their Values Ranges Defined in the Open IE Model for the Kazakh Language

Variables	*Features*	*Values*
x	The location of the analyzed word in a phrase	Shows a word position in a sentence, "minus" means the start of the count from the end of the sentence; 0 shows any other position of the word except the first three and the last three words in the sentence (43)
f	The feature of an auxiliary verb in the phrase	*aux* shows the existence of any of 35 auxiliary verbs of the Kazakh language in the analyzed phrase (44)
z	The grammatical case of the Kazakh noun	*Nom* – nominative, *Gen* – genitive, *Dat* – dative, *Acc* – accusative, *Ela* – local, *Ins* – instrumental, *Abl* – ablative (45)
a	The types of the Kazakh nouns declensions	*NSim* is a simple declension of nouns, *NPos* is a possessive declension of nouns (46)
n	The feature of the negative sentence	*me* and *emes* are signs of a negative sentence, represented by two different lists of words or particles (47)
c	The feature of plural suffixes	*tar, ter, dar, der, lar, ler* show the presence of a plural suffix with the same name in the analyzed word (48)
y	The derivational suffixes for verbs, nouns, participles, adverbials	*UnFu, FuCo* are features of a suffix of uncertain future tense and future conjecture tense in the analyzed word; *Psuf* and *Usuf* are features of one of 189 productive or one of 65 unproductive suffixes from specific lists in the analyzed verb; *NoN, NoV, Ncom, Nder* are features of the noun generation (*NoN* – from a noun, *NoV* – from a verb, *Nder* is a feature of some expression); *Part, ParP* are features of the participle generation by means of two different lists of suffixes; *VaP, Oad, Vad* are features of the verbal participle generation by means of three different lists of suffixes; *Vpas* is a feature of one of 20 verb suffixes in the analyzed word; *y* is a sign of the existence of suffix of the infinitive verb form; 0 is a sign of a verb stem (49)
d	The subjunctive action of the analyzed verb	*shi* shows a suffix of the subjunctive in the analyzed verb and 0 shows a lack of such suffixes (50)
m	A personal predicative or possessive flexion of the analyzed verb and verbal forms	*PrFl/PoF* shows a personal predicative/possessive flexion of analyzed participles, verbal adverbs, main and auxiliary verbs (51)
b	The supplementary semantics of the analyzed action	*mic* denotes the guessed action, *se* denotes the conditional mood and 0 denotes the lack of some supplementary semantics of the analyzed verb (52)

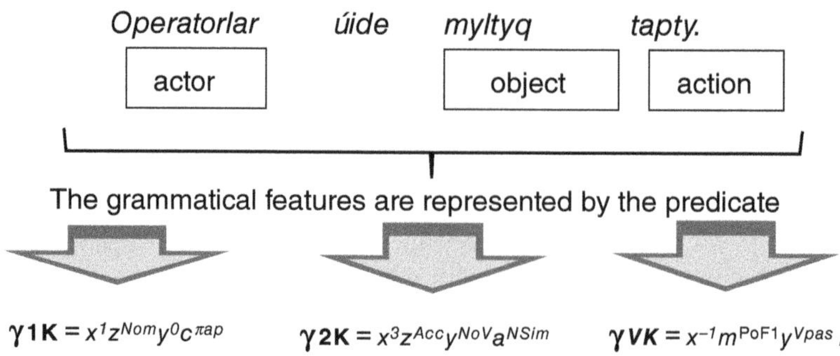

Figure 7.4 An example of fact identification in the Kazakh phrase. The predicate γ_{1K} identifies the grammatical features of the subject; the predicate γ_{2K} identifies the object; and γ_{VK} is the predicate of the fact.

Predicate γ_{VK} defines the combination of semantic and grammatical features of the central part of the fact triplet, namely the action or fact predicate:

$$\gamma_{VK} = \left(x^{-1} \vee x^{-2} \vee x^{-3}\right)\left(f^{tur} \vee f^{otur} \vee f^{jatyr} \vee f^{júr}\right) m^{PrF} z^{Vad} \vee \left(y^{Oad} \vee y^{FuCo}\right)$$
$$m^{PrFl} \vee y^{FuCo}\left(m^{PrFl} \vee \left(m^{PrFl} f^{edi}\right)\right) \vee y^{y}\left(f^{edi} \vee f^{eken}\right) \vee (y^{Vad} m^{PrFl}\left(p^{mic} \vee \left(p^{0}\right)\right) \vee$$
$$(m^{PoFl}\left(\left(y^{Vart} \vee y^{Vpa} \vee y^{Vpas} \vee \left(f^{edi}(n^{joq} \vee n^{emes} \vee n^{me} \vee n^{0}\right) \wedge\right.\right.$$
$$\left.\left.\left(y^{Part} \vee y^{Vad} \vee f^{otur} \vee f^{tur} \vee f^{jatyr} \vee f^{júr} \vee f^{ParP} \vee f^{UnFu}\right)\right)\right) \quad (56)$$

Figure 7.4 shows an example of the implementation of the model for the Kazakh sentence. In the Kazakh phrase «*Операторлар үйде мылтық тапты*», according to the formula (56), the verb «*тапты*» represents an action (long past tense). According to equation (54), the noun «*Операторлар*» is identified as a *subject* of the action or *subject of the fact*. The predicate γ_{2K} (55) identifies the noun «*мылтық*» as the *object* of the fact.

Chapter 8

The Kazakh-Russian parallel corpus of criminal texts

8.1 The problems of parallel corpora creation

Today, linguistic resources are not only an integral part of any linguistic research but also an important basis for the development of any natural language processing application such as machine translation (MT), information retrieval, text summarization, and human-machine dialogue. Such linguistic resources usually include dictionaries, thesauri, linguistic ontologies, monolingual, bilingual, and multilingual corpora. The process of their development includes dictionary research, analysis of the lexical structure of the language, consideration of textual characteristics, and examination of similar studies.

At the same time, one of the most urgent and progressive areas of development of linguistic resources is the design, creation, and development of high-quality text corpora (Rizun & Waloszek 2018). A corpus processed and systematized with the help of a concordancer allows for storing a huge amount of linguistic information essential for statistical analysis; diachronic changes and other research in spoken and written languages.

The existing corpora can be divided into specialized (genre, time, place), general, multilingual, teaching, historical or diachronic, monitoring, and others. The multilingual corpora are, in turn, divided into comparative corpora and parallel or translational corpora. As a rule, parallel corpora remain the most important when studying language and translation features, developing syntactic parsers, speech recognition tasks, etc.

In particular, the concept of parallel corpora is part of a broader and more complex concept such as MT. The quality of MT largely depends on the number of parallel sentences used in training. However, despite the rapid growth of a variety of software and practical applications, MT is still an unsolved task in computational linguistics.

Many bilingual and multilingual corpora have been created over the last decade, among which, from our point of view, the most interesting are: EUROPARL, the corpus of the European Parliament, with 20,000,000 words in 11 languages; CHEMNITZ GERMAN-ENGLISH TRANSLATION CORPUS with 1,000,000 words; KACENKA, the English-Czech corpus with 3,000,000 words; English-French Canadian Hansard, the English-French parallel corpus (Gale & Church 1993).

At the same time, there are quite a lot of linguistic corpora of the Kazakh language, among which the best known are as follows:

The Almaty Corpus of the Kazakh language (ACKL) contains more than 40 million words, 86% of which have grammatical parsing;

- Almaty Corpus of Kazakh;
- Kazakh text corpora on Sketch Engine (Kilgarriff et al. 2014);

DOI: 10.1201/9781003587514-8

- Open-Source-Kazakh-Corpus, created with the help of Wikipedia dump and including a collection of 20 million words (of which 600,000 are unique) (Chapaev & Turapbekov 2018);
- Kazakh Language Corpus (KLC) (Makhambetov et al. 2013).

At the same time, despite the existence of a large number of parallel multilingual corpora, the task of creating parallel corpora for the Kazakh language continues to be quite urgent. This task is considerably more difficult if we are talking about developing a parallel Kazakh-Russian corpus whose input language belongs to the Turkic language family and whose output language belongs to the Indo-European language family.

In order to realize their potential, modern parallel corpora must be aligned. Alignment implies matching certain fragments of the original text with corresponding fragments of the translated text.

Most of the works on parallel corpora distinguish directly or indirectly two levels of alignment: sentence alignment and lexical alignment. Usually, the task of automatic sentence matching, which involves comparing words in the source language with their equivalents in the translation, is very complex and time-consuming, because for many languages, sentences or words may not be matched "one to one". For example, several paragraphs in the source language may correspond to only one paragraph in the target language; also, some words may be deleted or replaced by distant synonyms or strong expressions, which may be completely different for different languages, etc.

We can divide existing sentence alignment methods into three categories. The first category of methods is based on identifying sentence and paragraph lengths (Gale & Church 1993). This approach is based on the hypothesis that sentence lengths in the original and translation are approximately the same.

The second group of alignment methods uses lexical information obtained from corpora (Kay & Roscheisen 1993). The methods of this group are very rarely used, due to the difficulty of accessing bilingual dictionaries and the complexity of automatic morphological analysis used to identify words in texts. Nowadays, most of the programs based on this group of methods use only texts on specialized topics, such as parliamentary speeches and legal texts (Fung & McKeown 1994).

The third group of parallel corpus text alignment algorithms is based on Part-of-Speech (POS)-tagging or morphological labeling contained in annotated corpora (Simard et al. 1992).

However, the implementation of any method from these three groups is associated with a certain amount of inaccuracies, so there is a growing interest in creating systems that use a mixture of all three methods. In particular, describes a hybrid parallel text alignment method combining fragment length dependencies and translation elements (Varga et al. 2007). The study is based on Hungarian, Romanian, and Slovenian.

The authors of the study (Sennrich & Volk 2011) showed that text alignment can be achieved without using additional language-specific resources. They used an alignment algorithm based on sentence length and trained the MT system on texts needing alignment. The MT system was used to translate parallel training corpus resources; alignment was then performed on the resulting automatic translation.

Another sentence alignment approach is described in (Li et al. 2010). In this paper, the authors proposed the Fast-Champollion algorithm for text alignment, which applies a combination of methods based on length and lexicon derived from the dictionary. The algorithm received the epithet "fast" because it optimized the process of dividing the input bilingual text into small alignment fragments. A review of the specialized toolkit InterText, used for parallel corpus alignment, was carried out in Vondricka (2014). The application is based on a hybrid alignment method. The same application was used to create the Kazakh-English corpus in the study (Zhumanov et al. 2017). The authors of the study used the Bitextor tool to generate a corpus based on multilingual websites. They loaded the entire website and applied a set of rules based mainly on HTML text structure and text block lengths (Rakhimova & Zhumanov 2017).

The authors of this paper (Grabar et al. 2018) aligned their texts at the sentence level, using punctuation marks for segmentation. At the same time, the approach needed manual fine-tuning. The Finnish and Russian language corpora based on this approach are aligned quite successfully (Harme 2018).

An additional challenge in creating an aligned binary parallel corpus is the choice of appropriate corpus content. There is now a large number of studies describing the extraction of parallel sentences from non-parallel or comparable information. For example, such information can be obtained using the well-known resource Wikipedia (Smith et al. 2010), which includes similar articles in different languages. Alternatively, such articles can be linked through "interwiki" links annotated on Wikipedia by users. However, the potential for parallel corpora even of such a global resource has not been fully explored to date (Lewoniewski et al. 2016).

Obviously, the problem of creating parallel aligned corpora has not been fully solved and universal alignment methods have not been defined yet. Moreover, it can be said that so far, in most approaches, the choice of alignment method directly depends on the language pair that is under study, the thematic direction, and the type of documents represented in the corpus (Rosen 2005).

8.2 Design of Kazakh-Russian criminal texts corpus

The developed corpus of Kazakh and Russian criminally related texts is a file structure, as shown in Figure 8.1.

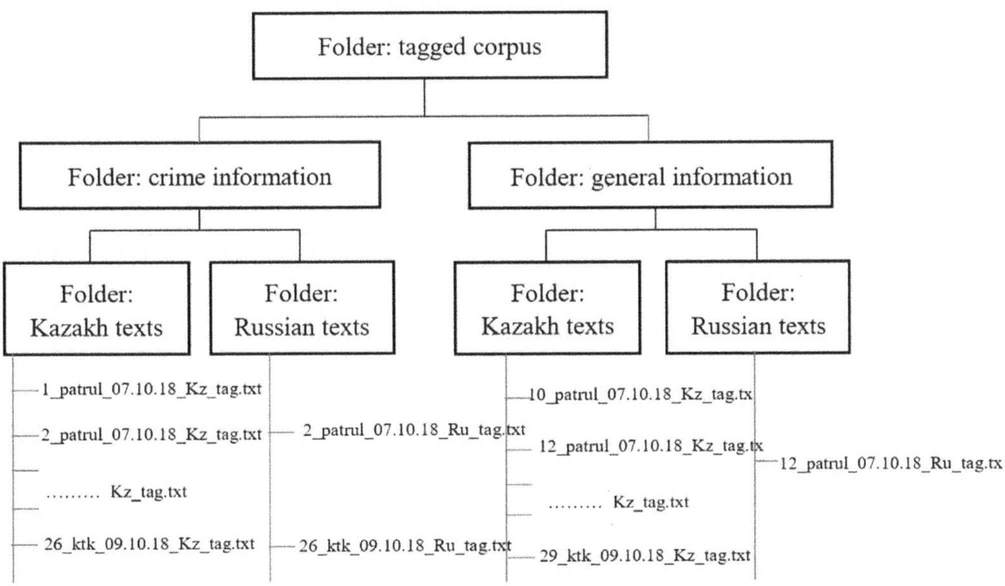

Figure 8.1 The file structure of the Kazakh-Russian crime-related texts corpus.

The name of the text file must correspond to the template:

Number_SourceName_Date_language_tag/row.txt

For example, the labeled text file of the text number 49 in the Kazakh language, obtained on the website of the news agency *Partrul* on September 7, 2018, must have a name: *49_partrul_07.09.18_Kz_tag.txt*

The criteria for the evaluation of a text corpus, in addition to its representativeness and size, are both the labelling system and the correctness of the encoding of the corpus metadata. Labeling is the addition of some extra-linguistic meta-information to a text corpus. This can be morphological (POS-tagging), syntactic, semantic, and other information. We use morphological, semantic, and temporal labeling to create corpora of criminally related information.

Using the manual labeling method increases its accuracy, but at the same time, it is labor-intensive and does not allow you to label large corpora. Conversely, the use of automatic labeling increases the number of errors, reduces accuracy, but allows large corpora to be labeled quickly enough.

In addition, in some cases, it is quite difficult to create algorithms for semantic, stylistic, and some other types of labeling. For this reason, in our study, some information, in particular, POS-tagging can be added to the corpus automatically, while semantic information is added manually. As a result, the percentage of error and multivalued annotation of the developed corpora should not exceed 5%.

The structural labeling of the corpus under development includes the following tags:

- the title of the text is highlighted with a tag:
  <head type=main> заголовок</head>
- if the text has subheadings they are highlighted with tags:
  <head type=h1> заголовок</head>
- the date of publication is highlighted:
  <date> </date>
- the site of the news agency from which the text was taken is highlighted with the tag:
  <site> </site>
- if there is an author, it is labeled with the tag:
  <author> автор < /author>

One of the main steps in the grammatical and semantic tagging of corpus texts is the selection of a set of tags or a set of word categories that will be applied to the tokens (tagset). Tagset represents the set of tags or word categories used for a given grammar tagging task, the choice of which determines the speed and accuracy of automatic processing. During tagset development, the following tag selection criteria must be taken into account:

- *conciseness* – short labels are more convenient than longer and more detailed ones;
- *perspicuity* – labels that are easy to interpret;
- *analysability* – labels should be easy to decompose into logical parts, easily readable by machine processing, and easily understandable by a human.

Based on the aforementioned criteria, the following tags were selected:

- tags *<s type=crim> sentence </s>* highlight sentences that have a criminal connotation;
- tag *<v type=crim> verb </v>* marks verbs that have a criminal meaning;

```
<head type=main> Полицейские Алматинской области изъяли у мужчины более 5 кг наркотиков </head>

<date> 06.10.2018 </date>

<site> patrul.kz</site>

<s type=crim> Задержание <a type=crim> подозреваемого </a> <v type=crim> произведено </v> <n type=crim> полицейскими </n> в ночное время на контрольном посту, действующем на 59 км трассы «Алматы - Бишкек». </s>

<s type=crim> В автомашине мужчины специально <v type=crim> обученная </v> на поиск <n type=crim> наркотиков </n> <a type=crim> служебно-розыскная </a> собака по кличке Таймас < type=crim> обнаружила </v> тайник с <n type=crim> наркотиками </n>. </s>

<s type=crim> «<n type=crim> Тайник </n> был установлен под одним из сидений автомашины Mercedes. </s> <s type=crim> <n type=crim> Полицейскими </n> было <v type=crim> изъято </v> 5 килограмм 360 грамм <n type=crim> гашиша </n>. </s> <s type=crim> <a type=crim> Задержанный </a> мужчина <v> помещен </v> под «<n type=crim> стражу </n> в Жамбылское районное подразделение <n type=crim> полиции </n>. </s>
```

Figure 8.2 Fragment of the labeled corpus file.

- tag *<n type=crim > noun </n>* marks nouns that have a certain criminal meaning;
- tag *<a type=crim > adjective and participle </a>* highlights adjectives and participles that have a certain criminal meaning.

In such a representation, the tag names (element types) *<s>, <v>, <n>, <a>* define the grammatical information of the part of speech and sentence as a syntactic unit. And the values of the attribute *type=crim* determine the semantic information of criminal relations. An example of such tagged text is shown in Figure 8.2.

8.3 Information technology for the Kazakh-Russian criminal texts corpus aligning

The task of creating a parallel corpus involves several stages. The first basic stage requires the use of specialized software tools and techniques to collect the text material of the corpus. In doing so, despite the fact that the Internet contains a huge number of bilingual and multilingual websites, selecting the right bilingual resources is an important part of developing a parallel corpus. This task is becoming more complicated due to the fact that two different languages, such as Kazakh and Russian, are being processed.

Four bilingual websites were selected for the text collecting: *zakon.kz, caravan.kz, kazlenta.kz, and nur.kz* (Khairova et al. 2018a). The selected sites are well-known and reliable portals of the Republic of Kazakhstan, one of the news areas of which is criminal news. The portals may contain news about criminal acts such as robberies, car thefts, murders, traffic accidents, and others. The texts of this very subject area represent the basic resource of the created corpus. In addition, these portals are bilingual and often contain closely related news publications in the Kazakh and Russian languages. As a result of scraping the above sites, 3,000 texts in two languages have been obtained: Russian and Kazakh. For the automatic collection (scraping) of the texts of the sites, we have developed a program that parses sites of a given structure and the required context.

id	head	url	text
3256	Месть за сестру:	https://www.inform.kz/	АЛМАТЫ. КАЗИНФОРМ - В специализи
3257	Чем чаще всего	https://www.inform.kz/	АСТАНА. КАЗИНФОРМ - Депутат Сена
3258	Сенаторы ратиф	https://www.inform.kz/	АСТАНА. КАЗИНФОРМ - Депутаты Сен
3259	115 тысяч кварти	https://www.inform.kz/	АСТАНА. КАЗИНФОРМ - 115 тысяч ква
3260	Сенатор вырази	https://www.inform.kz/	АСТАНА. КАЗИНФОРМ - Депутат Сена
3261	820 камер видео	https://www.inform.kz/	КОКШЕТАУ. КАЗИНФОРМ - 820 камер в
3262	Почему приоста	https://www.inform.kz/	АСТАНА. КАЗИНФОРМ - Вице-минист
3263	Задержан подоз	https://www.inform.kz/	ТУРКЕСТАН. КАЗИНФОРМ - Полицейс
3264	Сенатор рассказ	https://www.inform.kz/	АСТАНА. КАЗИНФОРМ - В Казахстане

Figure 8.3 The file structure of the Kazakh-Russian crime-related texts corpus.

At the next stage, criminally related texts were corrected manually. Thus, a corpus of more than 50,410 words was obtained (about 25,600 words belong to the Kazakh half of the corpus and about 24,800 words to the Russian half).

At the next stage, the structural organization of the corpus is determined. To date, there are three basic formats of corpora, defined depending on the pragmatic goals of the creators or users: (1) the traditional text format with references to the translation; (2) the presentation of texts in a tabular "mirror" form, more convenient for perception and comparison; and (3) the organization of a parallel corpus in the form of a database (DB).

For the created corpus, the third possible structure – a DB was defined as a data storage format. DB is the most convenient structure for storing a large amount of data, which are small text fragments, with the possibility of further permanent expansion and supplementation of the DB. A fragment of the table of the created DB, including ID, name, site address, and the text of the news article, is shown in Figure 8.3.

To perform POS-tagging of Russian corpus texts, we used *pymorphy2*[i] the Python package developed specifically for morphological analysis of Russian-language texts. The libraries of the package use the OpenCorpora dictionary and make hypothetical conclusions on unrecognized words.

The complexity of the structural and typological annotation of Kazakh texts is related to their belonging to the agglutinative languages. The agglutinative format, in which each agglutination (suffix or ending) carries only one semantic or morphological meaning, is opposed to the inflective format, in which each morpheme has several indivisible meanings at once (for example, case, gender, and number).

POS-tagging of Kazakh texts was performed by means of regular expressions based on the *RegexpTagger* class of the *nltk Python* library and a number of syntactic rules. For example, we can identify some types of Kazakh nouns using the list of regular expressions shown in Figure 8.4. Here, the tag *"_NNat"* defines the nominative case (атау) of the noun, the tag *"_NNil"* defines the genitive case (ілік), and the tag *"_NNba"* defines the dative case (барыс).

In order to increase the accuracy of POS-tagging, seven syntactic rules were additionally used. The basis for the development of such rules was the strict order of words in sentences of the Kazakh language. For example, "If a token follows words from a special list" – the token is marked as a verb:

$$\left[list\_1\ of\ words\right]\ tokeni\ =>\ tagtokeni='\_VV' \tag{57}$$

```
patterns=[(r'.*(шык|шы|пыр|мпыр|алар|ашыщ|лар|елер|ды) $',
'NNat'), ('r.*(мның|енің|рдың|дың,)$','NNil'), (r'.*(
да|те|та|нда|нде|ға|ге|қа|ке|на|не|тік|еге|ырға|рға}йға|ыға|аға|
шаға|сіз|мға|ға)$','NNba')]
```

Figure 8.4 Example of a regular expression allowing to identify some nominative, genitive, and dative nouns.

kz	ru
қылмыстық	криминал
мәйіті	трупы
мәліметтерге	данные
министрлігімен	с министерством
Оңтүстік	юг
орындарын	мест
өзара	взаимное
өзінің	его собственный
пиғылды	недобросовестный
Рудныйда	в Рудном
сату	продажа
сәттері	моменты

Figure 8.5 Fragment of the created Kazakh-Russian dictionary.

where list_1 of words = [қойды, қой, қалды, қал, салдым, салып, кетті, кетсеңші, бару, келу, шығу, жүру, түру, бар, кел, шық, жүр, қайт, шыққан, барған, түсті, түс, тұрындар, тұсын, көрме, …]

Next, several approaches to sentence alignment can be chosen. The first approach, based on the same length of sentences of the aligned texts, provides higher productivity. However, in our study, despite the advantages, this approach cannot bring accurate and objective results, as in the Kazakh language additional words are often used to express some semantic and morphological information, which fundamentally changes the length of the sentence. Because of the difference in the organization of grammar and semantics of inflective and agglutinative languages the use of sentence-length alignment in our parallel Kazakh-Russian corpus is not effective.

The second, more resource-intensive approach uses the lexical alignment of words. As a "lexical alignment tool", we used the created Kazakh-Russian dictionary, based on the English-Kazakh-Russian dictionary, which includes about 50,000 elements. Fragments of these dictionaries are shown in Figures 8.5 and 8.6, respectively.

To be able to make full use of this vocabulary-based method of automatic sentence alignment, we use the previously obtained results of POS-tagging of the texts of both languages. The use of correct morphological labeling allows us to correctly identify the correspondence between words, highlighting the reference tokens of the aligned sentences.

```
native###_туасынан, ·жаратылысынан, ·тумысынан###_прирождённый·
(прирожденный)¶
native###_табиғи, ·жаратынды###_природный¶
native###_тұнық, ·ұқыпты, ·кірсіз, ·пәк, ·мөлдір, ·кіршіксіз, ·бейкүнә, ·
әйнектей, ·ақ, ·мұнтаздай, ·таза, ·шайдай·ашық, ·мөлдір·бұлақ, ·дақсыз, ·саф,
ашық, ·адал, ·шын, ·нағыз, ·айна·дай, ·бәкізе, ·ғилман, ·жазықсыз###_чистый¶
native###_жергілікті·адам, ·туып-өскен, ·туған###_уроженец¶
native###_туған, ·бір·туған, ·тіған-туысқандар, ·туыстық, ·туып·өскен, ·
қарағым, ·шырағым###_родной¶
native·of·a·country·(·aborigine·)###_абориген###_абориген¶
nativity·(the·Nativity)###_рождество###_рождество¶
nativity###_дуниеге·келу, ·жаралу###_рождение¶
north·atlantic·treaty·organization·(NATO)###_°###_североатлантический·
союз·(НАТО)¶
North·Atlantic·Treaty·Organization·(NATO)###_°###_Североатлантический·
союз·(НАТО)¶
nato·(NATO; ·North·Atlantic·Treaty·Organization)###_°###_нато·(НАТО; ·
```

Figure 8.6 Fragment of the basic English-Kazakh-Russian dictionary.

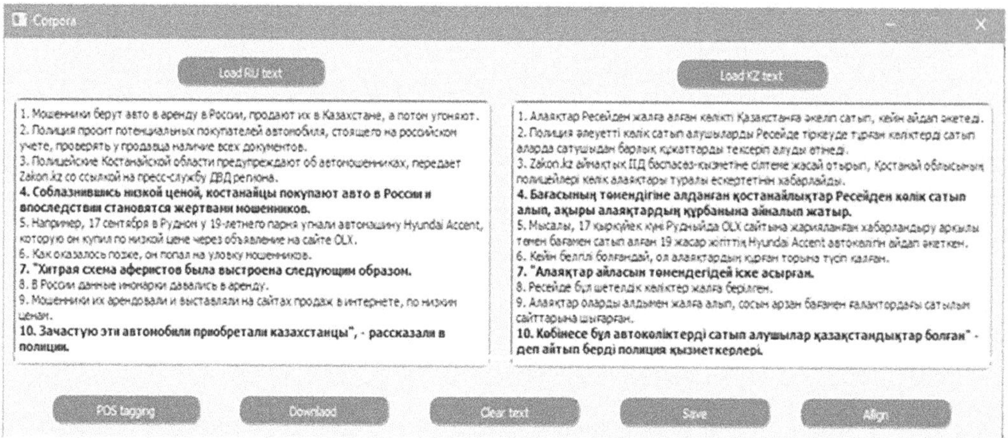

Figure 8.7 Fragment of the created Kazakh-Russian dictionary.

The created aligned parallel Kazakh-Russian corpus consists of criminally related texts collected from four Kazakh news sites for the period of May–December 2018. The corpus includes about 50,410 words.

To evaluate the accuracy of the automatic alignment of the corpus sentences we used expert evaluation of three experts, who used a specially designed application. The application allows the experts to select the text in any (Russian or Kazakh) language and automatically downloads a parallel file with the text in the opposite language (Kazakh or Russian, respectively). The sentences that did not receive a parallel equivalent in the opposite language after automatic alignment are highlighted in bold. While working with the corpus, the experts can mark the texts, save them with marks, or correct the aligned sentences manually. Figure 8.7 shows the user interface of the application used to work with the aligned parallel corpus.

The performed expert evaluation showed that the accuracy of automatically aligned sentences of the created parallel Kazakh-Russian corpus is about 60%, with a coefficient of agreement of 0.83. The other sentences were aligned manually.

After analyzing the results of the alignment, the following conclusions can be made about the causes of errors:

The greatest influence on the relatively low accuracy of the alignment of the created corpus comes from the large difference in the syntactic structures of the Kazakh and Russian languages, which globally leads to a mismatch in the number of sentences in the two parts of the corpus. Some sentences of the Russian text correspond to several sentences of the Kazakh text.

The result of the vocabulary alignment method largely depends on the quality of the translated dictionary used. However, due to the fact that Russian and Kazakh are in distant groups, some errors of polysemy are possible during dictionary creation.

The complexity and limitation of using comparable grammar for Kazakh and Russian require further work in the direction of contrastive linguistics.

The alignment of criminal texts requires that we should take into account proper names, titles, positions, and some patterns of semantic classes of words (currencies, dates, etc.), especially in news headlines.

All of these reasons should be considered and taken into account in further work with the aligned parallel Kazakh-Russian corpus of crime-related texts.

8.4 The rules-based algorithm of fact extraction from Kazakh text

POS-tagging of Kazakh texts was carried out using a developed tagger based on the RegexpTagger class of the NLTK Python package. Figure 8.8 shows a fragment of a regular expression that allows identifying some forms of nouns in Kazakh sentences:

The semantic markup of the Kazakh text corpus containing criminally significant information consists in highlighting and designating a fact triplet: subject → predicate → object. The corpus has a horizontal marking format. The use of the obtained tag names of morphological markup and some syntactic characteristics of words in a sentence as the values of the subject variables of equations (54)–(56) allows to extract the subject, object, and predicate facts from the sentences of the Kazakh language.

The subject of the action, designated by the label "_Sub", represents a person or an object that is the initiator of the action. The predicate is determined on the basis of the formula (54). The object of the action, designated by the label "_Ob", represents the person or object to which the action is directed and is determined on the basis of the formula (55). The core of the fact triplet is a predicate, denoted by the label "_Pred", which calls the action of the fact and is determined on the basis of the logical-linguistic equation (56). When marking, the following decision tree algorithm was used.

```
patterns=[(r'.*бен$','NN'), ('r.* пенен$','NN'),
('r.* басшылық$','NN'), (r'.* іпқону$','NN'),
(r'.* тармен$','NN'), (r'.* герлермен$','NN'),
(r'.* здар$','NN')]
```

Figure 8.8 A fragment of a regular expression that allows identifying some forms of nouns in Kazakh sentences.

The label "_Sub" is added to the word if the first, second, or third word in a sentence that has a plural suffix from the list [тар, тер, дар, дер, лар, лер], which is not preceded by suffixes of:

- genitive case from the list [ның, нің, дың, дін, тың, тің],
- directional-dative case [ға, ге, қа, ке, а, е, на, не],
- accusative case [ны, н, ні, ды, ді, ты, ті],
- locative case [да, де, нда, нде, та, те],
- ablative case [дан, ден, тан, тен, нан, нен],
- instrumental case [мен, менен, бен, бенен, пен, пенен].

1 If there is no word meeting condition 1 in the sentence, the label "_ Sub" is added to the word for which conditions 2 (a) and 2 (b) are met simultaneously:

 a there is a noun word-formation suffix from the list:

 - nominal formation of a noun [*ғай, гей, гер, ғи, ғой, дас, дес, дік, дық, кер, кес, қай, қар, қи, қой, қор, лас, лес,* лік, *лық, ман, паз, пана, сақ, тас, тес, тік, тық, хана, ша, шақ, ше, шек, ші, шік, шы, шық*];
 - verbal noun formation [*ақ, ба,* бе, *ғақ,* ғаш, *гек, гі, гіш, ғы, ғыш, дақ, дек, ек, ік, ім, іс, іш, к, кі, кіш, қ, қаш, қы, қыш, лақ, лек, м, ма, мақ, ме, мек, па, пақ, пе, пек, с, тақ, тек, уік, уық, ш, ық, ым, ыс, ыш*];
 - complex affix of noun formation [*герлік, гіштік, ғыштық, дастық, дестік, ділік, дылық, кеәтік, қорлық, ластық, лестік, лілік, лылық, паздық, сақтық, сіздік, сыздық, тастық, тестік, тілік, тылық, шақтық, шілдік, шілік, шылдық,* шылық];
 - expressive evaluation [*жан, ке, қан, сымақ, тай, ш, ша, шақ, ше, шік,* шық].

 b followed by no case suffix:

 - genitive case from the list [*ның, нің,* дың, *дін, тың, тің*],
 - directional-dative case [*ға, ге, қа, ке, а, е, на, не*],
 - accusative case [*ны, н, ні, ды, ді, ты, ті*],
 - locative case [*да, де, нда, нде, та, те*],
 - ablative case [*дан, ден, тан, тен, нан, нен*],
 - instrumental case [*мен, менен, бен, бенен, пен, пенен*].

2 The label "_ Obj" is added to the word if it is the first word from the beginning of the sentence that has a suffix:

 - directional-dative case [*ға, ге, қа, ке, а, е, на, не*],
 - accusative case [*ны, н, ні, ды, ді, ты, ті*],
 - after which there may be an ending of plurality [*тар, тер, дар, дер, лар, лер*].

3 The label "_Pred" is added to the word, if it is the last word of the sentence, with the suffixes [*п, ып, іп*] and the sentence contains a word beginning with [*тұр, отыр, жатыр, жүр*], followed by a suffix [*біз, бін, быз, бын, ды, міз, мін, мыз, мын, піз, пің, пыз, пын, сіз, сіздер, сіндер, сің, сыз, сыздар, сың, сыңдар, ті, ты*].

4 The label "*_Pred*" is added to the word if it is the last word of the sentence that has the suffix of the future presumptive tense [*ар, ер, ур, ір*] or the suffix of the adverbial participle [*а, е, у, і],* followed by the personal predicative suffix [*біз, бін, быз, бын, ды, міз, мін, мыз, мын, піз, пің, пыз, пын, сіз, сіздер, сіндер, сің, сыз, сыздар, сың, сыңдар, ті, ты*].

5 The label "*_Pred*" is added to the word if it is the last word of the sentence that has the suffix of the future presumptive tense [*ар, ер, ұr, ir*], and the sentence has an auxiliary verb [*edi, e*], after which there can be a personal predicative suffix [*біз, бін, быз, был, ды, міз, мін, мыз, мын, піз, пің, пыз, пын, сіз, сіздер, сіндер, сің, сыз, сыздар, сың, сыңдар, ті, ты*].

6 The label "*_Pred*" is added to the word if the sentence has an auxiliary verb [еді, екен], after which there can be a personal predicative suffix [*біз, бін, быз, бын, ды, міз, мін, мыз, мын, піз, пің, пыз, пын, сіз, сіздер, сіндер, сің, сыз, сыздар, сың, сыңдар, ті, ты*], and this word is the last word of the sentence, which has one of the following suffixes

- [*ді, дік, дің, дім, дің, ды, дык, дық, дым, дың, қ, ті, тік, тім, тің, ты, тык, тық, тым, тың*];
- [*а, ай, ал, ан, ар, арыс, ға, ғал, ғар, ғе, ге, гер, гі, гіз, гіздір, гіле, гір, гіт, ғы, ғыз, ғыздыр, ғызыл, ғыла, ғыр, ғыт, да, дан, дар, дас, дастыр, де, ден, дендір, дес, дiг, дік, дір, діргіз, дық, дыр, дырғыз, дырыл, е, ей, ел,* ен, *ер, й, іг, іғ, ік, ікіс, іл, іла, ілде, ілу, імсіре, ін, індір, ініс, іну, іңкіре, ір, ірде, іре, ірей, іріс, ірке, іркен, ірқе, іс, ісу, іт,* ке, *кер,* кіз, *кіле, кір, қа, қал, қан, қар, қе, қур, қыз, қыла, қыла, қыр, л, ла, лан, ландыр, лас, ластыр, лат, ле, лен, лендір, лес, лестір, лет, ліг, лік, лікіс, лін, ліс, лқа, лу, лығ, лық, лын, лыс, мала, меле, мсіре, мсыра, н, ні, ніл, ніс, ныл, ныс, ңгіре, ңғыра, ңкіре, ңқыра, ңра, ңре, р, ра, ре, с, са, сан,* се, *сен, сет, сетіл, сі, сін, сіре, стір, стыр, сы, сын, сыра, т, та, тан, тандыр, тас, те, тен, тендір, тес, тік, ттыр, тығ, тығс, тығыс, тық, тыр, тырыл, ура, ші, шы, ығ, ығыс, ық, ықыс, ыл, ыла, ылда, ылу, ылыс, ымсыра, ын, ындыр, ыну, ыныс, ыр, ыра, ырай, ырқа, ырқан, ырла, ыс, ысу, ыт*];
- [*азы, ақта, ал, ала, аңғыра, аура, бала, бе, беле, би, бі, бы, дала, ди, ді, ды, екте, ел, еңгіре, еуре, жи, жіре, жыра, зы, і, ін, ірей, іс,* іт, *қи, лі,* лы, *ма, мала, меле, ми, мсіре, мсыра, ңра, ңре, палапеле, пи, пі, пы, ра, ре, си, сіре, сый, сыра, т, ти, ті, ты, усіре, усыра, ши, ші, шы, ы, ын, ыра, ырай, ыс, ыт*].

7 The label "*_Pred*" is added to the word if it is the last word of the sentence that has the suffix [*п, ып, іп*], after which there is a personal predicative suffix [*біз, бін, быз, бын, ды, міз, мін, мыз, мын, піз, пің, пыз, пын, сіз, сіздер, сіндер, сің, сыз, сыздар, сың, сыңдар, ті, ты*]; suffixes [*мыс, міс*] may also be present in the word.

8 The label "*_Pred*" is added to the word if it is the last word of the sentence that has one of the following suffixes:

- [*ді, дік, дің, дім, дің, ды, дык, дық, дым, дың, қ, ті, тік, тім, тің, ты, тык, тық, тым, тың*];
- [*а, ай, ал, ан, ар, арыс, ға, ғал, ғар, ғе, ге, гер, гі, гіз, гіздір, гіле, гір, гіт, ғы, ғыз, ғыздыр, ғызыл, ғыла, ғыр, ғыт, да, дан, дар, дас, дастыр, де, ден, дендір, дес, дiг, дік, дір, діргіз, дық, дыр, дырғыз, дырыл, е, ей, ел, ен, ер, й, іг, іғ, ік, ікіс, іл, іла, ілде, ілу, імсіре, ін, індір, ініс,* іну, *іңкіре, ір, ірде, іре, ірей, іріс, ірке, іркен, ірқе, іс, ісу, іт, ке, кер, кіз, кіле, кір, қа, қал, қан, қар, қе, қур, қыз, қыла, қыла, қыр, л,* ла, *лан, ландыр, лас, ластыр, лат, ле, лен, лендір, лес, лестір, лет, ліг, лік, лікіс, лін, ліс, лқа, лу, лығ, лық, лын, лыс, мала, меле, мсіре, мсыра, н, ні, ніл, ніс, ныл, ныс, ңгіре, ңғыра, ңкіре, ңқыра, ңра, ңре, р, ра, ре, с, са, сан, се, сен,*

сет, сетіл, сі, сін, сіре, стір, стыр, сы, сын, сыра, т, та, тан, тандыр, тас, те, тен, тендір, тес, тік, ттыр, тыг, тыгс, тыгыс, тық, тыр, тырыл, ура, ші, шы, ыг, ыгыс, ық, ықыс, ыл, ыла, ылда, ылу, ылыс, ымсыра, ын, ындыр, ыну, ыныс, ыр, ыра, ырай, ырқа, ырқан, ырла, ыс, ысу, ыт];

- [*ган, ген, қан, кен, қон, га, ге, қа,* ке], [*атын, етін, йтын, йтін*].
- These suffixes may be followed by personal possessive endings of some verb forms [*дар, йік, йін, йық, йын, іздар, к, қ, м, ндар, ң, ңдер, ңіз, ңіздер, ңыз, сіздер, сің, сіңдер, сыздар, сың, сыңдар, ыздар*].

9 The label "*_Pred*" is added to the word if it is the last word of the sentence that has one of the suffixes:

- [*ді, дік, дік, дім, дің, ды, дык, дық, дым, дың, қ, ті, тік, тім, тің, ты, тык, тық, тым, тың*];
- [*а, ай, ал, ан, ар, арыс, га, гал, гар, ге, ге, гер, гі, гіз, гіздір, гіле, гір, гіт, гы, гыз, гыздыр, гызыл, гыла, гыр, гыт, да, дан, дар, дас, дастыр, де, ден, дендір, дес, діг, дік, дір, діргіз, дық, дыр, дыргыз, дырыл, е, ей, ел, ен, ер, й, іг, іг, ік, ікіс, іл, іла, ілде, ілу,* імсіре, *ін, індір, ініс,* іну, *іңкіре, ір, ірде, іре, ірей, іріс, ірке, иркен, ірқе, іс, ісу, іт, ке, кер, кіз, кіле, кір, қа, қал, қан, қар, қе, қур, қыз, қыла, қыла, қыр, л, ла, лан, ландыр, лас, ластыр, лат, ле, лен, лендір, лес, лестір, лет, ліг, лік, лікіс, лін, ліс, лқа, лу, лыг, лық, лын, лыс, мала, меле, мсіре, мсыра, н, ні, ніл, ніс, ныл, ныс, ңгіре, ңгыра, ңкіре, ңқыра, ңра, ңре, р, ра, ре, с, са, сан, се, сен, сет, сетіл, сі, сін, сіре, стір, стыр, сы, сын, сыра, т, та, тан, тандыр, тас, те, тен, тендір, тес, тік, ттыр, тыг, тыгс, тыгыс, тық, тыр, тырыл, ура, ші, шы, ыг, ыгыс, ық, ықыс, ыл, ыла, ылда, ылу, ылыс, ымсыра, ын, ындыр, ыну, ыныс, ыр, ыра, ырай, ырқа, ырқан, ырла, ыс, ысу, ыт*];
- [*азы, ақта, ал, ала, аңгыра, аура, бала, бе, беле, би, бі, бы, дала, ди, ді, ды, екте, ел, еңгіре, еуре, жи, жіре, жыра, зы, і, ін, ірей, іс, іт, қи, лі, лы, ма, мала, меле, ми, мсіре, мсыра, ңра, ңре, палапеле, пи, пі, пы, ра, ре, си, сіре, сый, сыра, т, ти, ті, ты, усіре, усыра, ши, ші, шы, ы,* ын, *ыра, ырай, ыс, ыт*].

These suffixes can be followed by personal possessive endings [*дар, йік, йін, йық, йын, іздар, к, қ, м, ндар, ң, ңдер, ңіз, ңіздер, ңыз, сіздер, сің, сіңдер, сыздар, сың, сыңдар, ыздар*].

If the last word of the sentence does not satisfy any of the conditions of paragraphs 3–9 of this algorithm, then the penultimate word and then the third word from the end of the sentence are checked for the same conditions.

To evaluate the results of the automatic extraction of facts from texts containing criminally related information, the following expert evaluation methodology was used. About one thousand facts were randomly selected from the automatically extracted facts and presented to the expert for evaluation. The expert evaluated the extracted fact as 1 if a triplet of the fact was identified correctly. That is, all three elements of the fact are correctly identified: the initiator of the action – subject, the subject or person to whom the action is directed – object, the action that unites all the participants – predicate. If at least one of the three fact elements was identified incorrectly, the expert evaluated this fact as 0 – incorrectly defined and extracted fact. Figure 8.9 shows the interface of the application used to evaluate the correctness of the aforementioned algorithm. The expert evaluation was performed by two experts.

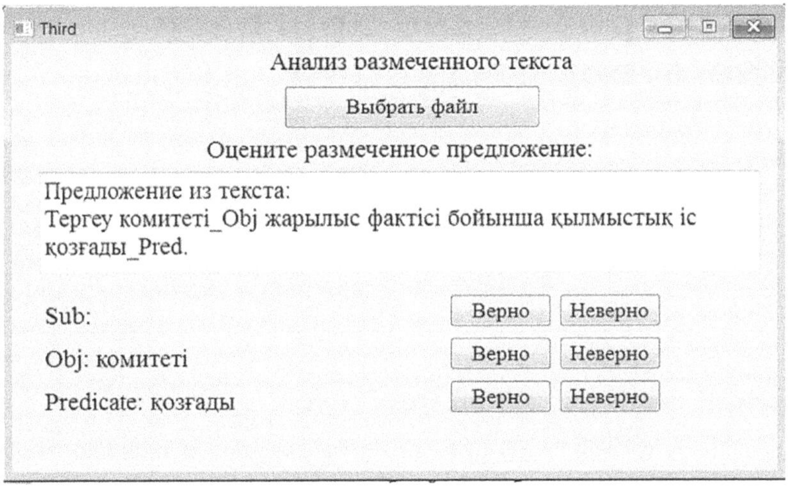

Figure 8.9 Interface of the application that allows the expert to evaluate the correctness of the application.

Table 8.1 Accuracy and Agreement of the Developed Model for the Corpus of Criminally Related Texts of the Kazakh Language

Corpus language	*Corpus size*	*Precision*	*Agreement*
Kazakh	225	71.0%	0.72

Table 8.1 shows the obtained coefficients of accuracy and agreement of the developed model for the corpus of criminally related texts in the Kazakh language.

Note

i https://nlpub.ru/Pymorphy

Chapter 9

Parallel corpus-based approach to crime event extraction

9.1 Methods of event extraction from texts

The existing methods related to EE tasks could be categorized into four groups, namely, (1) pattern matching algorithms, (2) machine learning methods, (3) deep learning models, and (4) unsupervised machine learning methods.

The first group exploits *pattern-based* event extraction (EE) approaches. Such an approach was first proposed in 1993 by Riloff et al. (1993) to extract terrorist events from domain-specific texts. Now there are quite a lot of pattern-based EE systems that are domain-specific for extracting various types of events. For example, a biomedical EE system TrigNER for the BioNLP 2013 EE task (Campos et al. 2014) or the Turku Event Extraction System (TEES) (Björne et al. 2017) are used in a variety of biomedical text mining tasks. There are systems for EE in the financial domain as well, some of which use EE methods based on lexical-semantic patterns (Hogenboom 2014). Additionally, recent trends of studies of EE in the terrorism and criminal domain are of considerable interest to our research. José A. Reyes-Ortiz (2019) presented an approach based on pattern matching techniques to extract criminal events from Spanish texts. To evaluate the process results, the author used a set of manually tagged newspapers with categories of specific events. Li et al. (2020) applied EE technology to the case description part in the Chinese legal text. The authors defined the event type, event arguments, and event arguments roles of the larceny case. Abdelkoui & Kholladi (2017) described the EE of criminal incidents from Arabic tweets. The author's approach is based on combining various indicators, including the names of places and temporal expressions that appear in the tweet messages.

However, the most recent papers devoted to EE tasks belong to the second group of approaches based on *machine learning* (ML). These approaches apply traditional ML classification algorithms, like Support vector machine (SVM), Maximum Entropy (ME), the nearest neighbor, and others. Most commonly, these algorithms utilize POS-tags, lemmatized words, the type of syntactic dependency between a trigger word and entity, and the dependent words and entity types as features of event classifications. More often, EE approaches based on ML algorithms were utilized in domain-specific areas, for instance, in the biomedical domain or finance and economic-connected domains. Some authors suppose simultaneously using pattern-based approaches and models of ML or deep ML for EE. In another paper (Pham & Ho 2014), the authors proposed a system that uses hybrid methods that combine both rule-based and ML-based approaches to solve GENIA EE. In this study on the ML step, the authors exploited N-gram features, frequency features, and dependency features. This paper (Sha et al. 2016) proposed a Regularization-Based Pattern Balancing method (RBPB) that includes using both event

DOI: 10.1201/9781003587514-9

patterns in a sentence to identify an event and the SVM classifier to define the trigger type. At the same time, these state-of-the-art systems, based on traditional ML methods, require many complex and hand-designed features. To generate these features, it is necessary to have professionals with linguistic knowledge and experts with domain knowledge. Additionally, these features often are represented by one-hot vectors, which cause data sparsity and feature selection problems (Xiang & Wang 2019).

On the other hand, according to Christopher Manning (2015), *deep learning* techniques can be successfully applied in various natural language processing (NLP) tasks related to classification, particularly with the classification of sentences, words, or full texts. Consequently, since the task of EE is related to the sentences and word classification issue, we can expect progress in applying deep learning techniques for extracting events from texts in the nearest future. Using convolutional neural networks (CNNs) and recurrent neural network models in EE in the last few years is illustrative in this regard. For example, to extract a biomedical event, Li et al. (2020) proposed to apply deep learning, namely, the CNN model, to capture the compositional semantic features of sentences with some patterns. Yagcioglu et al. (2019) employed a CNN and a long short-term memory recurrent neural network to detect cyber security events from a noisy short text. The graph neural networks use multiple neurons operating on a graph structure to enable deep learning in non-Euclidean spaces. Thus, in Liu et al. (2018b), the authors proposed to jointly extract multiple event triggers and arguments by attention-based graph convolutional networks. In Nguyen & Grishman (2018), the authors investigated a CNN and constructed a graph based on dependency trees to perform event detection. They proposed a pooling method that relies on entity mentions to aggregate the convolution vectors. Liu et al. (2018a), Liu et al. (2018b), have applied attention mechanisms in neural models in order to guide a neural model to unequally treat each component of the input according to its importance to the EE task. However, today usage of ML and deep learning is still a great challenge in practice. The main reason is the need to handle a large, annotated corpus for model training. Usually, obtaining such a corpus is a time-consuming and labor-intensive task, which involves a lot of domain and professional experts.

To avoid the necessity of the labeled corpus, some scholars leveraged *unsupervised learning* approaches. In these cases, they focused on open-domain EE tasks (Allan 2012). Open-domain EE approaches operate without predefined event schemas, and usually, this extraction aims at detecting events from a sentence or phrase and clustering similar events via extracted event keywords. However, in the case of the open-domain EE approaches, the accuracy of EE turns out to be rather low, and the events themselves are mostly vague and blurred.

While the EE has become a mature academic field, this task becomes challenging for the texts written in under-resourced and under-annotated languages. For that reason, in the last few years, studies addressing cross-lingual learning (CLL) for EE appeared (Subburathinam et al. 2019). Over the past decade, we have also seen the exploitation of the Multilingual Bidirectional Encoder Representations from Transformers (BERT) model (Fincke et al. 2021) and CNN (Lin et al. 2017) for cross-lingual relation and EE. Meanwhile, in most cases, cross-lingual EE approaches were based on multilingual versions of the ML models pre-trained on large multilingual corpora (Pelicon et al. 2021), and resource-rich and well-annotated language were exploited as the source language of the corpus. Typically, that was English (Subburathinam et al. 2019; Lin et al. 2017; Taghizadeh & Faili 2021). Moreover, EE requires a rich label space. That is an additional reason why gold-standard annotations for EE are publicly available only for a few languages (Getman et al. 2018). To fill this gap, when there are no well-annotated corpora for specific languages, we suppose that it may be possible to employ supplementary knowledge about the similarity of the syntactic and semantic patterns of the considered pair of languages to cross-lingual EE transfer (Lin et al. 2017).

9.2 Text mining applications in crime

Over the past several years, the number of research related to crime has grown significantly. To comprehensively include various existing tasks related to crime text information, we propose the following classification of Text Mining applications in crime: (1) crime text identification (or crime detection), (2) the crime event types classification; (3) crime pattern modeling and crime prediction; (4) hate speech detection; (5) crime information extraction (CIE), including crime entities (CE) identification; (6) crime-related event extraction (CREE). Even though sometimes these directions can overlap, Table 9.1 shows the generalized information about the existing approaches.

Perhaps most of the current studies relevant to the problems of crime-related text analysis, address the selection of such kinds of texts. The articles on crime text *identification* commonly described traditional clustering and topic identification approaches (Hossain et al. 2020; Karimi & Gharehchopogh 2020).

Nevertheless, much research not only distinguished between crime-related news/information and not-crime-related news/information but also focused on the *classification* of the crime event types (Salas et al. 2020; Santhiya et al. 2021; Moreno-Jiménez et al. 2017). Moreno-Jiménez et al. (2017) classified 1,000 news items from Annotated Crimes Corpus (Corpus Anotado de Delitos) in Mexico into types of crime (assault, homicide, kidnapping, and sexual abuse). Salas et al. (2020) selected two algorithms (SVM and neural networks) to multi-classify what type of crime news is reported. They processed crime articles from the Spanish corpus of Peruvian news. Santhiya et al. (2021) proposed a text-oriented decision support system that extracted English tweets under different crime categories, such as sexual harassment, rape, suicide, and others. Their crime classification tool is based on hybridized ML techniques combined with NLP techniques. Meanwhile, in the recent overview, Hassani et al. (2016) deduced that the most popular techniques typically chosen in the different applications for the crime event types classification are SVM and neural networks algorithms.

Besides the classification of the crime-related texts, we can also distinguish studies related to crime *pattern modeling* and crime prediction, which are often based on additional police-recorded crime data attributes. Chen's paper (Chen & Kurland 2018) aimed to solve the problem of identifying potential serial offending patterns using such variables in police-recorded crime event data as time, setting, and modus operandi. Joseph (2021) used the *K*-means clustering algorithm to extract patterns of crime-prone areas and crime types that possibly occur. In this research, the US Arrests data set was used, which included the district-wise number of arrests made in a year with various types of crimes, such as assault, murder, rape, etc.

Such a direction of research related to crime text information as *hate speech detection* in social media texts (Rangel et al. 2021; Siino et al. 2021; Miok et al. 2021; Qureshi & Sabih 2021; Mozafari et al. 2019) should be highlighted separately. Generally, the authors considered this term for numerous kinds of insulting user-created content on Twitter, blogs, and other social networks (Schmidt & Wiegand 2021). In the broader sense, the term hate speech refers to any communication that disparages a person or a group based on some characteristic, such as race, color, ethnicity, gender, sexual orientation, nationality, religion, or others (Nockleby 2000). The problem of hate speech detection was even considered at PAN 2021 hosted at CLEF 2021, where 66 approaches for this task decision were evaluated (Rangel et al. 2021). In general, the

Table 9.1 Overview of Approaches and Techniques Processed to Crime-Related Texts

Approaches and techniques	*Examples of the studies (references)*	*Methods*	*Dataset and processing language (if not English) or Regions*	*Effectiveness*
Crime texts identification (Crime detection)	Khairova et al. (2023)	Various clustering techniques (Grid-based, constraint-based, *k*-means clustering algorithm, and others)	The specialized Communities and Crime dataset	F-measure reaches 87%
The crime event types classification	Mullah & Zainon (2021), Ramponi et al. (2020)	Various ML techniques for classification (SVM and Neural Networks, and others)	Mostly, the specially annotated corpora: Annotated Crimes Corpus (Corpus Anotado de Delitos); Spanish corpus of Peruvian news (Zampieri et al. 2019a); English tweets dataset, Mexico (Zampieri et al. 2020)	The average obtained F-Score result of classification lies between 77.9% and 84%
The crime event types classification	Mullah & Zainon (2021), Ramponi et al. (2020)	Various ML techniques for classification (SVM and Neural Networks, and others)	Police-recorded crime event data, US arrests dataset	Quite low. On average, precision reaches 0.50 with recall 0.16
Crime pattern modeling and crime prediction	Nockleby (2000), Das & Das (2019)	Various classification and clustering algorithms with additional time and spatial characteristics	Police crime reports and witness narrative reports for the USA, UAE, and India, a corpus of domestic violence events (New South Wales Police Force). The newspaper reports on crime against women in Indian states, spatial-temporally tagged tweets about crime events in Spanish language, and News reports from Malayalam online papers.	Detection of some type of CE (for instance, Weapons) for police crime or witness narrative reports achieves up PR 0.96, RC 0.90, and more. While the F-measure was from 0.61 to 0.71 for CE identification in newspapers articles or social networks

(*Continued*)

Table 9.1 (Continued)

Approaches and techniques	*Examples of the studies (references)*	*Methods*	*Dataset and processing language (if not English) or Regions*	*Effectiveness*
Crime information extraction, including CE identification	Rahem & Omar (2014), Davani et al. (2019) Das & Das (2017)	Generally, rule-based language expression patterns combined with a dictionary, ontology, and thesaurus were utilized Less often, cauterization methods were used (graph-based clustering technique)	Labeled corpora or often manually labeling data from Twitter, Instagram, Yahoo!, and YouTube in English and Spanish, Dutch, Italian, Portuguese, Arabic, and some other languages	Accuracy achieved on average from 0.75 to 0.84, depending on a language. Some research showed that F-measure can achieve 0.9 on the good manually annotated tweets
Hate speech detection	Khairova et al. (2016, 2021), Siino et al. (2021), Qureshi & Sabih (2021)	Supervised machine learning classifiers, recurrent or convolutional neural networks, BERT model, sometimes with exploitation lexical resources	Online newspaper articles from the USA and India; structured reports of events according to actor, city, and country level; manually labelled tweets; the information from Malaysian National News Agency (BERNAMA); manually annotated subsets of the local news articles	F-measure of CE extraction of various types of ranges from 0.64 (person) to 0.96 (drugs name). F-measure of extraction of complete crime events (covering trigger, type, and arguments) that relevant very narrow domain ranges from about 0.6 (cybersecurity events) to 0.64 (hate crime). And only when researchers used manually labelled corpus for training precision can be achieved about 0.83.

problem of hate speech detection is solved by supervised ML classifiers (Qureshi & Sabih 2021) or, more often, by using recurrent or CNNs (Siino et al. 2021; Miok et al. 2021). In many cases, to address the problem, the advanced technology of additional transfer learning and the BERT model were applied (Mozafari et al. 2019).

Over the past few years, many papers dedicated to the issue of *crime information extraction* appeared, which considered the information extraction task about occurred or prospective crimes. Usually, either crime police reports or open sources of textual information were utilized as a dataset for the CIE task. However, obviously the best results were achieved when information was extracted from crime reports (Ku et al. 2008; Das & Das 2019). To analyze police and witness narrative reports, Ku et al. (2008) combined the large crime-specific lexicon and the algorithm to recognize the relevant entities based on some grammatical rules and patterns. Das and Das (2019) dealt with crime reports for the USA, UAE, and India. The authors demonstrated a graph-based clustering to extract paraphrases from the crime dataset for subsequent labeling of crime reports. Other studies considered particular types of criminal offenses based on textual information from open sources. Dasgupta et al. (2017) leveraged computational linguistics-based methods to extract different crime-related entities and events from crime-related news documents. They extracted the name of the criminal, the name of the victim, the nature of the crime, the geographic location, date and time, and the action taken against the criminal by using probabilistic classifiers and domain ontology to augment the accuracies of the extraction process. Rare research combined the use of police reports, newspaper articles, and victims' and witnesses' crime narratives.

The task of crime information extraction also includes *crime entities extraction* (Rahma & Romadhony 2021; Joseph et al. 2021; Das & Das 2019). To find five CE: crime type, victim, perpetrator, location, and time in Indonesian language texts, Rahma & Romadhony (2021) utilized ontology and rule-based methods. Joseph et al. (2021) gained information about places, the most used drugs, amount of each drug from reported news. They processed using NLP techniques like NER for extracting structured information. At the same time, Das & Das (2019) extracted classes named entities, such as states, streets, towns/cities, villages, and male forenames from online newspapers and websites that provide reports about crimes against women sorted according to the states.

Despite the large number of studies concerning crime-related texts generally, we can't say that there are many papers regarding the *CREE* task. However, the task of CREE from natural language texts had first arisen at the early DARPA Message Understanding Conferences (MUCs). The domain of MUC-3 and MUC-4 was Latin-American Terrorism, and the events extracted were associated with particular terrorist actions. In contemporary studies, criminal events are often defined as various types of events that refer to criminal activities. Typically, research studies consider the problem of CREE separately for various types of events (related to terrorism, cybercrime, crimes against the person, crimes related to transport, etc.). From this perspective, in particular, the works (Joseph et al. 2021; Rahem & Omar 2014) aimed to extract available drug crime and substance abuse information from online newspaper articles. Rahem and Omar obtained information about the nationalities of drug dealers, names of drugs, and the quantity and prices of drugs in the local market. Their extraction system was based on grammatical and heuristic rules and data from the Malaysian National News Agency (BERNAMA). In the paper by Yagcioglu et al. (2019), cybersecurity events detection was considered. Authors focused on such cybersecurity events as zero-day exploits, ransomware, data leaks, security breaches, vulnerabilities, etc. For their approach, they utilized a manually labeled dataset that included 2K tweets about crimes against women in India. Meanwhile, the study of Hossain et al. (2020)

aimed to predict violent events, such as Military Action by state actors or terrorist attacks by Non-State Actors (MANSA events). For evaluation of the approach, they used manually extracted, structured reports on events at the actor, city, and country levels.

Several studies performed the extraction of events connected exactly with a hate crime. According to the FBI's UCR Program1, a hate crime can be a criminal offense against a race, religion, disability, sexual orientation, ethnicity, gender, or gender identity. For instance, Davani et al. (2019) provided event detection and EE from news articles based on a crime acts taxonomy. Authors considered homicide and kidnapping events and such event attributes as the target of a crime event and the type of crime. For experiments, they manually annotated subsets of the main unlabeled local news articles corpus. Moreover, there are quite a lot of studies provided using crime EE to facilitate crime prediction. For instance, Han et al. (2021) focused on extracting hate crime events from New York Times news and then used the results to determine American national-level and state-level hate crime trends. To extract hate crime events, the authors applied deep-learning methods.

Despite the widespread development of approaches used for intellectual analysis of crime-related texts, the solutions presented in the extant literature are mainly based on the ML and deep ML models (Miok et al. 2021; Qureshi & Sabih 2021; Han et al. 2021). Such models, require the presence of large corpora, which should be previously balanced and manually tagged by experts under clear rules, and provided with language subtleties (Qureshi & Sabih 2021; Mullah & Zainon 2021).

9.3 Linguistic resources-based solutions

Following the conclusions made in Sections 9.1 and 9.2, it can be argued that for the evaluation and refinement of EE methods *corpora* are frequently utilized. These corpora should be specially annotated by semantic labels, which may describe event types, for instance, Sociopolitical events and event arguments, such as a person, organization, location, time, geopolitical entity, facility, vehicle, weapon, and others. Thus, the DEFT Richer Event Description Annotation Corpus, developed by the Linguistic Data Consortium, includes 158 documents as a prior training set and 202 additional documents as a test set (Rich ERE (Entity, Relation, and Event) Annotation Guidelines Overview). Now the corpus annotation scheme comprises 8,731 events and 10,319 entities and can be utilized to formally evaluate approaches to EE tasks from English, Chinese, and Spanish news articles and discussion forums.

Event-annotated corpora are most often focused on specific problem domains. So, one of the most developed are corpora of biomedical information. Ramponi et al. (2020) analyzed some public resources that provide manually annotated events in the biomedical field, including the GENIA event corpus, the BioInfer (biomedical information extraction resource) corpus, the gene regulation event corpus (GREC), the GeneReg corpus, and some others. Over the past few years, the use of linguistic resources for the study of *crime*-related topics has also intensified (Osathitporn et al. 2017; Rosa et al. 2018). The use of ontologies, corpora, thesauri, and structured lexical bases is still the most relevant for the hate speech detection task. Thus, a systematic and up-to-date review made by Poletto et al. (2021) showed that there are more than 64 annotated corpora and lexical resources (37 out of them are in English) that are centered on the notion of *hate* speech to date. For instance, the paper by Çöltekin (2020) introduced the first corpus of Turkish offensive language that consists of randomly sampled micro-blog posts from Twitter. A paper by Kumar et al. (2018) concerned the problem of the annotated corpus creation based on Hindi-English code-mixed data of Twitter and Facebook. The corpus is annotated using an aggression tag set. In the latest study by Battistelli et al. (2020), the methodology to build an ontology of the online hate speech domain in French was presented, but at the same time, unfortunately, the paper focused on modeling development aspects, while practical using of the ontology to annotate texts was not addressed. Furthermore, the popularity of that research field can be confirmed by it provided in the SemEval-2019 (Zampieri et al. 2019a) and SemEval-2020 (Zampieri et al. 2020) tasks as Task 6: Identifying and categorizing offensive language in social media (OffensEval) and Task 12: Multilingual offensive language identification in social media (OffensEval 2020) accordingly. To estimate different approaches to offensive language identification, automatic categorization of offense types, and offense target identification, the tweets collections in English (Zampieri et al. 2019a) and Arabic, Danish, English, Greek, and Turkish (Zampieri et al. 2020) were annotated according to the hierarchical taxonomy of the OLID ("Offensive Language Identification Dataset) schema (Zampieri et al. 2019b) were utilized. Apparently, there is a well-structured hierarchical system for detecting hate speech. However, there is no such general scheme for CREE yet.

At the same time, there are quite a lot of corpora focused on a subgenre of *legal* and *judicial* texts (the Cambridge Corpus of Legal English, The House of Lords Judgments Corpus, The Proceedings of the Old Bailey, JUD-GENTT, A Corpus of Malawi Criminal Cases) (Pontrandolfo 2019; Goźdź-Roszkowski 2021; Taylor 2020). In many cases, text mining tasks related to crime were based on the corpora of *newspaper* articles. In Ras's thesis (Ras 2017) authors used the corpus of British newspapers that comprised approximately 85,000 news articles to analyze corporate fraud news. Mukherjee & Sarkar (2020) proposed to exploit the corpus of newspapers written in the Bengali language to automatically get a picture of high crime-prone locations. However, as illustrated in the analysis by De Carvalho & Costa (2022), specific domain corpora with crime-related texts are applied for text mining applications less frequently than the corpora of newspaper articles. Adily et al. (2021) utilized the corpus of 492,393 domestic violence events provided by the New South Wales Police Force (Karystianis et al. 2018). The study by Gunawan et al. (2019) allowed creation of a specific domain corpus of pornography in the Indonesian language (Bahasa), which was proposed for the blocking technique of pornographic websites.

In addition, special mention should be made of the most current CREE approaches, which are based not only on the annotated corpora but also *ontologies* (or *specialized lexicons*). Thus, De Mendonça et al. (2020) proposed the Ontology-Based Framework for Criminal Intention Classification (OFCIC). They employed the Ontology of Criminal Expressions (OntoCexp) (De Mendonça et al. 2019) to select potentially crime-related posts on Twitter.

Thus, based on the results of related works analysis, we can conclude that the development of new linguistic resources, such as corpora, dictionaries, thesauri, and lexicons (i) for highly specialized problem domains (for example, related to crime) and (ii) for low-resource and under-annotated languages, is becoming the critical direction of increasing the power of CRE approaches application in multilingual social media space.

9.4 Types and subtypes of crime-related events

Following the studies (Nockleby 2000; Fincke et al. 2021; Lin et al. 2017; Pelicon et al. 2021), we determine and extract CRE from a corpus of news articles related to police and criminal activities. However, unlike previous research, despite the limited count of the event types, we consider not specific types of crimes (only drug crime or only traffic incidents, etc.), but the big group of events that relate to unlawful action (traffic accident, hate crime, police activities, and others).

Table 9.2 Event Types and Subtypes that We Consider

	Event type	*Event subtype*
1	TRANSFER	Movement, traffic accident
2	CRIME	Injure, offense
3	POLICE	Arrest, trial, PD

Specifically, we are interested in TRANSFER, CRIME, and POLICE types of events and their seven subtypes. Table 9.2 shows event types and subtypes considered.

Generally, in all these kinds of CRE, we can say about two participants and several attributes of the action or event. An agent is a participant that is an initiator of an event. The second participant of these event types is an object which, in a general way, is represented by a person, an organization, or a vehicle, to which the event action is directed.

Based on the COPLINK project (Dasgupta et al. 2017), to determine participants of CRE, we distinguish three different types of entities that can be involved in a criminal action. We employ semantic classes of people names, organizations names, and vehicles. However, various types and subtypes of CRE can involve various entity types in their capacity as agent and object. Additionally, all the types and subtypes of events we are considering have traditional TIME-ARG and PLACE-ARG attributes. Sometimes we look for the instrument or device to determine modus operandi, for example, a weapon applied to inflict harm. Additionally, on rare occasions, we can use an optional slot, WHY-ARG, to describe the reason for the event.

A CRIME CRE occurs whenever a person or an organization does something criminalized or unlawful. There are two subtypes of a CRIME event: INJURE and OFFENSE. An INJURE subtype of a CRIME CRE occurs whenever an action covers a person entity, so-called crimes against persons. This person can experience physical harm (be killed, be injured) or be affected by other criminal actions (be robbed, be tricked). Consequently, an object can be only the harmed person(s), whereas an agent of the subtype is the initiator of the attacking action, a person or an organization damaging to the physical harm.

An OFFENSE subtype occurs whenever an object of the criminal action isn't a person directly. In this case, an OFFENSE event can have two or one participant and some attributes of the event. The agent is the initiator of the offense action, a person or an organization damaging to some harm or doing an illegal activity. It is a necessary participant in the event. Nevertheless, an inanimate OBJECT, which is the second participant of this subtype, can either be or not in a certain phrase or sentence.

A TRANSFER CRE includes two subtypes, namely, MOVEMENT and TRAFFIC ACCIDENT. A MOVEMENT subtype of a TRANSFER Event occurs whenever an inanimate object or a PERSON is moved from one LOCATION to another. At the same time, we have suggested that moving something to steal or thieve is not a MOVEMENT CRE, it is exactly a CRIME CRE. Another subtype of a TRANSFER CRE is a TRAFFIC ACCIDENT, which occurs whenever a vehicle suffers an accident. In this case, an Agent should be a person or a vehicle that triggered the accident.

The last type of event that we have considered as CRE is a POLICE Event that occurs whenever the action is going to be done by police or officials. A POLICE CRE includes three subtypes, namely, ARREST, TRIAL, and PD. An ARREST is a subtype of a POLICE CRE, which occurs whenever the movement of a person is going to be constrained by a state actor (for instance, policemen or justice). In the case of an ARREST subtype, an agent can be well-defined as a person or an organization that was an initiator of the detention of another person, whereas an object is only a detained person.

A TRIAL is a subtype of a POLICE CRE, which occurs whenever a court or some government organization accuses a person or an organization of committing a crime. A PD (Police Department) is a subtype of a POLICE CRE, which occurs whenever a police officer implements official duties. The agent of a PD subtype should be exactly a policeman as a person or a PD as an organization.

9.5 A general methodology of a parallel corpus-based approach

Following the previous studies (Joseph 2021; Nockleby 2000; Fincke et al. 2021; Lin et al. 2017), we determine and extract three types and seven subtypes of CRE from the corpus of news articles relevant to police and criminal activities. An additional restriction is the use of a bilingual parallel corpus that includes aligned sentences in two low-resourced and under-annotated languages.

Our two-fold approach includes (1) the EPB method for CREE from the first part of the corpus (source language); and (2) cross-lingual CRE transfer technique for the second part of the corpus (target language). To implement this approach, in the *first* step, we use the EPB method for CREE to process texts in the source language. Following the approaches of Closed-domain Event Extraction (CdEE) (Nockleby 2000; Khairova et al. 2016), we sequentially determine the event trigger in the phrase describing the event, the event/trigger type, and identify the event arguments and their roles. This step involves the implementation of the following three stages:

(1.1) Application of the method of simultaneous CRE trigger detection and event/trigger type identification which is based on a multilingual synonyms dictionary with crime-related lexis (Salas et al. 2020) (for a detailed description of the method, see Section 9.5);
(1.2) Defining a schema for each CRE subtype that is based on the CRE types and subtypes discussed in Section 9.4. The schema describes particular classes of participants involved in events of this type, such as agents or objects. Additionally, since we consider police or criminal activity in the website news, we are always interested in the place and time of the event. Therefore, the PLACE-ARG and TIME-ARG attributes may also be relevant to the event we are parsing;
(1.3) Developing and usage the logical-linguistic equations (LLEs), and the predefined scheme of the event subtype to extract event arguments and identify their roles. The use of LLEs provides an opportunity to describe the roles of attribute participants that exist in a particular area via relations of grammatical and semantic characteristics of the words in the sentence (see Section 9.5 for a detailed description).

In the *second* step, we apply the cross-lingual CRE transfer technique to extract events from sentences in the target language (second part) of the corpus. The use of the technique is based on the hypothesis that the same event can be expressed by both a labeled sentence of the source language and an aligned sentence of the target language in the parallel corpus (see Section 9.5 for a detailed description). This step involves the implementation of the following two stages:

(2.1) Implementation of the POS-tag labeling of target language texts using morphological processing tools for a specific particular language;

(2.2) Using the shared semantic space of aligned sentences of the two languages, to apply knowledge about the annotation of the event of the parallel sentence in the source language to transfer the type, roles of the participants, and attributes of the event into the sentences of the target language. For this purpose, the patterns of the correspondence between POS-tags of a target language sentence and the possible roles of the event participants/attributes from an aligned source language sentence are utilized. An example of applying such patterns to the Kazakh language is shown in the Section 9.6.

Figure 9.1 shows the general scheme of the two-fold approach for crime-related event extracting from texts of a parallel corpus. We use the sentence *An unknown man was killed in the middle of the carriageway last night* in English as the source language only for making the example much clearer.

Our determination of a CRE trigger and identification of a trigger/event type is based on a multilingual synonyms dictionary (Salas et al. 2020). The lexis of the dictionary is obtained manually from texts on crime-related topics. Seven main thematic categories are determined for the terms, namely, movement, traffic accident, injure, offense, arrest, trial, and PD. This choice of categories comes from the fact that the information resources, from which the texts are taken, contained most data on three criminal areas: police, transfer, crime, and their subtypes mentioned above, thereby making our dictionary narrowly focused on crime-related topics.

All terms in the dictionary are separated into parts of speech, namely, nouns, verbs, and adjectives. Figure 9.2 shows a fragment of the dictionary, which now comprises about 600 main words (325 nouns, 120 adjectives, and 170 verbs) and more than 2,500 synonyms in four languages: English, Kazakh, Ukraine, and Russian. Each element <term> of the dictionary presents a word in a given part of speech with its synonyms, definitions, hyponyms, and hypernyms in four languages via child elements. A value of the elements <domain> of the dictionary indicates one of the seven aforementioned thematic categories.

Based on the statement that the main word, which most clearly expresses the occurrence of the event, is a verb (Santhiya et al. 2021), and consequently, a verb is the trigger of the event in a phrase or sentence, we find all verbs which occur both at the dictionary and in the texts of the first part of the corpus. The event/trigger type or the class of the event type is defined according to the value of the <DOMAIN> tag of the verb in our dictionary. For instance, the trigger verb *kill* in the sentence *An unknown man was killed in the middle of the carriageway last night* was classified as the event type “INJURE”, which matches the value <DOMAIN> tag of the lemma “kill” in the dictionary.

However, because our corpus contains a kind of crime news, in some instances, some phrases or sentences describe a CRE, but they are founded on semantic light verbs, like *mandate, report, assume, give,* and some others. To take into account that kind of sentence, we consider a set of special nouns that also can be triggers of the events. We exploited the list of about 1,000 nouns from our multilingual synonyms dictionary with criminal-related lexis. This list comprises, for example, such nouns as *killer, molestation, gunfire, assassination, detonation*, and others.

To extract participants and attributes of the event, we use LLEs that identify the respective roles of the event participants according to the predefined structure of the event subtype. The main mathematical means of the LLEs is the Algebra of Finite Predicates (AFP), which allows the modeling of various finite, deterministic, and discrete elements of the language system: sentences, phrases, collocations, words, grammatical and semantic characteristics, morphemes, etc.

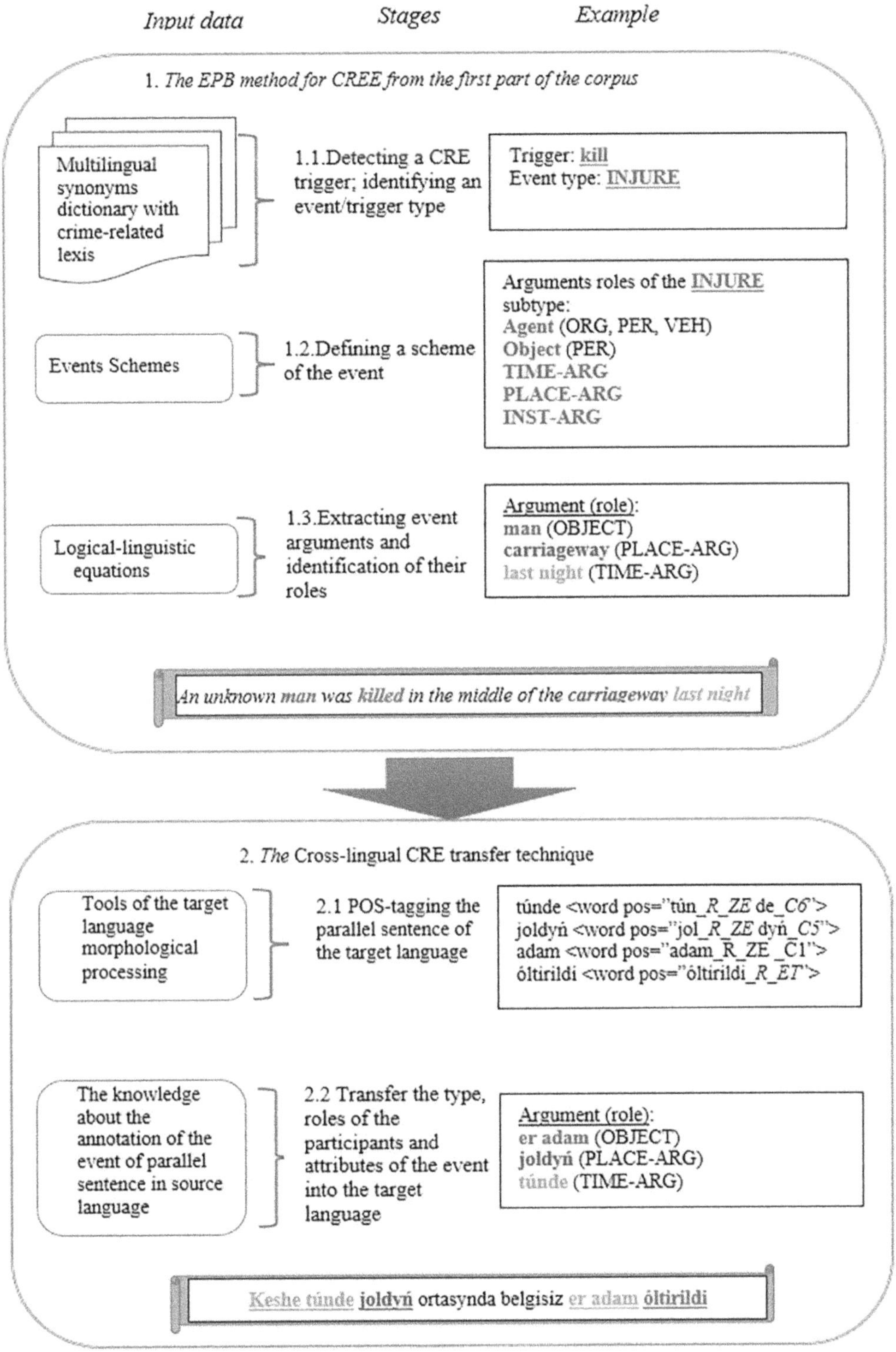

Figure 9.1 The scheme of the two-fold approach for crime-related event extracting from texts of a parallel corpus.

```
<vocabulary>
<nouns>
<term id="1">
<lemma lang="ru">стрельба</lemma>
<domain>OFFENSE</domain>
<synset lang="ru">обстрел, выстрел</synset>
<definition lang="ru">учебные занятия по ведению
<example lang="ru">Два человека получили ранения
<hypernims lang="ru">['приведение в действие', '
<hyponims lang="ru">['контрвыстрел', 'разряд', '
<lemma lang="en">shooting</lemma>
<synset lang="en">firing, fire, gunfire</synset>
<definition lang="en">the act of firing a projec
<example lang="en">his shooting was slow but acc
<hypernims lang="en">['actuation', 'propulsion']
<hyponims lang="en">['countershot', 'discharge',
<lemma lang="ka">атыс</lemma>
<synset lang="ka">ату, оқ жаудыру, атылыс</synse
<definition lang="ka">оқ атылғанда шығатын дыбыс
<example lang="ka">Алматының Ақбұлақ мөлтекаудан
<hypernims lang="ka">['іске қосу','қозғаушы күш'
<hyponims lang="ka">['қарсы атыс', 'ату', 'басын
<lemma lang="ua">стрілянина</lemma>
<synset lang="ua">стрільба, пальба</synset>
</term>
<term id="2">
```


Figure 9.2 The fragment of the multilingual synonyms dictionary with criminal-related lexis.

To describe a characteristic of the language element, the AFP applies a predicate variable x_i^a, where a is a value of the characteristic of ith element x (Reyes-Ortiz 2019):

$$x_i^a = \begin{cases} 1, \text{if } x_i = a \\ 0, \text{if } x_i \neq a \end{cases}, \left(1 \leq i \leq n\right) \tag{58}$$

where n is the amount of the elements. For example, for the Russian source language of our parallel corpus, a predicate variable x can characterize a grammatical case. In this way, x_i^{gen} will be equal to one if an ith word of the sentence has a genitive case, while the disjunction $x_i^{gen} \vee x_i^{nom} = 1$ means that the word i can have a genitive or nominative case in the Russian sentence.

Since many grammatical and semantic characteristics of various languages are different, particular LLEs should be established for each natural language. In the pilot implementation of our approach to CREE, we consider the source language of bilingual parallel corpus capacity as the Russian language.

As possible grammatical and semantic characteristics of words in Russian sentences, representing roles of event arguments, we identify a grammatical case of a noun, its animate or inanimate, a semantic class of the entities, and several features formalizing the passive voice in Russian.

Thus, we introduce a finite set of six predicate variables $M = \{x, y, z, m, l, f\}$, which can characterize the words in Russian sentences and represent the roles of participants and attributes of certain event.

At the next step of our model formulated in the previous studies (Björne et al. 2017), the predicate system S is introduced. The system includes predicates $P_i(x_i) \in S$, describing all possible values of the grammatical and semantic characteristics of the sentence words in a particular language.

The grammatical cases of nouns in the Russian language are specified via the predicate variable z:

$$P(z) = z^{nom} \vee z^{gen} \vee z^{dat} \vee z^{acc} \vee z^{ins} \vee z^{loc} \tag{59}$$

where *nom, gen, dat, acc, ins, loc* are nominative, genitive, dative, accusative, instrumental, and prepositional cases, respectively.

We can also specify semantic features of the nouns, such as animality via the predicate variable x:

$$P(x) = x^{anim} \vee x^{inan} \tag{60}$$

where *anim* is animate, *inan* means an inanimate noun.

We specify the semantic categories, which can be recognized at the Named Entity Recognition (NER) step, via the predicate variable y:

$$P(y) = y^{ORG} \vee y^{PER} \vee y^{LOC} \vee y^{VEN} \vee y^{TIME} \vee y^{TOOL} \vee y^{Others} \tag{61}$$

where ORG, PER, LOC, and VEH denote organizations, person names, locations, and vehicles, respectively; TIME and TOOL denote date and/or time and tools used in an action, respectively; others are used in case of impossible determination of the semantic attribute of a word.

To correctly select an agent as the initiator of the action and an object to which the action is directed, we introduce three additional predicate variables m, f, and l, that formalize the passive voice in the Russian language:

$$\begin{aligned} P(m) &= m^{Part} \vee m^{NOT_{Part}} \\ P(f) &= f^{aux} \vee f^{NOT_{aux}} \\ P(l) &= l^{suff} \vee l^{NOT_{suff}} \end{aligned} \tag{62}$$

Multidimensional predicate $P(x, y, z, m, l, f)$ defines the roles of event arguments via the predicate variables, describing grammatical and semantic characteristics of words in sentences:

$$\begin{aligned} &P(x, y, z, m, l, f) \rightarrow P(x) \wedge P(y) \wedge P(z) \wedge P(m) \wedge P(l) \wedge P(f) \\ &P(x, y, z, m, l, f) = \gamma_k(x, y, z, m, l, f) \times P(x) \times P(y) \times P(z) \times \\ &P(m) \times P(l) \times P(f) \end{aligned} \tag{63}$$

where $k \in [1, h]$, $h = 6$ is the number of roles of event arguments considered in the model. They are *agent, object, PLACE-ARG, TIME-ARG, INSTRUMENT-ARG, REASON-ARG*. The predicate $\gamma_k(x, y, z, m, l, f) = 1$ if the specified characteristics of words in the phrase, which represents a certain event, define one of the above roles, and $\gamma_k(x,y,z,m,l,f)=0$ if the conjunction of grammatical and semantic features of a word does not correspond to any of the roles. Then, relations between the characteristics of words in the sentence that do not describe any role of the event are excluded from the formula (6) by the predicate $\gamma_k(x,y,z,m,l,f)$.

We can specify the role of the agent of the event via the predicate γ_1. That is, the predicate γ_1 shows relations of grammatical and semantic characteristics of the words in Russian sentences that correspond to the agent role of the CRIME, TRANSFER, and POLICE events:

$$\gamma_1(x,z,m,l,f)=\left(y^{ORG}\vee y^{PER}\vee y^{VEN}\vee y^{Other}\right)\left(x^{anim}\vee x^{inan}\right)\wedge \left(z^{nom}\left(f^{NOTaut}l^{NOTsuff}\vee m^{NOTPart}\right)\vee z^{ins}\left(f^{aux}l^{suff}\vee m^{Part}\right)\right) \tag{64}$$

The event object is the second most core participant of the event after the agent. Typically, in traditional grammar, it is a noun phrase that denotes the entity acted upon or which undergoes a change of state of motion. In our specific crime-related domain, the object is more often a harmed person or a vehicle, which moves from one location to another, or something like this. We can also explicitly specify the role of the event object via the predicate γ_2:

$$\gamma_2(x,y,z,m,l,f)=\left(y^{ORG}\vee y^{PER}\vee y^{VEN}\vee y^{Other}\right)\left(x^{anim}\vee x^{inan}\right)\wedge \left(z^{acc}\vee z^{dat}\right)\left(f^{NOTsuff}l^{NOTsuff}\vee m^{NOTPart}\right)\vee z^{nom}\left(f^{aux}l^{suff}\vee m^{Part}\right) \tag{65}$$

In addition to the roles of participants of the event, we can identify other arguments via the LLESs. We distinguish the action attributes of PLACE-ARG and TIME-ARG via the predicates γ_3 and γ_4, respectively:

$$\gamma_3(x,y,z)=\left(y^{LOC}\vee y^{Other}\right)x^{inan}z^{loc} \tag{66}$$

$$\gamma_4(x,y,z)=y^{TIME}\vee x^{inan}\left(z^{loc}\vee z^{acc}\right) \tag{67}$$

In instances when there is not a word in a sentence, which satisfies these Equations (7)–(10), we suppose that a TIME-ARG or a PLACE-ARG or even an object or an agent is missing in this Event. For instance, in the sentence *Yesterday, in the center of the town, a deputy's car was burned,* the subject is missed.

Cross-lingual CRE transfer technique is based on the fact that the same event may be described in various languages. If we have an event type and event arguments roles, which are covered in a sentence of the first part of the corpus, and additionally, we have knowledge about the shared semantic space of aligned sentences in two languages, we can transfer the type and arguments roles of the event from the source language sentence to the target language sentence.

At the first step of the target corpus part processing, we POS-tag raw texts employing morphological processing tools of a particular language. Next, drawing on the knowledge about CRE in a sentence of the source part of the corpus, we tag an event type and event argument roles in an aligned sentence of the target corpus part. For this transferring, we found aligned sentences written in two languages in the two corpus parts and applied patterns of correspondence between morphological tags of the target language sentences and possible roles of the event participants and event attribute that we, in turn, can extract from the sentence of source corpus part.

9.6 Evaluation framework

The performance of the approach introduced in our paper has been ranked by traditional metrics. For each language of our parallel corpus, we calculated precision and recall individually. Considering the fact that we work with low-resource and under-annotated languages, and consequently, we do not have the corpora that include event annotation or corpora that can be used as the "gold standard", we are forced to employ experts to evaluate the results of our experiments. Nevertheless, our approach to computing recall and precision is based on the ACE (automatic content extraction) English Annotation Guidelines for Events [12] perspective on an event in general. In particular, the extent of an event is always the entire sentence within a trigger of the event occurs. Thus, calculating the recall of our experiment, we can assume that a sentence that comprises the trigger of a CRE describes this event.

Then following Santhiya et al. (2021) arguments that an event can include only event participants or additional attributes such as Time-ARG, PLACE-ARG, and INSTRUMENT-ARG, we consider two formats of the event. We tentatively call an event with includes a predicate and participants of the event a *short event*, and an event that comprises any of the event attributes in addition to the mentioned event element – as a *complete event*.

Thus, to evaluate the correctness of our CREE approach, five hundred automatically extracted and identified CRE were randomly selected from each part of the corpus (source and target languages). To avoid potential bias and subjectivity, we involve two experts to analyze the source language and two experts for the target language. The experts were asked to confirm for each of the CRE the correctness of its type, trigger, agent, object, and event attributes. The rating scale allowed three values and can be described as follows: If the "complete event" was extracted correctly the expert marked it "2"; If at least one of the attributes of the event was identified as incorrect but the trigger type and participants of the event were extracted correctly ("short event"), the expert marked it "1"; otherwise the expert marked extracted CRE as "0".

Then, we calculated the precision of short and complete CRE extraction for source and target languages separately. To increase the validation of our study we calculated the agreement of experts via Cohen's kappa coefficients.

In our experiments as a crime-related parallel corpus, we utilize the bilingual corpus of two low-resource and under-annotated languages, namely, Russian and Kazakh.

The corpus has been developed for more than three years (Ku et al. 2008), and now it includes row texts from four news websites on the Kazakhstan information Internet space zakon.kz, caravan.kz, kazlenta.kz, nur.kz for the period from April 2018 to June 2021. The choice of these bilingual sites stems from the fact that they provide a significant number of articles with criminal-related texts about various incidents, for example, robbery, murder, traffic accidents, and others.

Now, the volume of the parallel Kazakh-Russian corpus is not very large and accounts for about 22,000 aligned sentences. In order to align sentences in the corpus, we have applied the automatic text alignment application based on the translation dictionary, followed by manual validation (Ku et al. 2008).

Using verbs that occur both in the dictionary and in sentences as event triggers, we identify more than 30,000 crime-related events in the source corpus part. As previously mentioned, an event type is determined according to the value of the element <DOMAIN> of the trigger verb in the dictionary. For example, following the dictionary, the verb "stole" is a trigger for the offense subtype of CRE.

Table 9.3 The Distribution of Event Types in the Source Part of the Corpus

Event subtype	*Original verb*	*Lemmatized verb*	*Stemmed verb*
Injure	75	3,984	3,542
Offense	366	5,178	3,909
Movement	9	507	461
Traffic accident	139	2,351	2,909
Arrest	239	9,035	8,221
Trial	231	4,250	3,804
PD	294	7,433	6,723

Table 9.4 The Distribution of Events Found in the Source-Language Part of the Corpus into Seven Subtypes

Event type	*Event subtype*	*Trigger type*		
		Noun lemma	*Verb lemma*	*Noun + verb*
CRIME	Injure	456	3,984	298
	Offense	1,972	5,178	495
TRANSFER	Movement	132	507	69
	Traffic accident	611	2,351	104
POLICE	Arrest	947	9,035	498
	Trial	1,363	4,250	1,212
	PD	2,217	7,433	1,653

Table 9.3 shows the distribution of these events into seven subtypes. We simultaneously consider the distribution of original verbs in sentences, verbs lemmatized and stemmed at the stage of preprocessing.

The triggers of events are verbs. There is a distribution of the original form, lemmatized, and stemmed verbs.

The triggers of events are verbs. There is a distribution of the original form, lemmatized, and stemmed verbs. The study of a verb as an event trigger confirms the obvious fact that the recall of the EE from the text is mostly higher in the case of considering the match of the dictionary form to the verb lemma in a text than in the analysis of the verb stems in the text.

Taking into account the fact that a trigger can be not only a verb but also a noun, we considered about 500 nouns as triggers of events, determining the event type by the value of element <DOMAIN> of the noun in our dictionary.

Table 9.4 shows the distribution of events found in the source language part of the corpus into seven subtypes. We consider nouns, verbs, and noun + verb pairs as triggers separately.

The utilization of a noun + verb pair as an event trigger can enhance precision and simultaneously decrease recall of CREE compared to using nouns and verbs as triggers of events separately. For example, using the two-word trigger "court" + "sentenced" can improve the precision of the TRIAL event subtype identification compared to using only the verb "sentenced" as the event trigger. In total, about 4,350 events are extracted from the Russian part of the corpus. Figure 9.3 shows the sample of events extracted from the source language part of the corpus by applying verb + noun triggers.

In the next step, after selecting the events in the corpus and defining their types and subtypes, we identify the event arguments that include the participants and attributes of events described

File	sent number	Subtype of event	Trigger_noun	Trigger_verb
7670_ru_parsed	2	TRIAL	приговор	осуждены
7670_ru_parsed	2	TRIAL	УК	осуждены
1312_ru_parsed	13	TRIAL	УК	возбуждено
7887_ru_parsed	10	ARREST	показания	задержан
3708_ru_parsed	5	ARREST	задержанный	установлено
2596_ru_parsed	4	PD	полиция	обратились
1575_ru_parsed	9	INJURE	травма	умер
7854_ru_parsed	8	INJURE	ранение	нанесено
8704_ru_parsed	1	INJURE	убийство	подозревается
7991_ru_parsed	2	TRAFFIC_ACCIDENT	обгон	вылетел
9146_ru_parsed	11	TRAFFIC_ACCIDENT	наезд	совершил

Figure 9.3 The fragment extracted events from the source part of the corpus.

File	Sentence	Trigger of event	POS of trigger	Subtype of Event	Action	Agent	Object	PLACE-ARG	TIME-ARG	1st expert	2nd expert
8188_ru_parsed	0	убить	VERB	INJURE	убить	муж	женщина		с сентября	2	1
8704_ru_parsed	1	убить	VERB	INJURE	убить	сотрудник	жена	уральске		2	2
2555_ru_parsed	2	застрелить	VERB	INJURE	застрелить	полиция	подозреваем ого	нападение		1	1
2018_ru_parsed	2	застрелить	VERB	INJURE	застрелить	оппонент			3 апреля 1998 года	2	0
2485_ru_parsed	2	сбить	VERB	INJURE	сбить	автомашина	ребенок	зебра		2	1
6507_ru_parsed	3	сбить	VERB	INJURE	сбить	машина	супруг		в 9:00 утра 12 ноября	2	2
3402_ru_parsed	0	грабить	VERB	INJURE	грабить	мужчина	несовершен олетних	талдыкорг ане		2	2

Figure 9.4 The example of events, each of which includes trigger, subtypes, and arguments, are extracted from the Russian part of the corpus.

above. Using logical-linguistic Equations (64)–(67), we determine agent, object, and the attribute roles in each selected action. Figure 9.4 contains the sample of events extracted from the Russian part of the corpus, their subtypes, triggers, and arguments.

The target language of the crime-related parallel corpus that we utilize in our experiment is the Kazakh language. This language is quite difficult for automatic processing. We suppose that the main reason for this is the agglutinativeness and highly inflectional of Turkic languages. This means that a single root may produce hundreds of word forms in the Kazakh language. Each word-forming morpheme has its own specific morphological or semantic meaning (for example, person, case, number, time, mood, etc.). Therefore, it is difficult, if possible, to create a training corpus of sufficient size with enough labeled events.

For that reason, annotating the Kazakh part of the corpus is based on the fact that the same event may be described in various languages, and labeled metadata of a sentence of one language can be transferred to an aligned sentence of another language. Thus, we have employed

Table 9.5 The Patterns of the Kazakh Pos-Tagging Chunks that May Correspond to the Roles of the Event Arguments

Roles of event arguments	*POS-tags*	*Labels of cases*	*Label of possessive case*
Agent	R_ZE, R_ZEQ, R_BOS	-	-
Object	R_ZE, R_ZEQ, R_BOS	C4, C2, C3	S*
PLACE-ARG	R_ZE, R_ZEQ	C5, C6, C3	-
TIME-ARG	R_ZE	C6	-
INSTRUMENT-ARG	R_ZE	C7, C3	S*
Trigger of Event	POS-tags	Additional morphological information	
Action	R_ET	Not ET_KSE and not ET_ESM and not ET_ETU and not ET_ETB	

the knowledge about events and roles of the event arguments that are labeled in the Russian part of the parallel corpus to convey these labels to the Kazakh part of the corpus.

At the first step of the cross-lingual CRE transfer technique, we POS-tag Kazakh raw texts with morphological processing tools proposed by Makhambetov et al. (2013). Their method accounts for both inflectional and derivational morphology, including not fully productive derivation, and uses a standard HMM-based approach to disambiguate the Kazakh language.

As a result of morphological labeling, we have obtained tags with complex morphological information that include both the POS-tag of the word root and the labels of morphological information represented by each morpheme. For example, in the <word pos="qyzmetker_R_ZE ler_N1 i_S3 nen_C6"> tag of "qyzmetkerlerınen" Kazakh word "R_ZE" label means common noun; "N1" means the morpheme of a plural noun; "S3" means a possessive case of the third person of a singular/plural noun; and "C6" means an ablative case of a noun.

Next, taking as a basis the labeled texts of the Russian part of the corpus, we have labeled event types and roles of event participants and event attributes in the Kazakh part of the corpus.

In order to transfer labels from a source language sentence to the target language one, we create patterns of correspondence between morphological tags of the Kazakh sentence and possible triggers and roles of the event arguments, which we receive from the Russian sentence. Table 9.5 shows how morphological labels of the Kazakh text correspond to the possible roles of the event participants and event attributes. We base on the tagset.[1]

Here, R_ZE, R_ZEQ, R_BOS, and R_ET are POS-tags of noun, common; noun, personal; foreign word; and verb, accordingly. C2, C3, C4, C5, C6, C7 are cases of nouns. S* shows a possessive case.

As a result of cross-lingual CRE transfer, we identified triggers, participants, and arguments of the events related to criminal or police work news from the Kazakh language part of our parallel corpus. Figure 9.5 presents a sample of events, each of which includes triggers, subtypes, and arguments that are extracted from the Kazakh part of the corpus.

In total, more than 450 events were extracted from the Kazakh part of the corpus, 69 events of them belong to the ARREST subtype, 72 CRE belong to the TRIAL subtype, 94 events to

File	Sentence	Event	Subtype of Event	Action	Agent	Object	PLACE-ARG	TIME-ARG	1 expert results	2 expert results
2728_kz_parsed	40	POLICE	TRIAL	шығарды	сот	шешім	Ақтөбеде		2	2
7995_kz_parsed	8	POLICE	PD	іздеуге кіріседі	полицейлер	хабарламаны			1	2
8188_kz_parsed	0	CRIME	INJURE	алдап кетті	алаяқ	тұрғындарды			1	1
4703_kz_parsed	0	CRIME	INJURE	берді	Ақтауда				0	0
3977_kz_parsed	7	CRIME	OFFENSE	жасаған		наурызда			0	0
5111_kz_parsed	4	POLICE	ARREST	ұстады	полицейлер	ұрлаушыны	Көкшетауда		2	2
2481_kz_parsed	0	TRANSFER	TRAFFIC ACCIDENT	қағып кетті	Қарағандыда				0	0
8413_kz_parsed	1	CRIME	INJURE	пышақтап тастады	Оралда				0	0

Figure 9.5 The example of events, each of which includes triggers, subtypes, and arguments, are extracted from the Kazakh part of the corpus.

Table 9.6 The Precision of CREE from Parallel Corpus

	Source language (Russian)	*Target language (Kazakh)*
Short CRE	76.30%	61.50%
Complete CRE	73.00%	55.76%

the INJURE subtype, 34 events belong to the TRAFFIC ACCIDENT subtype, 4 events belong to the MOVEMENT subtype, 102 CRE belong to the PD subtype, and 89 events belong to the OFFENSE.

Evaluation of the experiment results was carried out by two experts for each of the languages. Every one of them has more than ten years of experience in editorial or publishing activities. As we mentioned in Section 9.6, the experts ranked 500 randomly selected CREs that were automatically extracted from each part of the corpus (source and target languages) as "0", "1", "or 2". That enabled us to calculate *precision* for short and complete types of events by following a traditional equation:

$$precision = \frac{tp}{tp + fp}, \tag{68}$$

Here calculating the precision of extraction for the so-called "complete" events, we consider a true positive (*tp*) event that is marked as 2. And the false positive (*fp*) is the number of events that include attributes but were not marked by experts as "2".

According to our definition of a *complete event*, it includes event attributes additionally to event participants, in other words, a complete event comprises a short event plus event attributes. Bearing this in mind, for the so-called *short event*, we consider true positive (*tp*) as the number of events that are marked both "2" and "1". And the false positive (*fp)* is the number of events that were marked by experts as "0".

Table 9.6 shows the precision of CREE from the source and target languages of the parallel corpus, which are Russian and Kazakh, respectively.

To compute the *recall* of CREE, we based on our preceding assumption (Section 9) that if a sentence includes an event trigger, it should describe some CRE. We verify how many events were extracted from 500 randomly selected sentences with criminal-related trigger verbs from

Table 9.7 The Recall and F1-Measure of Event Extraction from Parallel Corpus

	Source language (Russian)	*Target language (Kazakh)*
Recall CRE	94.80%	72.40%
F_1 short CRE	84.55%	66.51%
F_1 complete CRE	82.48%	63.00%

Table 9.8 Comparison to the State of the Art Focusing on: Various Languages, the Range of the Event Extraction Types, and Event Arguments that Were Extracting

Approaches and techniques	*PR*	*RC*	*F_1*	*Languages*	*Types of CRE*	*Arguments of CRE*
[8]	0.79	0.72	0.76	English	Cyber-security	Event subtypes
[52]	0.82	0.83	0.82	English	Hate crime	Only individual attributes
[24]	0.88	0.86	0.87	Malaysian	Drug-Related	Only individual attributes
[25]	0.64	0.68	-	Arabic	MANSA event	Short CRE
[9]	0.62	0.59	0.61	Indonesian	Various types	Complete CRE
PaCo-based approach	*0.76/0.73*	*0.94*	*0.85/0.82*	*Russian*	*Various types*	*Short CRE/ complete CRE*
	0.62/0.56	*0.72*	*0.67/0.63*	*Kazakh*		*Short CRE/ complete CRE*

the corpus and calculate *recall* by applying the following traditional equation separately for Kazakh and Russian languages:

$$recall = \frac{tp}{tp + fn}. \tag{69}$$

In this case, we consider both the short and the complete event types as true positive (*tp*) CREE.

Table 9.7 presents the recall and F_1-measure of CREE from the parallel corpus for Russian and Kazakh languages, respectively.

Our analysis showed a decrease in the precision and obviously recall of target language processing compared with the source language. Most likely, the main reason for this is the agglutinativeness and polysemy of the morphology of the Kazakh language. Furthermore, the precision, and, consequently, F1-measure of "short" CRE extraction is higher than the "complete" CRE extraction, although only slightly.

Table 9.8 compares the effectiveness of the proposed PaCo-based approach with other methods of CREE, focusing on various languages, the range of the EE types, and event arguments involved in the events.

Comparing the obtained recall, precision, and F_1 measure with preceding research (Joseph 2021; Lin et al. 2017), we can approve that despite gaining not very high coefficient values, our results are comparable for the target language (Kazakh) and sometimes better for the source language (Russian).

Table 9.9 The Confusion Matrix of the Experts' Assessment: Extraction of Short CRE

	Source language (Russian)		*Target language (Kazakh)*	
First expert	*Second expert*			
	"0"	*"1"*	*"0"*	*"1"*
"0"	93	36	164	72
"1"	15	256	7	257

Table 9.10 The Confusion Matrix of the Experts' Assessment: Extraction of Complete CRE

	Source language (Russian)		*Target language (Kazakh)*	
First expert	*Second expert*			
	"0"	*"2"*	*"0"*	*"2"*
"0"	117	8	192	11
"2"	28	347	48	249

However, in our case, we extract events that consist of all possible information about CRE (complete CRE), namely, a type/subtype, trigger, agent, object, Time-ARG, PLACE-ARG, and INSTRUMENT-ARG.

Furthermore, unlike previous studies (Joseph 2021; Nockleby 2000; Sha et al. 2016; Fincke et al. 2021), which considered only one specific type of event, for instance, hate crimes (Fincke et al. 2021), and so on, we address a wide range of types and subtypes of CRE and calculate the extraction precision for all crime related event types together.

An additional advantage of our approach is an opportunity for EE from the texts in low-resource and under-annotated languages. To be able to refer to the results of experiments in the future, they must be as objective and accurate as possible. Generally, assessing the validity of experiments that are performed on a particular corpus is carried out either with the involvement of experts or by comparison with the so-called "gold standard", i.e., the preliminarily annotated corpus.

Since the fact that our study concerns low-resource and under-annotated languages, we can't validate the results of experiments based on semantically pre-annotated corpora. For that reason, for research results evaluation, the experts' opinions were used. First, two native speaker experts independently assessed the short and complete CRE identification correctness and then the level of agreement of their opinions was checked using Cohen's kappa coefficient (Rahem & Omar 2014).

We calculated Cohen's kappa coefficients for two levels of events (short and complete CRE) in Russian and Kazakh languages separately. As previously mentioned, experts were asked to evaluate the results of the extraction, while the evaluation scale considered three possible options: 1 if short CRE was correctly identified, 2 if complete CRE was correctly identified, and 0 if at least one of the event participants or the subtype of the event trigger was incorrectly identified. While it is worth noting that in calculating the coefficient agreement of short CREs, we considered correct events that were noted by the expert either 1 or 2.

Tables 9.9 and 9.10 present the confusion matrix of the experts' assessment of the CREE from the Russian-Kazakh parallel corpus. In the tables, the rows present the decision of the first

Table 9.11 Cohen's Kappa Coefficients of Agreement

	Source language (Russian)	*Target language (Kazakh)*
Short CRE	89.80%	84.20%
Complete CRE	92.80%	88.20%

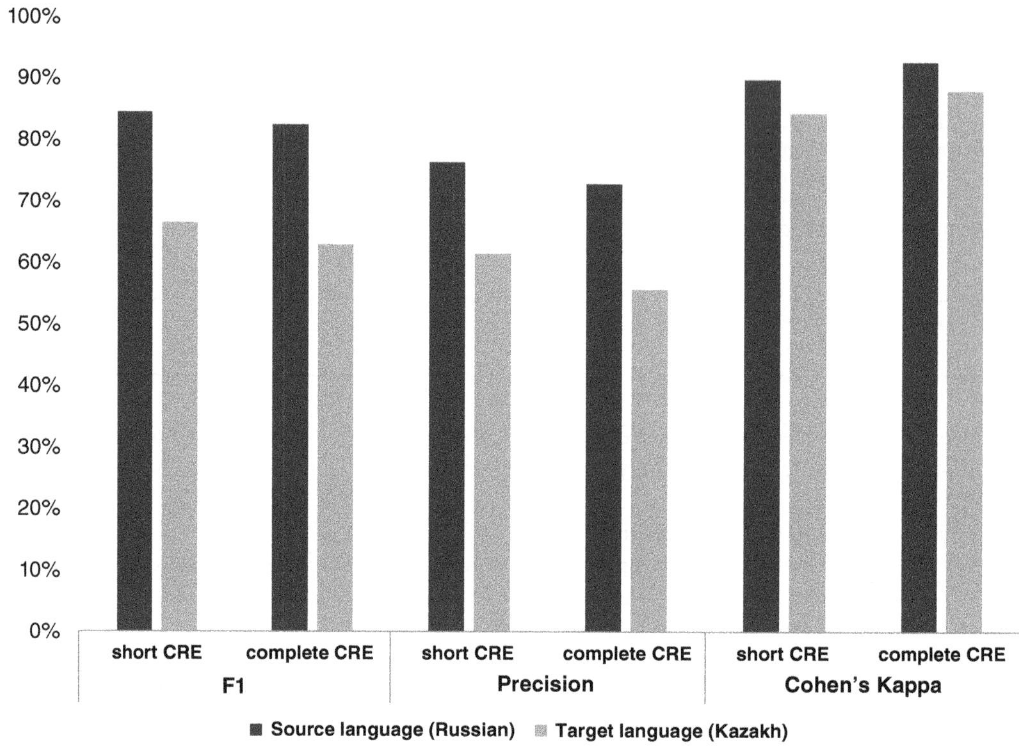

Figure 9.6 Summary of the experiment's evaluation metrics.

expert, and the columns, the decision of the second one for short and complete CREE of source and target parts of the parallel corpus.

Table 9.11 presents Cohen's kappa coefficients for *short* and *complete* CRE of two languages separately that are calculated based on this matrix. The commonly accepted scale for estimating Cohen's kappa coefficient is as follows (Rahem & Omar 2014): from 0.81 to 0.99 — near perfect agreement; from 0.6 to 0.80 — substantial agreement; from 0.41 to 0.60 — moderate agreement; and from 0.21 to 0.40 — fair agreement. Based on the scale, we can claim that values of Cohen's kappa coefficients contribute to increasing validation of our study. However, despite the fact that the values of the agreement coefficients look promising, further study must continue to handle increasing semantically annotated corpora for validation of obtained results.

The experiment's evaluation metrics are summarized in Figure 9.6.

Note

1 tagset.

Chapter 10

Conclusion

The second section of the monograph presents an analytical review of existing problems concerning the technology of searching for illegal information in text data. The current state and prospects of the development of formalization and information search methods in unstructured and semi-structured text arrays are considered, as well as the existing possibilities of using information extraction (IE) methods to extract criminally related information. On the basis of the analysis, a general approach to formalization and identification of CRE has been developed.

The third section studies the relationship between linguistic formalisms in natural-language texts and the real meaning of a criminally or socially significant event in society. The gnoseological aspects of information processes of identification of semantic (lexical) and grammatical identifiers of criminality are considered. On the basis of this analysis, a method of generating structured machine-readable information based on an unstructured text is presented. Also, the third section deals with the specific features of extracting crime-related event (CRE) from texts. In particular, we consider the technology of searching semantically close short text fragments, the implementation of which allows to increase the completeness of the information retrieval system of CRE.

The fourth section considers the mathematical description of the developed logical-linguistic model of fact extraction from arrays of semi-structured texts and shows the specific features of the implementation of this model for the texts of Russian and English languages. Also, we give a method for formalizing the grammatical ways of expressing the urging fact in English, the use of which will make it possible to identify texts of a certain urgent-aggressive orientation.

In the fifth section, the analysis of existing problems of automatic processing of the Kazakh language and the specific features of its formalization is considered. We have developed a logical-linguistic model of Open IE for the Kazakh language based on the analysis of possibilities for formalizing factual information in the texts of the Kazakh language. The use of the developed model allows extracting elements of the triplet of fact from the sentences of the Kazakh language on the basis of relations of grammatical and semantic categories of sentence words.

The sixth section focuses on the elements of information technology for the identification and analysis of criminally related information in the text corpus. In particular, we describe the technology for the formation of the Kazakh-Russian parallel corpus of texts on criminal topics. The method of alignment of the created corpus of texts on criminal topics, based on the identification of facts, is considered and the developed application, which allows working with the corpus, is described. In addition, the section provides the structure and tagset of the created corpus of the Kazakh and Russian languages.

DOI: 10.1201/9781003587514-10

In general, the use of technology for the identification of criminally related information in multilingual text arrays, which aspects are given in the monograph, will increase the efficiency of semantic analysis of the texts of the Kazakh language, and the natural language as a whole.

Further work on the practical implementation of the developed set of models, methods, and technologies will make it possible to automate the extraction by state authorities of information that has elements of criminal meaning from external textual data sources such as social networks, electronic media, forums, blogs, and other electronic resources.

Thus, in this study, we focused on the pattern-based EE approach that gives the opportunity to extract crime-related events from news articles that were published in low-resource and under-annotated languages.

First, *the major methodological contribution* of the work is the introduction of the two-stage method to extract criminal and police-related events from a bilingual parallel corpus, which is composed of two low-resource and under-annotated languages.

In this study, we demonstrated how logical-linguistic equations, which represent roles of the event participants according to the predefined structure of the event subtype, and the cross-lingual CRE transfer strategy could be successfully used for crime-related event extraction (CREE) based on the parallel corpus.

As already noted, there are a large number of different techniques for event extraction (EE). Most of them exploit pattern-based (Rahma & Romadhony 2021; Pham & Ho 2014) and machine learning (ML) methods (Khairova et al. 2016, 2021; Riloff 1993). The main reason for the absence of a unified standard approach for EE lies in the fact that ML approaches need large, semantically annotated corpora but a pattern-based EE approach is a time-consuming and labor-intensive task that must involve a lot of domains. Therefore, the *additional methodological contribution* of our research is the enhancement of the pattern-based EE method (Rahma & Romadhony 2021; Moreno-Jiménez et al. 2017; Khairova et al. 2019), which is based on the multilingual synonyms dictionary with crime-related lexis and logic-linguistic equations. These equations allow us to represent the event's argument roles via the relationship between the grammatical and semantic characteristics of the words in a sentence.

Regarding EE from the terrorism and criminal domain texts, on the one hand, this domain can be considered well-researched (Björne et al. 2017; Moreno-Jiménez et al. 2017; Khairova et al. 2019), but on the other hand, many of the involved studies consider the problem of CRE separately for various types of crime events (related to terrorism, cybercrime, crimes against the person, crimes related to transport, etc.) (Joseph 2021).

Enhancing the pattern-based EE method (Rahma & Romadhony 2021; Khairova et al. 2019; Joseph 2021), we address the challenge of increasing the number of various event types related to police and criminal activities that can be extracted from news articles simultaneously.

As explained in Section 9 for modification of mentioned cross-lingual technique, we propose to simultaneously use the (1) preliminary POS-tag labeling of target language texts; and (2) the patterns of the correspondence between POS-tags of target language sentences and possible roles of the event participants/attributes that are transferred from an aligned source language sentence. This modification allows us to handle the bilingual parallel corpus. The research (Abdelkoui & Kholladi 2017) fairly states the EE task becomes more difficult for texts written in low-resourced and under-annotated languages.

Additionally, gold-standard annotations for EE are publicly available only for a few languages. Usually, in such corpora there are only in English (Wang et al. 2020) and some other European languages. In our study, we *modify the cross-lingual CRE transfer technique* for processing the second part of the corpus (target language), based on supplementary knowledge about the semantic similarity patterns of the considered pair of languages (Abdelkoui & Kholladi 2017).

The incremental *practical contribution* of the research is the following. Unlike major studies on the detection and extraction of CRE in news articles, which analyzed only one certain type of crime (Fincke et al. 2021; Lin et al. 2017), we consider the big group of events that relates to unlawful action. In order to detect these events, we have predefined the structure of three event types, namely, TRANSFER, CRIME, and POLICE several subtypes (see Table 9.2). Every subtype structure includes about two participants and several attributes of the action or event. Thus, one of the practical contributions is distinguishing seven different subtypes of events that can be involved in a criminal action that allows obtaining facts related to police and criminal activities clearly and more accurately.

We should also highlight the practical contribution that was produced by the cross-lingual CRE transfer technique for transferring labeled metadata from a sentence of one language into an aligned sentence of another language. Based on the technique, diverse EE applications for low-resourced and under-annotated languages can be designed. As explained in Section 9.5 and summarized in Table 9.6, applying this technique for the Russian-Kazakh aligned corpus allows us to extract CREs from news articles in the Kazakh language. Every identified event comprises event type, roles of event participants, and event attributes extracted from the Kazakh part of the corpus. Our experiment showed the precision of CREE in the Kazakh part of the corpus is 61.50% for short CRE that includes the correctly identified trigger, subtype/type, agent, and object, and 55.76% for complete CRE that includes extra correctly identified roles of the attributes of the event. We obtained the patterns of POS-tags chunks of Kazakh texts that can represent the event participants (agent, object) and event attributes (PLACE-ARG, TIME-ARG, and INSTRUMENT-ARG). Even though the obtained precision is lower than the average result of the EE approach (Lin et al. 2017), we have extracted CRE from texts in the Kazakh language for the first time. Since this language is a low-resource and under-annotated language, we had little capacity to involve extra-linguistic resources to process the Kazakh language.

Next, the event subtype distributions obtained as a result of the experiments can contribute to the development of social research in regions. For instance, in our illustrative experiment on the dataset comprising texts on news articles of the Kazakh region (Table 9.4), CRE related to police activities appeared the most frequently (about 63%), and only about 12% and about 7% of events relate to directly suffered persons and traffic accidents, respectively. Including such handling for web news articles into various content analysis stages allows us to compare distributions of crime types of events by different countries and over different time periods.

Finally, it is worth mentioning the result of the research part concerning the problem of an event trigger identification in a sentence. Traditionally, the main verb of the sentence is considered an event trigger in pattern-based EE approaches (Campos et al. 2014; Björne et al. 2017). However, based on the multilingual synonyms dictionary with criminal-related lexis (see Figure 29) and the conducted experiments, we demonstrate that the precision of CREE increases when a pair of a noun and a verb are considered as a trigger of the event. Additionally, as summarized in Table 9.3, we considered the impact of the verb form (original form, verbs lemmatized, or stemmed verb) on the EE recall. We realize that we conducted experiments only on one text corpus. However, the non-contradiction of observed results to the general natural language processing (NLP) knowledge looks promising and allows us to expect our findings to be confirmed on other corpora.

In Table 10.1, we summarize the methodological and practical contributions of our research.

Table 10.1 Summary of Research Contributions

Type of contribution	*Contribution*
Methodological and theoretical contributions	• Developing the two-stage method of extracting criminal and police-related events from a bilingual parallel corpus composed of two low-resource and under-annotated languages, we address the challenges of crime-related events extraction from not special domain documents (like news articles) described by Hogenboom (2014). • Enhancing the pattern-based event extraction method (Liu et al. 2018; Subburathinam et al. 2019; Fincke et al. 2021) we address the challenge of increasing the number of various event types related to police and criminal activities that can be extracted from news articles simultaneously. • Modifying the cross-lingual CRE transfer technique, we address the methodological challenges mentioned by language semantic similarity patterns researchers (Davani et al. 2019).
Practical contributions	• Predetermining the structure of seven subtypes of events allows extracting facts related to police and criminal activities from news websites clearer and more accurate. • Based on the modified cross-lingual CRE transfer technique, diverse EE applications for low-resourced and under-annotated languages can be designed. For example, we efficiently extracted CREs from news articles in the Kazakh language and obtained the patterns of POS-tags chunks of Kazakh texts that can represent event structures. • The event subtype distributions obtained as a result of the experiments can contribute to the development of social research in regions (see Table 9.4). • Using the special NLP approaches such as applying a pair of noun + verb as an event trigger instead of only verb, as well as lemmatization of text verbs, allows increasing the facts extracting recall.

References

Abdelkoui, F., Kholladi, M.-Kh. 2017. Extracting Criminal-Related Events from Arabic Tweets: A Spatio-Temporal Approach, *Journal of Information Technology Research (JITR)* 10(3): 34–47.

About Wolfram|Alpha's Knowledge Base Covers an Immense Range of Areas. [Online]. Available: wolframalpha.com/about.

Adily, A., Karystianis, G., Butler, T. 2021. Text Mining Police Narratives for Mentions of Mental Disorders in Family and Domestic Violence Events, *Trends and Issues in Crime and Criminal Justice* 7(629): 1–6.

Agichtein, E., Gravano, L. 2000. Snowball: Extracting Relations from Large Plaintext Collections, *Proceedings of the 5th ACM International Conference on Digital Libraries*. San Antonio, Texas, 2000: 85–94.

Akbik, A., Loser, A. 2012. Kraken: N-ary Facts in Open Information Extraction, *Proceedings of the Joint Workshop on Automatic Knowledge Base Construction and Web-scale Knowledge Extraction*: 52–56.

Allan, J. 2012. *Topic Detection and Tracking: Event-Based Information Organization*. Berlin: Springer: 12.

Angeli, G., Premkumar, M.J., Manning, C.D. 2015. Leveraging Linguistic Structure for Open Domain Information Extraction, *Proceedings of the 53rd Annual Meeting of the Association for Computational Linguistics*: 344–354.

Answers. Asking a Question on WikiAnswers. Wikipedia: Reference desk. [Online]. Available: https://en.wikipedia.org/wiki/Wikipedia:Reference_desk.

Baeza-Yates, R. 1996. Visualizing Large Answer It Text Databases, *Workshop on Advanced User Interfaces*. Gubbio, Italy, May 1996, ACM Press: 101–107.

Baeza-Yates, R., Ribeiro-Neto, B. 1999. *Modern Information Retrieval*. (Vol. 463, No. 1999). New York: ACM press.

Barzilay, R., McKeown, K.R. 2001. Extracting Paraphrases from a Parallel Corpus, *Proceedings of the 39th Annual Meeting on Association for Computational Linguistics*. Stroudsburg, PA, USA: 50–57.

Battistelli, D., Bruneau, C., Dragos, V. 2020. Building a Formal Model for Hate Detection in French Corpora, *24th International Conference on Knowledge-Based and Intelligent Information & Engineering Systems* 176: 2358–2365.

Björne, J., Ginter, F., Salakoski, T. 2017. The Biomedical Event Extraction Downstream Application, *EPE*: 17–24.

Blondel, V., Gajardo, A., Heymans, M., Senellart, P., Dooren, P. 2004. A Measure of Similarity Between Graph Vertices: Applications to Synonym Extraction and Web Searching, *SIAM Review* 46(4): 647–666.

Bolla, R.A. 2014. Crime Pattern Detection Using Online Social Media, *Masters Theses*: 7321p.

Campos, D. et al. 2014. *Source Code for Biology and Medicine* 9(1): 1–13.

Chapaev, D., Turapbekov, B. 2018. *Building Kazakh Language Open Source Corpora Using Wikipedia Resources. Suleyman Demirel University Bulletin*. Turkey: Suleyman Demirel University: 153–160.

Chen, H. et al. 2004. Crime Data Mining: An Overview and Case Studies, *IEEE Computer Society Press Los Alamitos, CA, USA* 37(4): 50–56.

Chen, P., Kurland, J. 2018. Time, Place, and Modus Operandi: A Simple Apriori Algorithm Experiment for Crime Pattern Detection, *Proceedings of the 9th International Conference on Information, Intelligence, Systems and Applications*, Zakynthos, Greece: 1–3.

Cohen, K., Johansson, F., Kaati, L., Mork, J.C. 2014. Detecting Linguistic Markers for Radical Violence in Social Media, *In Terrorism and Political Violence* 26(1): 246–256.

Cohn, M.A., Mehl, M.R., Pennebaker, J.W. 2001. Linguistic Markers of Psychological Change Surrounding, *In Sychological Science* 15(10): 687–693.

Çöltekin, Ç. 2020. A Corpus of Turkish Offensive Language on Social Media, *Proceedings of the 12th Conference on Language Resources and Evaluation (LREC)*: 6174–6184.

Crestan, E., Pantel P. 2010. Web-Scale Knowledge Extraction from Semi-Structured Tables, *WWW '10 Proceedings of the 19th International Conference on World Wide Web*: 1081–1082.

Das, P., Das, A.K. 2017. A Two-Stage Approach of Named-Entity Recognition for Crime Analysis, *Proceedings of International Conference on Computing, Communication and Networking Technologies*: 1–5.

Das, P., Das, A.K. 2019. Graph-Based Clustering of Extracted Paraphrases for Labelling Crime Reports, *Knowledge Based Systems* 179: 55–76.

Dasgupta, T. et al. 2017. Crimeprofiler: Crime Information Extraction and Visualization from News Media, *Proceedings of the International Conference on Web Intelligence*, ACM: 541–549.

Davani, A.M. et al. 2019. Reporting the Unreported: Event Extraction for Analyzing the Local Representation of Hate Crimes, *Proceedings of the 9th International Joint Conference on Natural Language Processing (EMNLP-IJCNLP):* 5753–5757.

De Boom, C., Canneyt, S.V., Bohez, S., Demeester, T., Dhoedt, B., 2016. Learning Semantic Similarity for Very Short Texts, *Pattern Recognition Letters* 80: 150–156.

De Carvalho, V.D.H., Costa, A.P.C.S. 2022. Exploring Text Mining and Analytics for Applications in Public Security: An In-depth Dive into a Systematic Literature Review, *SciELO Preprints*, 10.51359/2965-4661.2023.259008.

De Mendonça, R.R. et al. 2019. OntoCexp: A Proposal for Conceptual Formalization of Criminal Expressions, *16th International Conference on Information Technology-New Generations* (ITNG 2019): 43–48.

De Mendonça, R.R. et al. 2020. A Framework for Detecting Intentions of Criminal Acts in Social Media: A Case Study on Twitter, *Information* 11(3): 154, https://doi.org/10.3390/info11030154.

Duc-Thuan, V., Bagheri, E., 2016. Open Information Extraction. *Encyclopedia with Semantic Computing and Robotic Intelligence* 1(1): 1630003.

Duncker, K. 1936. Lernen und Einsicht im Dienst der Zielerreichung, *Acta Psychologica, Hague* 1: 77–82.

Etzioni, O., Banko, M., Soderland, S., Weld, D. 2008. Open Information Extraction from the Web. *Communications of the ACM 51*. New York, NY, USA: 68–74.

European Guide to good Practice in Knowledge Management – Part 1: *Knowledge Management Framework CWA 14924-1*. March 2004. [Online]. Available: https://www.cencenelec.eu/.

Fader, A., Soderland, S., Etzioni, O. 2011. Identifying Relations for Open Information Extraction, *Proceedings of the Conference on Empirical Methods in Natural Language Processing*. Edinburgh, Scotland, UK: 1535–1545.

Fillmore, Ch. 1971. Verbs of Judging: An Exercise in Semantic Description. In Charles J. Fillmore and D. Terence Langendoen (eds), *Studies in Linguistic Semantics, NY*: 273–290. New York: Holt, Rinehart and Winston: 273–290.

Fillmore, Ch. 1977. The Case for Case Reopened. In P. Cole and J.M. Sadock (eds) *Syntax and Semantics, Volume 8: Grammatical Relations*. New York: Academic Press: 59–81.

Fillmore, Ch. 1985. Frames and the Semantics of Understanding. *Quaderni di Semantica* VI: 222–254.

Fincke, S., Agarwal, S., Miller, S., Boschee, E. 2021. Language Model Priming for Cross-Lingual Event Extractio, *arXiv preprint* arXiv:2109.12383.

Fung, P., McKeown, K. 1994. Aligning Noisy Parallel Corpora Across Language Groups: Word Pair Feature Matching by Dynamic Time Warping, *Proceedings of the First Conference of the Association for Machine Translation in the Americas (AMTA-94)*. Columbia, Maryland, USA: 81–88.

Gale, W.A., Church, K.W. 1993. A Program for Aligning Sentences in Bilingual Corpora, *ACL'93 29th Annual Meeting*. USA (NJ) 19(1): 75–102.

Gamallo, P., Garcia, M. 2015. Multilingual Open Information Extraction, *Portuguese Conference on Artificial Intelligence*: 711–722.

Gamallo, P., Garcia, M., Fernandez-Lanza, S. 2012. Dependency-Based Open Information Extraction, *Proceedings of the Joint Workshop on Unsupervised and Semi-Supervised Learning in NLP*: 10–18.

Gashteovsk, K., Gemulla, R., Del Corro, L. 2017. MinIE: Minimizing Facts in Open Information Extraction, *Proceedings of the Conference on Empirical Methods in Natural Language Processing*: 2630–2640.

Gatterbauer, W., Bohunsky, P., Herzog, M., Krupl, B., Pollak, B. 2007. Towards Domain-Independent Information Extraction from Web Tables, *Proceedings WWW-07*. Banff, Canada: 71–80.

Getman, J., Ellis, J., Strassel, S., Song, Z., Tracey, J. 2018. Laying the Ground- Work for Knowledge Base Population: Nine Years of Linguistic Resources for TAC KBP, *Proceedings of the 11th International Conference on Language Resources and Evaluation (LREC-2018).*

Goźdź-Roszkowski, S. 2021. Corpus Linguistics in Legal Discourse, *International Journal for the Semiotics of Law* 34: 1515–1540, https://doi.org/10.1007/s11196-021-09860-8.

Grabar, N., Kanishcheva, O., Hamon, T. 2018. Multilingual Aligned Corpus with Ukrainian as the Target Language, *SLAVICORP, Prague*: 53–57.

Gunawan, D. et al. 2019. Building the Pornography Corpus for Bahasa Indonesia Based on TRUST+™ Positif Database, *International Conference on ICT for Smart Society (ICISS), IEEE* 7: 1–7.

Han, L., Kashyap, A., Finin, T., Mayfield, J., Weese, J. 2013. UMBC EBIQUITY-CORE: Semantic Textual Similarity Systems, *Proceedings of the Second Joint Conference on Lexical and Computational Semantics* 1: 44–52.

Han, S. et al. 2021. American Hate Crime Trends Prediction with Vent Extraction. *arXiv preprint* arXiv:2111.04951.

Harme, J. 2018. Last Year but Not Yesterday? Explaining Differences in the Locations of Finnish and Russian Time Adverbials Using Comparable Corpora, *SLAVICORP*, Prague: 60–63.

Hassani, H., Huang, X., Silva, E., Ghodsi, M. 2016. A Review of Data Mining Applications in Crime, *Statistical Analysis and Data Mining: The ASA Data Science Journal* 9(3):139–154.

Hitzler, P., Krötzsch, M., Rudolph, S. 2010. *Foundations of Semantic Web Technologies*. CRC Press. Boca Raton, FL: 427 p.

Hogenboom, F. 2014. Automated Detection of Financial Events in News Text, *ERIM PhD Series in Research in Management, 326 ERIM Reference Number: EPS-2014-326-LIS, SIKS Dissertation Series No. 2014-41.*

Hossain, K.T. et al. 2020. Forecasting Violent Events in the Middle East and North Africa Using the Hidden Markov Model and Regularized Autoregressive Models, *The Journal of Defense Modeling and Simulation* 17(3): 269–283.

Itskov, F.E., Shabanov-Kushnarenko, Yu.P., Sharonova, N.V. 1992. Ob osnovnykh svoystvakh predikata ekvivalentnosti i yego ispol'zovanii v teorii intellekta. *Metody analiza i sinteza sistem: nauch.-tekhn.* sb. Severodonetsk: Izd. KHIRE.: 22–27.

Jakobson, R., Shifters & Verbal Categories. 1990. In on Language. edited by R. Linda Waugh and Monique Monville-Burston, Harvard University Press, Cambridge, London, England: 386–392.

Jones, R., Ghani, R., Mitchell, T., Riloff, E. 2003. Active Learning with Multiple View Feature Sets, *ECML 2003 Workshop on Adaptive Text Extraction and Mining*: 203–233.

Joseph, J.G. et al. 2021. Automatic Information Extraction and Inferencing System from Online News Sources for Substance Abuse Cases, *CEUR Workshop Proceedings of the International Semantic Intelligence Conference, ISIC:* 516–520.

Joseph, N. 2021. *Crime Analysis Based on K-Means Clustering*. Preprint.

Jungnickel, D. 2008. Graph, Networks and Algorithms. *Algorithms and Computation in Mathematics* (5), Springer Berlin Heidelberg, New York: 650 p.

Jurafsky, D., J.H. Martin. 2008. *Speech and Language Processing: An Introduction to Natural Language Processing, Computational Linguistics, and Speech Recognition*. 2nd ed. Upper Saddle River, NJ: Prentice Hall: 1024. ISBN-13: 978-0131873216.

Karimi, M., Gharehchopogh, F.S. 2020. An Improved K-Means with Artificial Bee Colony Algorithm for Clustering Crimes, *Journal of Advances in Computer Research Quarterly* 11(3): 61–82.

Karystianis, G. et al. 2018. Automatic Extraction of Mental Health Disorders from Domestic Violence Police Narratives: Text Mining Study, *Journal of Medical Internet Research* 20(9): E11548, https://doi.org/10.2196/11548.

Katz, J., Fodor, J. 1964. The Structure of a Semantic Theory. In *The Structure of Language: Readings in the Philpsophy of Language*. edited by *Keith J.* Englewood Cliffs, NJ: Prentice Hall: 479–518.

Kay, M., Roscheisen, M. 1993. Text Translation Alignment, *Computational Linguistics* 19(1): 121–142.

Khairova, N., Kolesnyk, A., Mamyrbayev, O., Mukhsina, K. 2019. The Aligned Kazakh-Russian Parallel Corpus Focused on the Criminal Theme, *CEUR Workshop Proceedings*: 116–125.

Khairova, N., Lewoniewski, W., Wecel, K. 2017. Estimating the Quality of Articles in Russian Wikipedia Using the Logical-Linguistic Model of Fact Extraction, *Conference Proceedings of BIS 2017. Part of the Lecture Notes in Business Information Processing Book Series*, Poland, Poznan: 28–40.

Khairova, N., Lewoniewski, W., Węcel, K., Mamyrbayev, O., Mukhsina, K. 2018a. Comparative Analysis of the Informativeness and Encyclopedic Style of the Popular Web Information Sources, *Business Information Systems*. Springer, Cham 320: 333–347.

Khairova, N., Mamyrbayev, O., Mukhsina, K., Kolesnyk, A. 2020a. Logical-Linguistic Model for Multilingual Open Information Extraction. *Cogent Engineering* 7(1): 1714829.

Khairova, N., Mamyrbayev, O., Rizun, N., Razno, M., Ybytayeva, G., 2023. A Parallel Corpus-Based Approach to the Crime Event Extraction for Low-Resource Languages, *IEEE Access* 11: 54093–54111. doi:10.1109/ACCESS.2023.3281680.

Khairova, N. F., Petrasova, S., Gautam, A.P.S. 2016. The Logical-Linguistic Model of Fact Extraction from English Texts. In G. Dregvaite, R. Damasevicius (eds), *Information and Software Technologies: 22nd International Conference, ICIST 2016, Druskininkai, Lithuania, October 13–15, 2016, Proceedings* (Vol. 639, pp. 625–635). Cham: Springer. https://doi.org/10.1007/978-3-319-46254-7_51

Khairova, N., Petrasova, S., Lewoniewski, W., Mamyrbayev, O., Mukhsina, K. 2018b. Automatic Extraction of Synonymous Collocation Pairs from a Text Corpus. FedCSIS, *Proceedings of the Federated Conference on Computer Science and Information Systems* 15: 485–488.

Khairova, N., Petrasova, S., Mamyrbayev, O., Mukhsina, K. 2020b. Open Information Extraction as Additional Source for Kazakh Ontology Generation, ACIIDS 2020, *Lecture Notes in Artificial Intelligence 12033, Intelligent Information and Database Systems – 12th Asian Conference*, ACIIDS 2020, Phuket, Thailand, 23–26 March: 86–96.

Kilgarriff, A., Baisa, V., Bušta, J., Jakubíček, M., Kovář, V., Michelfeit, J., Rychlý, P., VíSuchomel, V. 2014. *The Sketch Engine: Ten Years On, Lexicography*. Berlin, Heidelberg: Springer: 7–36.

Kobayashi, N., Inui, K., Yuji, M. 2007. Opinion Mining from Web Documents: Extraction and Structurization. *Journal of Japanese Society for Artificial Intelligence, Special Issue on Data Mining and Statistical Science* 22(2): 227–238.

Ku, C.H., Iriberri, A., Leroy, G. 2008. Crime Information Extraction from Police and Witness Narrative Reports, *Proceedings of the 2008 IEEE Conference on Technologies for Homeland Security:* 193–198.

Kumar, R., Reganti, A.N., Bhatia, A., Maheshwari, T. 2018. Aggression-Annotated Corpus of Hindi-English Code-Mixed Data, *Proceedings of the 11th Language Resources and Evaluation Conference (LREC)*, arXiv preprint arXiv:1803.09402.

Lewoniewski, W., Węcel, K., Abramowicz, W. 2016. Quality and Importance of Wikipedia Articles in Different Languages, *International Conference on Information and Software Technologies*. Poznan, Poland: 613–624.

Li, L., Liu, Y., Qin, M. 2020. Extracting Biomedical Events with Parallel Multi-Pooling Convolutional Neural Networks, *IEEE/ACM Transactions on Computational Biology and Bioinformatics* 17(2): 599–607.

Li, P., Sun, M., Xue, P. 2010. Fast-Champollion: A Fast and Robust Sentence Alignment Algorithm, *Proceedings of the 23rd International Conference on Computational Linguistics: Posters*, Beijing, China: 710–718.

Li, Q., Zhang, J., Zhang, Y. 2020. Event Extraction for Criminal Legal Text, *2020 IEEE International Conference on Knowledge Graph (ICKG):* 573–580.

Lin, Y., Liu, Z., Sun, M. 2017. Neural Relation Extraction with Multi-Lingual Attention, *Proceedings of the 55th Annual Meeting of the Association for Computational Linguistics* 1: 34–43.

Liu, X., Chen, Y., Liu, K., Zhao, J. 2018a. Event Detection Via Gated Multilingual Attention Mechanism, *32nd AAAI Conference on Artificial Intelligence*: 4865–4872.

Liu, X., Luo, Zh., Huang, H. 2018b. Jointly Multiple Events Extraction via Attention-Based Graph Information Aggregation, *Proceedings of the 2018 Conference on Empirical Methods in Natural Language Processing*.

Liyuan, L., Xiang, R., Qi, Z., et al. 2017. Heterogeneous Supervision for Relation Extraction: A Representation Learning Approach, *Proceedings of the 2017 Conference on Empirical Methods in Natural Language Processing*: 46–56.

Luckicgev, S. 2009. Graphical Notations for Rule Modeling. In A. Giurca, D. Gašević, K. Taveter (eds), *Handbook of Research on Emerging Rule-Based Languages and Technologies. Open Solutions and Approaches*, 1, New York: Hershey: 76–98.

Makhambetov, O., Makazhanov, A., Yessenbayev, Z., Matkarimov, B., Sabyrgaliyev, I., Sharafudinov, A. 2013. Assembling the Kazakh Language Corpus, *Proceedings of the Conference on Empirical Methods in Natural Language Processing, Kazakhstan*: 1022–1033.

Manning, C.D., Raghavan, P., Schütze, H. 2008. *Introduction to Information Retrieval.* Cambridge: Cambridge University Press. ISBN: 978-0-521-86571-5. https://doi.org/10.1017/CBO9780511809071

Manning, Ch.D. 2015. Computational Linguistics and Deep Learning, *Computational Linguistics* 41(4): 701–707.

McCulloch, W.S., Pitts, W. 1943. A Logical Calculus of the Ideas Immanent in Nervous Activity, *Bulletin of Mathematical Biophysics* 5: 115–133, https://doi.org/10.1007/BF02478259.

Melchuk, I.A. 2000. Course of General Morphology. Morphological Means, *Languages of Russian Culture, Vienna, Wiener Slawistischer Almanach* 3(3): 367p.

Meloy, J.R. 2011. Approaching and Attacking Public Figures: A Contemporary Analysis of Communications and Behavior. In J.R. Meloy, J. Hoffmann (Eds.), *Threatening Communications and Behavior: Perspectives on the Pursuit of Public Figures*. Washington, DC: The National Academies Press: 75–101. ISBN: 978-0-309-15141-0. https://doi.org/10.17226/13091

Meloy, J.R., Hoffmann, J., Guldimann, A., James, D. 2012. The Role of Warning Behaviors in Threat Assessment: An Exploration and Suggested Typology, *Behavioral Sciences & the Law* 30(3): 256–279.

Meloy, J.R., Hoffmann, J., Roshdi, K., Guldimann, A. 2014. Some Warning Behaviors Discriminate Between School Shooters and Other Students of Concern, *Journal of Threat Assessment and Management* 1(3): 203–211.

Meloy, J.R., Mohandie, K., Knoll, J.L., Hoffmann, J. 2015. The Concept of Identification in Threat Assessment, *Behavioral Sciences & the Law* 33(2–3): 213–237.

Miller, G.A., Beckwith, R., Fellbaum, C., Gross, D., Miller, K.J. 1990. Introduction to WordNet: An On-line Lexical Database, *International Journal of Lexicography* 3(4): 235–244.

Miok, K., Skrlj, B., Zaharie, D., Robnik-Sikonja, M. 2021. To BAN or Not to BAN: Bayesian Attention Networks for Reliable Hate Speech Detection, *Cognitive Computation*: 1–19.

Mooney, R.J., Bunescu, R. 2005. Mining Knowledge from Text Using Information Extraction, *Newsletter. ACM SIGKDD Explorations Newsletter – Natural Language Processing and Text Mining* 7(1): 3–10.

Moreno-Jiménez, L.-G. et al. 2017. Criminal Events Detection in News Stories Using Intuitive Classification, *Proceedings of Mexican International Conference on Artificial Intelligence, MICAI*: 120–132.

Mozafari, M., Farahbakhsh, R., el Crespi, N. 2019. A BERT-Based Transfer Learning Approach for Hate Speech Detection in Online Social Media, *Proceedings of the International Conference on Complex Networks and Their Applications*: 928–940.

Mukherjee, S., Sarkar, K. 2020. Analyzing Large News Corpus Using Text Mining Techniques for Recognizing High Crime Prone Areas, *Proceedings of the 2020 IEEE Calcutta Conference* (CALCON): 444–450, https://doi.org/10.1109/CALCON49167.2020.9106554.

Mullah, N.S., Zainon, W.M. 2021. Advances in Machine Learning Algorithms for Hate Speech Detection in Social Media: A Review, *IEEE Access* 9: 88364–88376.

Nguyen, T.H., Grishman, R. 2018. Graph Convolutional Networks with Argument-Aware Pooling for Event Detection, *Proceedings of the 32nd AAAI Conference Artificial Intelligence*: 5900–5907.

Nirenburg, S., Raskin, V. 2004. *Ontological Semantics.* Cambridge, MA: The MIT Press: 420p.

Nivre, J. et al. 2016. Universal Dependencies v1: A Multilingual Treebank Collection, *Proceedings of the 10th International Conference on Language Resources and Evaluation (LREC 2016)*, Paris, France, May. European Language Resources Association (ELRA): 62–69.

Nockleby, J.T. 2000. Hate Speech. In L.W. Levy, K.L. Karst et al. (eds), *Encyclopedia of the American Constitution*, 2nd ed. New York: Macmillan: 1277–1279.

Osathitporn, P., Soonthornphisaj, N., Vatanawood, W. 2017. A Scheme of Criminal Law Knowledge Acquisition Using Ontology, *Proceedings of the 18th IEEE/ACIS International Conference on Software Engineering, Artificial Intelligence, Networking and Parallel/Distributed Computing (SNPD)*: 29–34.

Pasca, M., Dienes, P. 2005. Aligning Needles in a Haystack: Paraphrase Acquisition Across the Web, *Proceedings of the Second International Joint Conference: Natural Language Processing*, Korea: 119–130.

Paul, K.D. et al. 2013. Using Behavioral Indicators to Help Detect Potential Violent Acts: A Review of the Science Base. *RAND Corporation*: 258p.

Pedersen, T., Patwardhan, S., Michelizzi, J. 2004. WordNet: Similarity – Measuring the Relatedness of Concepts, *Proceedings of Demonstration Papers at HLT-NAACL*: 38–41.

Pelicon, A., Shekhar, R., Škrlj, B., Purver, M., Pollak, S. 2021. Investigating Cross-Lingual Training for Offensive Language Detection, *PeerJ Computer Science* 7(559), https://doi.org/10.7717/peerj-cs.559.

Pham, X.-Q., Ho, B.-Q. 2014. Combination of Rule-Based and Machine Learning for Biomedical Event Extraction, *Proceedings of the CONF-IRM.*

Phillips, W., Riloff, E. 2002. Exploiting Strong Syntactic Heuristics and Co-Training to Learn Semantic Lexicons, *Proceedings of the Conference on Empirical Methods in Natural Language Processing (EMNLP)*: 22–32.

Poletto, F. et al. 2021. Resources and Benchmark Corpora for Hate Speech Detection: A Systematic Review, *Language Resources and Evaluation* 55(2): 477–523.

Pontrandolfo, G. 2019. *Corpus Methods in Legal Translation Studies. Law, Language and Communication Series*. Routledge. ISBN: 978-1-138-47967-2.

Qureshi, K.A., Sabih, M. 2021. Un-Compromised Credibility: Social Media Based Multi-Class Hate Speech Classification for Text, *IEEE Access* 9: 109465–109477.

Rahem, K.R., Omar, N. 2014. Drug-Related Crime Information Extraction and Analysis, *Proceedings of International Conference on Information Technology and Multimedia (ICIMU), IEEE*: 250–254.

Rahma, F., Romadhony, A. 2021. Rule-Based Crime Information Extraction on Indonesian Digital News, *Proceedings of the 2021 International Conference on Data Science and Its Applications (ICoDSA)*: 10–16.

Rakhimova, D., Zhumanov, Z. 2017. Complex Technology of Machine Translation Resources Extension for the Kazakh Language. *Advanced Topics in Intelligent Information and Database Systems*. Springer International Publishing, Almaty, Kazakhstan.

Ramponi, A., Plank, B., Lombardo, R. 2020. Ä Cross-Domain Evaluation of Edge Detection for Biomedical Event Extraction, *Proceedings of the 12th Language Resources and Evaluation Conference*: 1982–1989.

Rangel, F. et al. 2021. Profiling Hate Speech Spreaders on Twitter Task at PAN 2021, *CLEF 2021 Labs and Workshops, Notebook Papers.*

Ras, I.A. 2017. A Corpus-Assisted Critical Discourse Analysis of the Reporting on Corporate Fraud by UK Newspapers 2004–2014, *PhD Thesis, University of Leeds.*

Reyes-Ortiz, J.A. 2019. Criminal Event Ontology Population and Enrichment using Patterns Recognition from Text, *International Journal of Pattern Recognition and Artificial Intelligenc*e 33(11): 1940014.

Rich ERE Annotation Guidelines Overview, Linguistic Data Consortium, Philadelphia, PA, USA, August 23, 2021 [Online]. Available: https://catalog.ldc.upenn.edu/LDC2016T23.

Riloff, E. 1993. Automatically Constructing a Dictionary for Information Extraction Tasks, *Proceedings of the 11th National Conference of Artifical Intellegence*: 811–816.

Rizun, N., Waloszek, W. 2018. Methodology for Text Classification using Manually Created Corpora-based Sentiment Dictionary, *Proceedings of the 10th International Joint Conference on Knowledge Discovery, Knowledge Engineering and Knowledge Management (IC3K 2018)*. 1: KDIR, Poland: 212–220.

Rosa, F.F., Jino, M., Bonacin, R. 2018. Towards an Ontology of Security Assessment: A Core Model Proposal, *Information Technology-New Generations* (738): 75–80.

Rosen, A. 2005. In Search of the Best Method for Sentence Alignment in Parallel Texts, *Computer Treatment of Slavic and East European Languages.* Third International Seminar, Bratislava, Slovakia: 174–185.

Salas, A.H., Morzan-Samam, J., Nunez-del-Prado, M. 2020. Crime Alert! Crime Typification in News Based on Text Mining, *Lecture Notes in Networks and Systems* 69: 725–741.

Santhiya, K., Bhuvaneswari, V., Murugesh, V. 2021. Automated Crime Tweets Classification and Geo-Location Prediction Using Big Data Framework, *Turkish Journal of Computer and Mathematics Education* (TURCOMAT) 12(14): 2133–2152.

Schank, R.C. 1972. Conceptual Dependency: A Theory of Natural Language Understanding. *Cognitive. Psychology* 3(4): 552–631.

Schmidt, A., Wiegand, M. 2021. A Survey on Hate Speech Detection Using Natural Language Processing. *Proceedings of the Fifth International Workshop on Natural Language Processing for Social Media*: 1–10.

Sennrich, P., Volk, M. 2011. Iterative, MT-based Sentence Alignment of Parallel Texts, *Proceedings of the 18th Nordic Conference of Computational Linguistics (NODALIDA 2011)*, Switzerland: 175–182.

Sha, L. et al. 2016. RBPB: Regularization-Based Pattern Balancing Method for Event Extraction, *54th Annual Meeting of the Association for Computational Linguistics*: 1224–1234.

Shinzato, K., Sekine, S. 2013. Unsupervised Extraction of Attributes and Their Values from Product Description, *6th International Joint Conference on Natural Language Processing, IJCNLP:* 1339–1347.

Shyam Varan Nath. 2006. Crime Pattern Detection Using Data Mining, *IEEE/WIC/ACM International Conference on Web Intelligence and Intelligent Agent Technology Workshops* 4: 41–44.

Siino, M. et al. 2021. Detection of Hate Speech Spreaders Using Convolutional Neural Networks, *CLEF 2021 Labs and Workshops, Notebook Papers.*

Simard, M., Foster, G.F., Isabelle, P. 1992. Using Cognates to Align Sentences in Bilingual Corpora, *Proceedings of the 4th International Conference on Theoretical and Methodological Issues in Machine Translation (TMI 1992)* Montreal, Canada: 67–81.

Sint, R., Schaffert, S., Stroka, S., Ferstl, R. 2009. Combining Unstructured, Fully Structured and Semi-Structured Information in Semantic Wikis, *Proceedings of the 4th Semantic Wiki WorkShop (SemWiki) at the 6th European Semantic Web Conference*, ESWC.

Smith, J.R., Quirk, C., Toutanova, K. 2010. Extracting Parallel Sentences from Comparable Corpora using Document Level Alignment, *Proceedings of the Human language Technologies/North American Assosiation for Computational Linguistics*: 403–411.

Smrž, P., Mrnuštik, M. 2011. Decipheer-D4.1.1-WP4-BUT State of Art of Event Detection Methods-PU. *Report. Brno University of Technology.*

Subburathinam, A. et al. 2019. Cross-Lingual Structure Transfer for Relation and Event Extraction: *Proceedings of EMNLP-IJCNLP*: 313–325.

Taghizadeh, N., Faili, H. 2021. Cross-Lingual Adaptation Using Universal Dependencies, *ACM Transactions on Asian and Low-Resource Language Information Processing* 20(4): 1–23, https://doi.org/10.1145/3448251.

Taylor, A.V. 2020. MWCC: A Corpus of Malawi Criminal Cases, *NLLP@ KDD*: 39–47.

Tseng, Y.-H., Lee, L.-H., Lin, S.-Y., Liao, B.-S., Liu, M.-J., Chen, H.-H., Etzioni, O., Fader, A. 2014. Chinese Open Relation Extraction for Knowledge Acquisition, *Proceedings of the 14th Conference of the European Chapter of the Association for Computational Linguistics* 2: 12–16.

U.S. National Library of Medicine. National Institutes of Health. MeSH (Medical Subject Headings) [Online]. Available: http://www.nlm.nih.gov/mesh/.

Varga, D., Halacsy, P., Kornai, A., Nagy, V., Nemeth, L., Tron, V. 2007. Parallel Corpora for Medium Density Languages, *Amsterdam Studies in the Theory and History of Linguistic Science Series* 4(292): 247p.

Vishal, G., Lehal, G.S. 2009. A Survey of Text Mining Techniques and Applications, *Journal of Emerging Technologies in Web Intelligence* 1(1): 60–76.

Vo, D., Ebrahim, B. 2016. Open Information Extraction, *Encyclopedia with Semantic Computing and Robotic Intelligence* 1(1).

Vondricka, P. 2014. Aligning Parallel Texts with InterText, *Proceedings of the 9th International Conference on Language Resources and Evaluation (LREC'14)*: 1875–1879.

Wang, X., Zhang, Y., Chen, Y. 2018. *A Survey of Truth Discovery in Information Extraction.*

Wang, X., Wang, Z., Han, X., Jiang, W., Han, R., Liu, Z., Li, J., Li, P., Lin, Y. and Zhou, J., 2020. MAVEN: A massive general domain event detection dataset. *arXiv preprint arXiv:2004.13590.*

Westphal, C. 2009. Data Mining for Intelligence, Fraud and Criminal Detection. *Advanced Analytic & Information Sharing Technologies.* New York: CRC Press Taylor & Francis Group: 440p.

Wilks, Y.A. 1975. A Preferential, Pattern-Seeking Semantics for Natural Language Inference. *Artificial Intelligence* 6: 53–74.

Wilks, Y.A. 1979. Machine Translation and Atificial Intelligence. In B.M. Snell (ed), *Translating and Computer.* Amsterdam: North Holland: 27–43.

Wong, Y.W., Widdows, D., Lokovic, T., Nigam, K. 2009. Scalable Attribute-Value Extraction from Semi-structured Text, *2009 IEEE International Conference on Data Mining Workshops*: 302–307.

WordNet. *A Lexical Database for English.* Princeton University. [Online]. Available: http://wordnet.princeton.edu/.

Wu, H., Zhou, M. 2003. Synonymous Collocation Extraction Using Translation Information, *Proceedings of the 41st Annual Meeting on Association for Computational Linguistics*, Stroudsburg, PA, USA (1): 120–127.

Xiang, W., Wang, B. 2019. A Survey of Event Extraction from Text, *IEEE Access* 7: 173111–173137.

Yagcioglu, S. et al. 2019. Detecting Cybersecurity Events from Noisy Short Text, *arXiv preprint* arXiv: 1904.05054.

Yahya, M., Whang, E.S., Gupta, R., Halevy, A. 2014. ReNoun: Fact Extraction for Nominal Attributes, *Proceedings of the Conference on Empirical Methods in Natural Language (EMNLP)*: 325–335.

Zampieri, M. et al. 2019a. SemEval-2019 Task 6: Identifying and Categorizing Offensive Language in Social Media (OffensEval), *Proceedings of the 13th International Workshop on Semantic Evaluation (SemEval-2019), Association for Computational Linguistics (ACL):* 75–86.

Zampieri, M. et al. 2019b. Predicting the Type and Target of Offensive Posts in Social Media, *Proceedings of the Annual Conference of the North American Chapter of the Association for Computational Linguistics: Human Language Technology* (NAACL-HLT) 1: 1415–1420.

Zampieri, M. et al. 2020. SemEval-2020 Task 12: Multilingual Offensive Language Identification in Social Media (OffensEval 2020), *Proceedings of the 14th International Workshop on Semantic Evaluation.*

Zhumanov, Z., Madiyeva, A., Rakhimova, D. 2017. New Kazakh Parallel Text Corpora with Online Access, *Conference on Computational Collective Intelligence Technologies and Applications.* Almaty, Kazakhstan: 501–508.

Appendices

Appendix A. Classification of the main word-forming verb affixes of the Kazakh language.

қыла/ -кіле, ғыла/-гіле, ңқыра/-ңкіре, -іңкіре ңғыра/-ңгіре, мсыра/- мсіре, ымсыра/- імсіре (and their phonetic variants), ылда/-ілде, ырла/-ірде	Verbal affixes (or voice affixes) added to verbal stems	Ес- ңгіре-у Са- ңғыра-у
-ла /-ле (-да /-де, -та /-те (in all phonetic variants), -лан/-лен (дан /-ден, -тан /-тен, лат/-лет), -лас/-лес, -ландыр/-лендір, -ластыр/-лестір (in all phonetic variants)	The most productive affixes; The main verb-forming index from other parts of speech	Көңілсіз-де-н-у Әлсіз-де-н-у
-ла /-ле, -а/-е, -лық/-лік,- ық/-ік, -шы/-ші (in all phonetic variants)–іғ, -ліг, -тығ, -діғ, -ре), -ыра, -іре, -ыла, -іла	Can be either nominative or verbal	Үр-ле-у Тісте-ле-у Түй-ре-у
ай/-ей, й, ар/-ер, р, ра/-ре, ыр/-ір,		Көг-ер-т-у үлк-ей-т-у Кішір-ей-т-у
-зы, -азы, -ма, -бе, -ды/-ді, -ы/-і, ты/-ті, лы/-лі, ра/-ре, -шы/-ші, ын, ін, ал, ел мала /-меле, -палапеле, -бала/-беле, -ақта/-екте, -дала/-ала сыра/-сіре, мсыра/-мсіре, усыра/-усіре, жыра/-жіре, аңғыра/-енгіре, ңра/-нре ыра/-сіре, аура/-еуре,	Unproductive affixes	
сы/-сі , сын/-сін, са/-се, сан/-сен	N – formal indicator of reflexive voice	
-лық/-лік ық/-ік дық/-дік тық/-тік,-тығ –лығ -ығ іғ		Соқ-тық Соқ-тығ-у
қар/-кер қыр/-кір ғар/-гер ғыр/-гір қа/-ке ға/-ге қа/-ке, қан/-кен ан/-ен, ғал/-қал ырқа /-ірке лқа ырқан /-іркен	Affixes –л и –н of the reflexive voice must be added	
ғы/-гі ғыт/-гіт ға/-ге қы/-кі -т, ыт/-іт	Affix –т of the causative voice	
бы, бі, пы, пі		
сый, си, ырай, ірей, ыс, іс, жи, ши	Figurative verbs, of various movements, also mean changes in the appearance and facial expressions of the subject	
ди, ти, ми, пи, би, қи ки ыс іс	Figurative verbs	

Appendix B. Classification of auxiliary verbs of the Kazakh language with concretization of the action type.

Auxiliary verbs	The type of action
қой with the verbal participle with *–а [-е, -й]* *қойды*	Fast action
қал) with the verbal participle with *–а [-е, -й]* *қалды*	Completed sudden action
сал with the verbal participle with *–а [-е, -й]* *салдым* *салып*	Completed action
кет with main verbs (*отыр жат жығыл*) with the verbal participle with *–а [-е, -й]* *отыра кетті* *қисая кетсеңші*	Action performed haphazardly
бару *келу* *кетушығужүру* *тұру* with the verbal participle in *–а [-е, -й]* *ала бар, ала қел, ала шық, ала жүр, ала қайт, шыққан, барған*	Associated action
түс with the verbal participle with *–а [-е, -й]* *түсті*	Strengthening and extending the action
бер with the verbal participle with *–п* *беру*	Action lasting for an unlimited period of time
тұр *тұрыңдар* *тұсын*	Temporary action, with the meaning of "for now"
көр with the verbal participle with *–а [-е, -й]* *көрменті* *көрме* —request Combined with a compound verb stem of the perfect form *жоғалты ала көрме* *кетіп қала көрме*	Attempted action, meaning "to try"
жазда with the verbal participle with *–а [-е, -й]* *жаздады* It may be combined with the analytic perfect form, in which case the second component of the compound verb takes the form of a verbal participle with *–а [-е, -й]* *жоғылтып ала жаздады* *жығылып қала жаздады*	An action not performed for any reason. "Almost ..."
Алу with the verbal participle with *–а [-е, -й]* *алады* *алмадым* - negation *алмайды*- negation	Possibility or impossibility (in the negative form)
болу with the past verbal participle with *–ған(- ген, - қон,- кен)* *өлген болып жатты* *таныаған болып* *жатқан болып* *қалған болды да*	The person was pretending
кел(in the third person) with the main verb on the suffix *– ғы (- гі, -қы,- қі)* *келеді* *келді* *болғым келеді* *бейімдегісі келді*	The optative form

Appendix C. The main word-forming voice suffixes of Kazakh verbs.

Suffix	Voice	Example
–н, –ын, –ін	Reflexive	*Жу–ын–у , ора–н–у Көр–ін, көр–ін–ді*
–лан, –лен, –дан, –ден, –тан,| –тең	Reflexive	*Намыс–тан–у, шат–тан–у*
–сын, –сін, –қан, –кен	Reflexive	
–л, –ыл, –іл	Reflexive	They form both the passive and the reflexive voice *бу–ыл–у, түй–іл–у*
–лык, –лік, –дық, –дік, –тік, –ық, –ік, –лыг, –іг, –ліг	Reflexive	*Бу–лыг–у, іл–іг–у*
–с, –лас, –лес	Reflexive	*Орна–лас–у, қате–лес–у*
–л, –н	Passive	*Жина–л–ды*
–ыл, –іл, –ын, –ін	Passive	*Оқ–ыл–ды*
–лын, –лін, –ныл, –ніл	Passive	*Же–лін–у, Қолда–ныл–у, пайдала–ныл–у*
–с, ыс, –іс	Reciprocal	
–лас, –лес, –дас, –дес, –тас, –тес	Reciprocal	*Мұн–дас–у, сыр–лас–у, қас–тас–у*
–ылыс, –ныс, –ыныс, –iнiс –тыгыс и др.	Reciprocal and reflexive	*сапыр–ыл–ыс–у, байла–н–ыс–у, ұг–ын–ыс–у соқ–тыг–ыс–у,*
–стыр, –стiр, –ластыр, –лестiр	Reciprocal and causative	*жара–с–тыр–у, таны–с–тыр–у*
–ландыр, –тендір, –лендір	Reflexive and causative	*Индустрия–лан–дыр, коллектив–тен–дір, ірі–лен–дір*
–дастыр	Causative	*Колхоз–дас, колхоз–дас–тыр, колхоз–дас–тыр–ыл*
–т, –ыт, –іт, –дыр, –дір, –тыр, –гыз, –гіз, –қыз, –кіз, –ар, –ер, –ыр, –ір, –қар, –кер, –гыр, –дар, –сет	Causative	
–гыздыр, –гіздір, –дыргыз, –діргіз	Complex affixes	
–ындыр, –індір, –ландыр, –лендір, –тандыр, –дендір и	Reflexive + causative	
–ылыс, –лыс, –ініс, –ліс , –ыгыс, –тыгс, –тыгыс, –лікіс, –ықыс, –ікіс, –ныс, –ніс, –ыныс, –ініс	Reflexive + reciprocal	
–лін, –лын, –ніл	Reflexive + passive	
–тырыл, дырыл, –гызыл, –сетіл	Causative + passive	
–ттыр	Causative + reciprocal	
–арыс, –іріс	понудительный	
–стыр, –стір, –ластыр, –лестір	Reciprocal+causative	

Appendix D. Formalization of the grammatical formulation of the Kazakh mood.

Imperative

Person	Number	Word stem features	Affix	Example
1	sin.	To the stem of the verbal participle or the verb with–a, –e	–йын –йін	шақыр–а–йын көтер–е–йін ен–е–йін ки–е–йін
1	pl.	To the stem of the verbal participle or the verb with –a, –e	–йық –йік	тарт–а–йық қос–а–йық жат–а–йық
2	sin.	Matches the main form of the verb		жет өт қорға
2	sin. Polite	Adding an affix to the verb stem	–ңыз –ңіз	тында–ңыз кейіме–**ңіз**
2	pl.	Adding the plural affix to the singular form after the affix ң	–дар –ң–дар –ң–дер	таста–ң–дар ойла–ң–дар
2	pl. polite	The plural affix is added to the polite singular form	–ңыз–дар –ңіз–дер	тоқта–ңыз–дар жәрдемдесі–ңіз–дер
3	sin.	Adding an affix to the verb stem	–сын –сін	бер–сін тапсыр–сын
3	pl.	The 3rd person has no plural form		
		The addition of affixes to the imperative defines the action as urgent	–шы, –ші	Ала—йын–шы, Айт–шы, айты–ңыз–шы

The present particular tense of the indicative mood

Person	Number	Word stem features	Auxiliary verb	Example
1	sin., pl.	Verbal participle with –п	отыр, тұр, жатыр, жүр	мен жазып отыр–мын, біз жазып отыр–мыз
2	ед., pl.	Verbal participle with –п	отыр, тұр, жатыр, жүр	сен келе жатыр–сың, сендер келе жатыр–сың–дар
2	sin., pl.	Verbal participle with –п	отыр, тұр, жатыр, жүр	көріп тұр–сыз, көріп тұр–сыз–дар
3	sin., pl.	Verbal participle with –п	отыр, тұр, жатыр, жүр	катысып жүр

(Continued)

(Continued)

The present transitive tense of the indicative mood

Person	Number	Word stem features	Affixes	Example
1, 2, 3	sin., pl.	Verbal participle with –а, –е, –й, –и	Personal verb flexions: –мын, –сыз, –сың, –мыз, –міз, –сыңдар, –сендер, –сіздер, –сыздар, –ды, –ай–ды	(ол бар–а–ды), колхозшылар егін жинайды

The future presumptive tense of the indicative mood

Person	Number	Word stem features	Affixes
1, 2, 3	sin., pl.	Verbal participle with –ар, –ер, –ір, –ир	Personal verb flexions: –мыз, –міз, сыз, –сың, –сыңдар, –сендер, –сіздер, –сыздар

The indefinite future tense of the indicative mood

Person	Number	Word stem features	Affixes	
1, 2, 3	sin., pl.	глаголы на –мақ, –мек –пақ, –пек, –бақ, –бек	Personal verb flexions: –мыз, –міз, сыз, –сың, –сыңдар, –сендер, –сіздер, –сыздар может быть: –шы, –ші	бар–мақ–пын), ол театрға бар–мақ, сат–пақ–шы–мын, жолық–пақ–шы–мын. сен аудармақ –сың, сендер аудармақ –сың–дар, сіз аудармақ –сыз, сіздер аудармақ –сыз–дар, олар аудармақ

Person	Number	Features of formation	Auxiliary verb	Examples
1, 2, 3	sin., pl.	Auxilary verb takes personal flexions	Еді, екен	бітірменші еді, әңгімелеспекші едім

(Continued)

(Continued)

The past tense of the indicative mood

Person	Number	Word stem features	Affixes	Examples
		Verbal participle with –п	Personal verb flexions: –пін, –піз, –сің –сіндер, –сіз –сіздер, –ті –ті, –ты. (3d person); –мыс, –міс (also can be added)	жүргізіппіз, жүргізіпсің, жүргізіпті, жеңіптіміс, қайтып келіптіміс

The simple past tense of the indicative mood

Person	Number	Word stem features	Affixes
		Past participle with ған, ген қан, кен, ға, ге, қа, ке	Personal verb flexions: – мын, –мін –быз, –сың –сыңдер

недавно прошедшее (окончательное) время изъявительного наклонения

		Word stem features	Affixes	
		Verb stem	Possessive affixes: –ды, –ді, –ты, –ті Plural form adds **–к, –қ, –м, –ң**	көрін–ді–м, көрін–ді–к, Сен көрін–ді–ң, сіздер көрін–ді–ніз–дер, ол [олар] көрін–ді

Person	Number	The main word of the predicate	Auxilary verb	
		Noun	[емес/ жоқ] еді	етікші еді
1	sin., pl.	Verbal participle with –п, причастие на ған, ген, қан, кен	[емес/ жоқ] едім, [емес/ жоқ] едік	Мен алған емес едім, біз алған емес едік
2	sin., pl.	Verbal participle with –п, причастие на ған, ген, қан, кен	[емес/ жоқ] едің, [емес/ жоқ] едіндер, [емес/ жоқ] едіңіз, [емес/ жоқ] едіңіздер	Сен алған емес едің, сендер алған емес едіңдер, сіз алған емес едіңіз, сіндер алған емес едіңіздер
3	sin., pl.	Verbal participle with –п, причастие на ған, ген, қан, кен	[емес/ жоқ] еді	Ол алған емес еді, олар алған емес еді

The unfinished past tense of the indicative mood

(Continued)

(Continued)

Person	Number	The main word of the predicate	Auxilary verb	Examples
1	sin., pl.	State verbs (отыр, тұр, жатыр, жүр)	[емес/ жоқ] едім, [емес/ жоқ] едік	Келе жатыр едім, Біз келе жатыр едік
2	sin., pl.	State verbs (отыр, тұр, жатыр, жүр)	[емес/ жоқ] едің, [емес/ жоқ] едіңдер, [емес/ жоқ] едіңіз, [емес/ жоқ] едіңіздер	Сен келе жатыр едің, Сендер келе жатыр едіңдер, Сіз келе жатыр едіңіз, Сіздер келе жатыр едіңіздер
3	sin., pl.	State verbs (отыр, тұр, жатыр, жүр)	[емес/ жоқ] еді	Ол келе жатыр еді, Олар келе жатыр еді
1,2,3	sin., pl.	Participle with атын, етін, йтын, йтін	[емес/ жоқ] едім, [емес/ жоқ] едік, [емес/ жоқ] едің, [емес/ жоқ] едіңдер, [емес/ жоқ] едіңіз, [емес/ жоқ] едіңіздер, [емес/ жоқ] еді	танымайтын еді, еститін еді

The past intention form of the indicative mood

		The main word of the predicate	Auxilary verb	Examples
1,2,3	sin., pl.	Participle with мақ, мақшы	[емес/ жоқ] едім, [емес/ жоқ] едік, [емес/ жоқ] едің, [емес/ жоқ], [емес/ жоқ] едіңіз, [емес/ жоқ] едіңіздер, [емес/ жоқ] еді	Жазбақшы едім, жазбақшы едік, жазбақшы емес едік, жазбақшы едің, жазбақшы едіңдер, жазбақшы едіңіз, жазбақшы едіңіздер, жазбақшы емес едіңіздер, жазбақшы еді

Compound subjunctive

(Continued)

(Continued)

Person	Number	The main word of the predicate	Auxilary verb	Examples
1,2,3	sin., pl.	Participle with –ар, –ер, –р	едім, едік, едің, едіңіз, едіңіздер, еді	Айтар едім, айтар едің, айтар едік, айтар едіңіздер

The optative mood of the passive type

Person	Number	Word stem features	Affixes	Examples
1	sin., pl.	Past participle with ғай, гей қай, кей	–мын, мыз –быз	
2	sin., pl.	Past participle with ғай, гей қай, кей	–сың сыз –сындар, сыздар	
3	sin., pl.	Past participle with ғай, гей қай, кей	–	

Person	Number	The main word of the predicate	Auxilary verb	
1, 2,3	sin., pl.	Word stem with–ғай, –гей, –қай, –кей	едім, едік, едің, едіңіз, едіңіздер, еді	Бітіргей едім, жеткей еді

The optative mood of the affirmative type

Person	Number	The main word of the predicate	Affixes	Auxiliary verb
1,2,3	sin., pl.	Word stem with –ғы, –гі, –қы, –кі	possessive affixes: – мыз, –міз, –ң –ңыз –ңіз –сы –сі	келеді тында–ғы–м келеді, тында –ғы–ң келеді, тында–ғы –ларыңыз келеді, тында –ғы–сы келеді

Person	Number		Auxiliary word	Auxiliary verb
1, 2, 3	sin., pl.	Word stem with, –са, –се	игі	едім, едік, едің, едіңіз, едіңіздер, еді Ал–са игі едім, Ал–са игі едіңіз, Ал–са игі еді

Conditional mood

(Continued)

(Continued)

Person	Number		Possible personal flexions:	
1	sin., pl.	Word stem with –са, –се	–м [шы],–қ[шы], –к[шы]	Ал–са–м, Ал–са–қ бер–се–к, айтса–м–шы, Айтса–қ–шы
2	sin., pl.	Word stem with –са, –се	–ң[шы], –ңыз[шы], –ңіз[шы], (+–дар[шы], –дер[шы])	Ал–са–ң, ал–са–ңыз, ал–са–ң–дар, ал–са–ң–дар, айтса–ңыз–шы
3	sin., pl.	Word stem with –са, –се	–	Ал–са, бер–се

Person	Number		Possible personal flexions:	Auxilary word
1, 2, 3	sin., pl.	Word stem with –са, –се	–м,–қ, –к, –ң, –ңыз, –ңіз,	екен, еді, ғой мен көр–се–м екен, мен көр–се–м еді, мен көр–се–м ғой, сіздер көр–се–ңіз–дер екен, сіздер көр–се–ңіз–дер еді, сіздер көр–се–ңіз–дер ғой

Index

Note: **Bold** page numbers refer to tables and *italic* page numbers refer to figures.

For Product Safety Concerns and Information please contact our EU
representative GPSR@taylorandfrancis.com
Taylor & Francis Verlag GmbH, Kaufingerstraße 24, 80331 München, Germany

www.ingramcontent.com/pod-product-compliance
Ingram Content Group UK Ltd.
Pitfield, Milton Keynes, MK11 3LW, UK
UKHW052049230926
475702UK00025B/966
9781032957890